Long Way ON A Little

An earth lover's companion for enjoying meat, pinching pennies, and living deliciously

SHANNON HAYES

Left to Write Press *Richmondville, NY*

10 9 8 7 6 5 4 3 2 1

ISBN 978-0-9794391-2-4
Library of Congress Control Number: 2012912547

Book design and production: Jill Shaffer
Cover and interior illustrations © 2012 Jill Weber
Photography: Bob Hooper and Shannon Hayes
Editor: Damon Lee Fowler
Proofreading and indexing: Steve Hoare

Left To Write Press
270 Rossman Valley Rd
Richmondville, NY 12149
www.ShannonHayes.info
www.GrassfedCooking.com
518.827.7595

Left to Write Press is distributed by Chelsea Green Publishing Company

Quantity Sales: Special discounts are available on quantity purchases for groups and individuals. Please visit www.GrassfedCooking.com or www.ShannonHayes.info for details, or call Left to Write Press directly.

U.S. TRADE BOOKSTORES and WHOLESALERS:
Please contact Chelsea Green Publishing, 85 North Main Street, Suite 120, White River Jct., Vermont 05001. Orders: 800.639.4099; offices: 802.295.6300.

About Left to Write Press:

Left to Write Press is an initiative of Shannon Hayes and Bob Hooper, who wanted to publish books completely on their own terms, so they could earn a decent return on Shannon's writing without selling their souls. We are now on our third book, and we've managed to stick to our guns to keep it written, published, edited and designed locally and regionally. And we even managed to do it on recycled paper. Left to Write Press expresses our agenda for an ecologically sound, socially just world, where everyone is well-fed and happy. Now stop reading this small print, and start enjoying our book!

For Bob —
May our life together taste better than ever.
I love you.

Simple and Perfect Pork Roast, p. 130.

Contents

The Best Steak, Cooked Indoors, p. 67.

The Best Steak, Cooked Outdoors, p. 66

Beef Kebabs, p. 68

CHAPTER SIX

Pork

Turkey: Straightforward, Simple and Delicious, p. 156

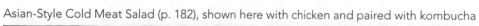

Asian-Style Cold Meat Salad (p. 182), shown here with chicken and paired with kombucha

Salt-curing duck for confit, p. 158; Grilled Jerk Chicken Hearts, p. 226

CHAPTER NINE

Heads, Tails, and Other Under-Appreciated Treasures

Super Slow Roasted Beef, p.78

Foreword

No one is better positioned to understand the critical role that food plays in the history and well-being of a society than farmers and everyday cooks. Those whose business it is to routinely provision a nation's table have an intimate relationship with food that few others can boast. Unfortunately, they seldom put a lot of thought into the importance of their place in society, let alone history. They have a job and they do it; they don't often write about it.

Conversely, those who do write about it all too often have little more than an academic understanding of what is really involved in bringing dinner from the earth to the table.

Shannon Hayes is a shining exception, a rarity among food writers. She has an intimate relationship to the subject that few others can claim, a practical knowledge and understanding that runs well beyond academic, for this scholar and teacher is also an experienced farmer and accomplished everyday cook.

The cream beyond all that is that Shannon is an engaging writer who knows how to tell a story. And there's no story more important in the telling than a recipe, for its success or failure in practice rests on how well it is presented in theory. Shannon's fresh, casual approach is like a neighbor sharing across the backyard fence—a really smart neighbor who knows what she's talking about. Wise without being condescending, thorough without being tedious, economical without being simplistic, her comfortable style says, "This is really good, and a lot easier than you think. You can do it, but don't worry: I'm right here by your elbow every step of the way."

When Shannon asked me to edit the recipes that follow, we immediately agreed that their most important element was that comfortable, neighborly tone. Where a step needed clarity or detail, we worked hard to provide it without compromising that quality.

I knew from the beginning that working with Shannon would be a lot of fun, as comfortable and refreshing as a long visit with an old friend. And so it was. What I didn't realize, however, was how much I would learn. In her introduction, she says that writing this book revolutionized her kitchen, changing her entire approach to cooking and eating the meat provided by the gentle creatures from her pastures. I freely and humbly confess that working with her has in turn revolutionized my own kitchen, and invite you to let her do the same for yours. Revolution has never tasted better.

Damon Lee Fowler
Spring Chicken and Lamb Season, 2012
Savannah, Georgia

ACKNOWLEDGMENTS

The creation of this book has been touched by more people than I can possibly count. I owe thanks to all our customers at Sap Bush Hollow Farm, who are forever helping me to understand what needs to be investigated in the world of sustainable meat; who support my family's farm, which, in turn, supports this cookbook writing habit.

A couple customers in particular bear mentioning for extra thanks:

Rebecca Eckel, our local physician and long-time customer, who looked into our eyes and not at a monitor, and in doing so, quickly set our family on a path to healing, and helped me realize how to make this book helpful for all those readers who may be coping with diabetes; and

Joellyn Kopecky, who burst into our kitchen with radiance and love and introduced our family to a way of eating that has improved our health immeasurably.

I owe thanks to the grassfed farmers across the country, who continue to share their enthusiasm for the peaceful critters who walk the earth with us, and for the blessings they bring to our plates.

I also would like to express my thanks to the folks at Chelsea Green, who have found a way to support my work as an independent writer/self-publisher, while enabling me to join forces with the quality authors among their ranks.

Thanks are due to the friends who came to sit around my table while I experimented with recipes; and most especially to my daughters, Saoirse (8) and Ula (5), child victims of my culinary queries. You've grown to be so open-minded about the foods that I serve you, and amazingly diplomatic about the ones you don't like (but seriously, when you say "It's delicious" and then eat only your salad, I can see right through it).

I owe deep thanks to Damon Lee Fowler, who let me persuade him to become my editor, thus infusing this book with his sincere passion for food and culture. Damon is a rare soul who is willing to direct his gastronomic passion toward what is important and needed before what is trendy, and the love he brings to his work comes through on every page of this book.

A heap of thanks needs to go out to Steve Hoare of Black Dome Press, my proofreader and publishing counselor, who does everything from determining when a colon should be a semi-colon, to helping me calculate costs and pricing and streamline my production process. Thanks for so many years of assistance with my projects, Steve!

Jill Shaffer Hammond deserves a load of accolades, too. She is my book designer extraordinaire, who repeatedly maintains a state of grace and equanimity as I give her a mountain of impossible design concepts that I want incorporated into the work, make her adhere to them, then decide that none of them work and go back to the beginning . . . then repeat. Ad nauseum. In the end, she still manages to make me look good, and continues to help me out. Wow!

I'd also like to express my deep appreciation to Jill Weber of Frajil Farms, who used vivid colors and creative lines to capture the warmth and charm of our way of life for the cover art and illustrations in this volume. They bring so much to the final book—thank you!

As is forever true, I must express my appreciation for my mom and dad, Jim and Adele Hayes, of Sap Bush Hollow Farm. Not only do you make room for me on the land and in the cutting room, but you tolerate my extreme recipe testing needs and don't even complain when 5 lbs of filet mignon suddenly go missing from inventory for "recipe testing." As you can see in the beef chapter, I was telling the truth. . . .

And finally, I need to thank Bob, my best friend and amazing husband, who does absolutely everything else to make books like this a reality: he washes the dishes after every recipe test, critiques every flavor, copy edits every bit of writing, fills every book order, snaps every photograph, sets up every cooking workshop, and prepares every presentation that I take on the road. He makes me coffee every morning after I sign off from writing, discusses all my ideas with me, handles the grocery shopping for my ingredients lists, and does all the necessary bookkeeping after. He makes this self-publishing adventure a practical and fun reality, and he makes my life a joy.

Introduction

In school, we learned the story of our nation through history books—notoriously dry volumes chronicling momentous battles, pivotal decisions made by leaders, and notable popular movements that shaped our culture. But there is also a flavorful side of history that textbooks typically fail to acknowledge: the role of the hearth and kitchen. No history unfolds, no revolution succeeds, without a kitchen fire to fuel it. The thrift and ingenuity of colonial women inspired a uniquely American cuisine that enabled the rebellious boycott of British goods; westward pioneers plied the frontier carrying beans, pork bellies, and cornmeal; the industrial revolution moved the open hearth to the iron cook stove; immigrants carried their cultural histories to their tables; and Freedom Marchers celebrated with Dr. Martin Luther King, Jr. over racks of spareribs and his beloved pecan pie. A profound human history is recorded not only in classical texts, but in cookbooks.

A perusal of the cookbooks published since the American Revolution will tell another, less heroic side of our story, as well. As industrialization beckoned us from a life of travails, Americans started drifting toward passive consumerism; increasingly, cookbooks featured recipes that relied heavily on canned and processed foods as primary ingredients. As our affluence increased and our regard for thrift and prudence slackened, cookbooks offered recipes for removing calories and fat from our diets. Livestock production became increasingly industrialized, and we became ever more ignorant concerning where meat comes from, the true costs of its production and, moreover, how to use it wisely. Cookbooks reflected our finicky penchant for using only prime steaks and roasts of animals, thus relegating enormous amounts of the useful animal to "by-product."

The countercultural movements of recent decades tell their stories through cookbooks, too. Environmentalists and social activists alerted us to issues of confined livestock production, farm waste pollution, equitable food distribution, animal cruelty, etc., and the first vegetarian cookbooks emerged, laying the foundations of the "sustainable cuisine" movement.

My own part in reflecting history through writing cookbooks is rooted in this movement, though my family has raised meat for sixty-five years. I came of age as a writer just as the local food movement was gaining its foothold, and it was moving beyond the idea that sustainable cuisine was synonymous with vegetarianism. Meat, when raised responsibly on green pastures, is part of an ecologically benign and even beneficial food production system.

My first cookbook, *The Grassfed Gourmet Cookbook*, was regarded as an unusual volume because my culinary knowledge came less from gourmet training than from an intimate knowledge of livestock farming. In the book, I argue that the way the animals and the land are treated are essential "ingredients" for good food. The publication of *The Grassfed Gourmet* tied me forever to the "locavores," a movement fueled by a cadre of ecologically concerned food writers who have sought to describe food not just as something to eat, but as a critical element of our communities. They have

The health benefits of grassfed meat and dairy products

Grassfed meat and dairy products have a lot to recommend them. They're better for the environment, they are a great way to restore our local food system and local economies, and they have superior flavor. But the benefits don't stop there. Grassfed meats are a good source of omega-3 fatty acids, which are essential to healthy heart and brain function, and have even been shown to retard the growth of a number of different cancers. The meat and dairy products from grassfed animals are also a source of conjugated linoleic acids, or CLAs, a critical nutrient for battling and preventing cancer. In fact, grassfed meat and dairy products are shown to be three–five times higher in CLAs than conventional meat and dairy. They are also significantly higher in Vitamin E than other conventionally grown products.

Vitamin E, a nutrient that many Americans are deficient in, is an important antioxidant that also helps with hormone regulation and supports heart, respiratory, brain, prostate and breast health.

When we make an effort to expand our culinary repertoire to include bone broth, rendered animal fats and grassfed organ meats, the nutritional bonuses keep coming. Bone broth is a great source of proteinaceous gelatin and electrolytes, and the fats and organ meats are important sources of the fat-soluble vitamins essential to our health: A, D, E, and K, all which are critical to our body's ability to absorb the other nutrients it requires.

The great news about grassfed products is always growing. To learn more about the most up-to-date health findings, be sure to visit eatwild. com, a comprehensive web resource devoted to disseminating the good news about going grassfed.

Food waste in America

Food waste in the United States generates some staggering statistics. Food activists Danielle Nierenberg and Abby Massey wrote in *USA Today* that, each day, the average American discards 1 ½ pounds of food. Rather than going to the compost pile to generate new soil for future production, nearly all of it winds up in landfills or incinerators, fueling 34 percent of our methane emissions. And that's just the household food waste; up the figures if you calculate the post-market waste from supermarkets, restaurants, cafeterias and cafés. A study reported in *Environmental Science and Technology* estimates our food wastes add up to 350 million barrels of oil per year, almost 1 million barrels each day.

illustrated the many ways that food production can help enhance local economies, gain community food security, rebuild social relationships, protect and revitalize our open spaces, and reduce our carbon footprint and fossil fuel consumption. Better still, a locally centered diet can free other communities around the world to grow their own food, rather than export cash crops to satiate distant appetites for exotic nourishment. The sustainable cuisine movement clearly comprehends that, while history books may record history, cookbooks and cooks can actually shape the future.

And change is definitely in order. Revolutionary ideals (and, of course, the love of good food) have fired my passion for writing cookbooks, and this volume is no exception.

I have been thrilled to see my meat customers and my readers, after a lifetime with factory farmed meats and groceries, use my previous cookbooks (*The Grassfed Gourmet Cookbook* and *The Farmer and the Grill*) as tools to create a more sustainable diet. But my experience selling my family's meats and the time I spend in our on-farm butcher shop have taught me that we have not come nearly far enough in rebuilding and rethinking our food system.

Even with my family farm's earth-conscious customer base, the waste is appalling. In conversations, I glean confessions about the waste at home: bits of steaks, chops and roasts that are discarded because no one in the household makes use of the leftovers; thawed meats discarded before they spoil "as a precaution"; frozen meat with a little package-wear tossed out for the same reason; bones cut from roasts or steaks sent to the trash without being boiled for broth. I see the waste every time I step into the cutting room: mountains of bones and organ meats are discarded because no one will make use of them. I see it accumulate in our unsold meat inventory: bins of beef shanks, lamb necks, chicken soup parts, lard, tallow, pigs' feet and skin filling the freezers.

The emerging enthusiasm for locally produced foods, and a growing awareness of the importance of pasture-based farming is restoring the viability of more small family farms nationally. But a deeper change needs to happen. At this point in the local food revolution, small family farmers are still a niche; the nation is largely fed by factory farms. Those of us on the land often hear that our efforts, however noble, are of marginal social value—we could never truly feed our country. We can only hope to satisfy the hunger of a few well-heeled health nuts and environmental zealots.

I believe those statements are true—*if* Americans continue to eat as they currently do, *if* we continue to be wasteful with our food. We grass-based farmers could not possibly raise enough steaks, pork chops and chicken breasts to satisfy our

Legumes and grains

Long Way on a Little represents the fourth book in my writing career, and it has taken the longest amount of time for me to write (four years). I initially thought that this would be a breeze to produce, because I assumed that the easiest, most economical way to prudently use grassfed and pastured meats was to pair them with grains and legumes. Thus, I began this project writing recipes that prominently featured them. After soaking them in yogurt or whey to neutralize their phytic acid, they would be cooked in meat broth, increasing their nutrient density, then paired with smaller volumes of meat. The recipes were delicious. But during this time, for some reason, my family began developing health problems: weight gain, fungal infections, digestive disorders, cavities. While these may have seemed like normal, part-of-life afflictions to the rest of America, we didn't feel that living organically and locally-centered agrarian lives should subject us to so many maladies. Through a process of elimination, we discovered that none of us can tolerate grains and legumes as a steady part of our diet. Since I test all of the recipes in my home kitchen before publishing them, I had to

rewrite much of what appears in the coming pages. If my family couldn't eat it and I couldn't test it, then I wasn't including it in the book. We learned that there are millions of Americans confronting grain and legume intolerances. So I decided, rather than abandoning this book project and living off beef and greens, I'd challenge myself to develop recipes that made ecological sense through the prudent use of meat and leftovers, but that also were free of grains and legumes.

The vast majority of recipes in this book do not contain any grains or legumes. However, as I mentioned, a lot of the grain and legume dishes are *really* delicious. Furthermore, I know that there are still millions of folks who seem able to eat these foods with no problems. Thus, I winnowed out all but the very best grain and legume dishes—those dishes that are so delicious that even my grain-intolerant family will willingly suffer consequences for them on rare occasions. The bulk of the recipes that are here, however, represent how we eat on a daily basis. These are the dishes that we have enjoyed the most while our health and vitality were restored. Whether you can take pleasure in grains and legumes or not, I am certain your family will find them delicious.

What's with the carbohydrate profiles?

If you've just read the sidebar on grains and legumes, you are aware that my family endured a health crisis during the time I was writing this book. Among the most troubling was the discovery that my husband, Bob, had developed a rare form of insulin-dependent diabetes (neither type 1 nor type 2). Insulin dependency is a manageable life condition, but it does require that a person knows exactly how many carbohydrates he or she is ingesting at every meal. In order to test these recipes on my family, I had to look up the carbohydrate count on every single ingredient. Since diabetes is becoming a national issue, I decided to include these notes in the book for anyone else who might need the information. Please be aware, however, that these may not be absolutely accurate. I used the USDA food database, where the carbohydrate counts are based on average figures taken from a variety of samples. Actual figures may vary, especially if you are working with naturally variable farm-fresh foods. I'm certain that whole raw milk from a grassfed cow is going to have a different carb count than a cup of milk from a grocery store carton, for example. Further, there is some debate as to whether all the calculations on the USDA database are entirely accurate. Still, I found it the most reliable among the databases I perused, and the calculations seemed to result in accurate insulin dosing for Bob, so these are the numbers we've chosen to use. If exact carbohydrate counts are critical to your health, I encourage you to review the figures yourself and make any adjustments you think may be necessary before preparing the recipes.

nation's protein requirements, even if our numbers increased dramatically. However, each beast that gives its life for our sustenance offers far more quality nourishment than most Americans are willing (or know how) to eat.

Those folks with both feet firmly planted in the local food movement might feel entitled to wag our fingers and pat ourselves on the back for our ethical food choices. But even those of us with green halos need to do more. At the start of this book project, my own refrigerator bore testimony to this fact: it was a haven for moldy leftovers. But, like those in the local food movement, I believe we can show the rest of the country that a great transition *can* happen. We can move away from the polluting industrial farming system, break our oil habit, cool down the planet and live vibrant community-centered lives rich with delicious food. All of this is possible, but we have to go deeper than eating homegrown tomatoes and grassfed rib eye steaks.

Long Way on a Little is my culinary exploration of this issue. In the coming pages, as I've done in all of my books, I've provided recipes to cook every cut of meat readily available on grassfed and pasture-raised beef, lamb, pork and poultry (even the prime cuts!) The difference is that I've examined every piece of meat for its potential as a primary meal, and then as a secondary meal. Thus, every primary

Slow cookers, pressurecookers and microwaves

When it comes to ecologically sensible cooking, we must remember that the tools we select for the job can also help to conserve resources. Slow cookers, pressure cookers and microwaves are three modern technologies that are revered for just this purpose. I've got opinions on all of them, and as you use this book it may be helpful to know them so that you can make adjustments according to your own opinions.

Slow cookers: I don't know how civilization advanced without them. (Well, I guess there *was* the Dutch Oven.) I love my slow cooker, and if a recipe requires any kind of moist-heat cooking, I will almost always find a way to pull out my Crock-Pot and use it. Slow cookers enable you to prepare a meal for energy costs of less than 25 cents per day, and you can even do it while you are outside or away from home with the added security that it doesn't have an open flame. The recipes in this book that call for a slow cooker will work with any pot that holds six quarts or more.

Pressure cookers: I once read that using a pressure cooker resulted in cooking foods too quickly at high temperatures (above the boiling point) that can be nutritionally "dangerous." However, I never found any studies that corroborate this statement, the energy and time savings are amazing, and the flavor of the grains, legumes and vegetables out of the pressure cooker are terrific—better, in my opinion, than if they were boiled in water. For this reason, in the few recipes that call for legumes in this book, I do turn to the pressure cooker. While writing this book I experimented repeatedly with the pressure cooker on meat, and I simply could not be sold on it, no matter how my ecological sensibilities and my quest to find faster ways to cook meals tried to persuade me. I found meat cooked in a pressure cooker to be too stringy and devoid of flavor. Thus, the pressure cooker comes into play with grains, legumes and root vegetables. If these food items are mainstays in your diet, it is worth the investment.

Microwave ovens: There are two camps when it comes to microwaves. One believes their use of radiofrequency electromagnetic energy could quite possibly result in reconfiguring perfectly good food into the demons of hell. The other argues that they are perfectly safe, that there is no research to confirm the demons-of-hell argument, and that they are extremely energy efficient. The microwaves emitted by the oven cause the water molecules in food to rotate, which causes it to heat quickly. Call me a superstitious Luddite, but I'm sticking with the demons-of-hell camp on this one. While studies may suggest the food is safe, it just doesn't taste good, and all those microwaves and bouncing water molecules just make me skittish. We do have a microwave in our house, but we never use it for food. We use it to heat a hot-pack that goes into a thermal carrying case for keeping potluck dishes warm. It is rarely used, and I do not require it for any of my recipes.

If you are looking for more ways to conserve energy in your kitchen, I recommend Alexandra Zissu's *The Conscious Kitchen*, published in 2010 by Clarkson Potter.

cut recipe, be it for a loin roast or a whole chicken, comes with recommendations for recipes to use the leftovers, which are found in Chapter 8, "Leftovers and Soups."

I've also delved deeply into the use of "Bones and Fat" in Chapter 3, in which I take you through the techniques for making good broth and rendering fat. If you are unfamiliar with these techniques, I urge you to read these pages carefully, as many of the recipes throughout the book assume you will have both bone broth and rendered fats on hand (although, in most cases, butter can be substituted for lard or tallow). My reasoning for this is threefold: many of the recipes that include bone broth would typically be written in more conventional cookbooks with wine as the liquid base. Unless you are bottling your own, wine is considerably more expensive to cook with than homemade broth. Thus, if you invest the time in making it, broth represents a financial savings. Secondly, as they are some of the most nutrient-dense foods imaginable, both fat and broth offer rewards when you recover and use them. Because they increase the nutrient density of your dishes, you are likely to satisfy more hungry bellies on less food. And finally, from the standpoint of meat cutting room waste, it is simply a matter of more prudently using all the gifts we farmers have taken from the gentle creatures who roam our fields.

Interestingly, the best salves, soaps and ointments from days gone by were also made with livestock fats. In researching this book, I learned that skin care need not be dependent upon expensive, ecologically problematic, imported ingredients. The unused fats from our livestock are a treasure trove of fat-soluble vitamins, as nourishing to the skin as they are to our bodies. Thus, I've also included a selection of recipes for incorporating the fats into skin-care products. I've discovered that making and using these products has not only helped ease the strain on my household budget, but has become a pleasant micro-enterprise to supplement my family's income.

Chapter 9, "Heads, Tails and other Under-Appreciated Treasures," is a foray into what most Americans consider the grisly side of prudent meat consumption. I, too, fell into this camp, balking at the very idea of cooking a pig's head or skewering a chicken's heart. The thought of tackling this chapter, frankly, filled me with dread. Having written it, I've come through the fog, and the recipes included are some of my family's favorites. While heads, tails and organ meats do not represent as much waste from an animal as the bones and fat, their concentration of minerals and fat-soluble vitamins makes discarding them a huge waste of nutritional value. And, handled properly, they are fantastic.

Long Way on a Little represents the single greatest learning curve I've climbed in my understanding of grassfed meats and how to most thoroughly use them. It represents four years of studying cookbooks from the Great Depression and World War II eras, of experimenting in the kitchen, of writing and rewriting until I could outline a new cuisine for my family that minimizes our waste and maximizes our nutrition and our enjoyment. I hope you will find it useful in your own kitchen, and that you will join me in what has now become a permanent learning path, of perpetually exploring how we can use our food choices to heal the planet and change the course of history in this country, and how, ultimately, each of us can find the delicious trail to going *a long way on a little*.

CHAPTER ONE

Meat and Planet Earth

t heralds a new era in food writing when the first chapter of a cookbook entails a discussion of ruminant animals' digestion, the methane it produces, and discourse about carbon dioxide, nitrous oxide, fossil fuels, grass, manure, cow farts and sheep burps. Like it or not, these are essential elements of the making of your food, so step into your barn boots and spend a little time mucking through the details so you understand how they impact quality and flavor. After all, it can leave a bad taste in your mouth when what you eat causes ecological havoc. Food is infinitely more pleasurable and tastier when you know you are eating in harmony with nature.

I am settling at my desk to write this book following another winter of speaking at a series of sustainable farming conferences. For about two decades, attendance at these events has been predominantly composed of seasoned farmers and ranchers seeking better ways to improve their livestock operations. But, in recent years, an ever-growing population of twenty-something environmentalists has packed the rooms to talk about raising their first batch of pastured chickens, study pasture management, learn how to butcher a lamb, hone their charcuterie skills, and figure out how to grill a tasty steak. They dress simply, carry refillable water bottles and travel mugs, wear their hearts on their sleeves and exude love for community, culture, livestock and the earth through their every pore. While a phalanx of dooms-dayers despond about our impending fossil fuel shortage and climate crisis, I can't help but be filled with hope at the joyous energy this next generation is breathing into our country's new sustainable future.

What strikes me about so many of these folks is that they eat meat and have reconciled the intertwining of their lives with livestock and their love of the earth.

Not long ago, that seemed an unlikely balance to strike. Those who professed love of the earth and all her creatures presumably eschewed burgers, protested animal agriculture, relished their plates of beans and rice, and hogged the blanket bearing the environmentalist label all to themselves, leaving us livestock farmers out in the cold.

Today, my world, admittedly insular, is populated by fellow farmers, earth-lovers and meat-eaters. Vegans don't spend much time at my market stall perusing the steaks and sausages, they don't come out to the farm to visit, and I don't think very many of them live here in pasture-rich Schoharie County, where you can't throw an adzuki bean without hitting a livestock farmer. Thus, I had become lulled into the mistaken belief that the "all-meat-is-bad" banners were finally being sent to the compost pile.

Not so.

Livestock Farming: Scourge of the Planet or Victim of Bad Research?

In 2006, the UN Food and Agriculture Organization released a study which concluded that livestock production is responsible for more greenhouse gas emissions than all forms of transportation combined. Celebrating this proclamation, the group People for the Ethical Treatment of Animals (PETA) outfitted a Hummer with a driver wearing a chicken suit and a banner decrying meat as the top cause of global warming (*NY Times*, Aug 29, 2007). Around that time, I was invited to speak about the virtues of grassfed livestock farming at a permaculture gathering in New York City, and my hosts and I were bombarded with protesting e-mails and phone calls. The anti-meat campaign was (and still is) alive and well.

The ecologically concerned animal rights activists have an important campaign. In raising issues about animal welfare within the food system, they have helped to improve the overall treatment of livestock. They've pushed those of us who choose to farm to learn to speak more clearly about how and why we do what we do. They've helped the public understand that "factory farming" is inherently a violation of the earth, the spirits of the animals, and the humans who are imprisoned by the system. Whether intentionally or not, they've created a space where small-scale sustainable pasture-based farmers can come forward and make our voices heard. And it is important that we do that, because oversimplified arguments about the role of meat in the future of our planet still abound.

The damning 2006 FAO study is a prime example of such misinformation. This report accuses the livestock industry of generating 18 percent of all greenhouse gas emissions, including carbon dioxide, nitrous oxide and methane. When I first perused the study, I assumed it was wagging a finger at the big ol' mean factory

What do all the labels mean?

Free range. The *free-range* label implies that animals had *access* to an outdoor area. While some farmers use the term to describe grassfed meats, technically this term does not mean they were raised on pasture, or that grass was included in their diet (although it may have been).

Grassfed. In October 2007, the USDA released an official definition of grassfed, saying that it is meat that comes from animals whose diet is derived solely from forage, with the exception of milk consumed prior to weaning (forage includes grasses, forbs, cereal crops in the pre-grain state, and browse). According to the USDA, animals must have continuous access to pasture during the growing season. Hay, haylage, baleage, silage, non-grain crop residue and other roughage sources also may be acceptable feed sources. This is a "voluntary standard" for production, wherein livestock producers have the option of requesting official USDA verification of their grassfed claims. This definition has stirred some controversy among farmers in the movement, and some organizations are working to come up with a new, more strict, definition of *grassfed* and to have an inspection and certification program similar to what has been adopted by the organic industry. Naturally, I have some opinions on these issues, discussed in my editorial, "Some personal thoughts on the grassfed labeling issue," in the next sidebar.

Pasture-raised or pastured. Pasture-raised animals are animals that are raised on pastures, of course. The definition includes meat and dairy products from grassfed ruminants like sheep, cows, buffalo and goats. Unlike "grassfed," however, the term also applies to animal products from omnivorous critters like pigs and chickens. Pigs and chickens need an additional protein source in their diets, which is often administered in the form of grains containing soy or fish meal. They cannot subsist on grass alone, although they will happily graze, and they will get a portion of their protein requirement in the form of bugs as they hunt about. So while the definition of pastured or pasture-raised can apply to grassfed ruminants, the term grassfed cannot apply to all pastured animals. Technically, pigs and chickens are said to be pastured or pasture-raised, and lamb and beef are grassfed (although the terms are often mistakenly used interchangeably in casual conversation).

farms; *certainly* they weren't implicating us earth-loving small-scale farmers. After all, it is widely known that small-scale farming benefits local communities socially and economically, that they safeguard the local food supply, that they protect land resources for the future. But our green halos were about to be tarnished.

The culpability for "livestock's long shadow" was laid squarely at the feet of *small farmers*, who were accused of generating nearly three-quarters of that 18 percent. Further, the authors suggest that for the solution we look to fossil-fuel-dependent, un-natural, inhumane and ecologically devastating "intensive" (a.k.a. "factory") farming systems for our meat supply: "The principal means of limiting livestock's impact on the environment must be to reduce land requirements for livestock. This involves intensification of the most productive arable and grassland used to produce feed or pasture." In this case, intensification refers to industrialized food production methods. This is a fascinating conclusion, considering that small farmers have been raising livestock for the last 10,000 years, and the current spike in greenhouse gas emissions really started getting underway following the industrial revolution.

How could these diligent analysts come to such counterintuitive conclusions? British researcher Simon Fairlie, author of *Meat: A Benign Extravagance*, has assiduously dissected and reexamined the study's findings to illuminate its problems and biases.

For starters, small-scale livestock farmers world-wide took the statistical blame for problems that were tangentially related to them. In the FAO study, 34 percent of the total emissions ascribed to livestock farming were attributed to the release of carbon dioxide from the devastating deforestation of the Amazon. And that is being counted as an "extensive" (a.k.a "small-scale") farming practice. But roads are being cleaved into the Amazon not by farmers, but by international logging interests seeking exotic woods for the export market. Once the roads are opened and the loggers have cleared the trees, reports Scott Wallace for *National Geographic* in his story "Farming the Amazon," an unsavory mix of characters move in and wreak further damage. While farmers and ranchers are part of the mix, so are miners, squatters,

Some personal thoughts on the grassfed labeling issue.

In October 2007, after heated debates and fierce commentary, the USDA adopted an official definition for grassfed meat. It is a touchy subject for many of us farmers.

Let me explain by first offering a little history behind the grassfed movement. The word *grassfed* was originally a term that farmers came up with years ago in an effort to explain to the public how we raise our animals. There wasn't an official council on the subject, it just became a word that we all adopted. And typically, those of us who were bandying it about had an unspoken agreement about what it meant. Grassfed implied that our animals ate grass from our fields in the growing season, and the stored grass during the winter or dry season in the form of hay, haylage, baleage, or stockpiled forage (extrathick nutrient-dense grasses left on the stem in the field).

We *graziers* opted for this system of raising ruminants (sheep, cows, goats, buffalo, etc.) for

ethical, environmental and economic reasons. It was generally accepted practice, therefore, that we didn't use hormones or antibiotics. They didn't make sense in our small farming system. It was also generally accepted that we conscientiously managed our pastures for optimum grass nutrition, and that our animals were rotated to fresh fields regularly. We didn't put a bunch of fancy stickers on our meat packages making these claims. If you wanted to know what was or what wasn't in the meat, you just asked us. That's because, if you were buying this meat, you *could* ask us, because you knew us. Even if you couldn't make it to the farm or opted to do mail order, you could still call up the farmer and get your questions answered. Relationships and trust were the foundation of the movement.

Then, wouldn't you know it, this whole grassfed thing took off. Organic and natural foods are currently the fastest-growing segment of the food industry; and grassfed has been the fastest-growing segment of the organic/natural sector. Grocery store chains, middlemen, and brokers clamor for a piece in this suddenly hot market. In an effort to protect

speculators, land thieves and hired gunmen. Destruction of the Amazon rainforest is thus a complicated picture. As Fairlie points out, climate analysts typically don't allocate emissions from deforestation and burning to "livestock," as it is not the primary cause of the problem. Certainly, your local small-scale pasture-based livestock farmers have nothing to do with destruction of rainforests; on the contrary, by providing locally raised, grassfed meat, they help obviate the demand for imported beef.

Next, the 2006 FAO study considers nitrous oxide from livestock farming, which it estimates to be 5.5 percent of total greenhouse gas emissions. In his analysis of the findings, Fairlie argues that even if we got rid of all the world's livestock, this figure would not disappear. The human race would still require food, and growing it requires nitrogen, an essential nutrient whether the crop is homegrown tomatoes or industrially grown broccoli. Without livestock, rather than getting nitrogen from manure or blood meal, we'd simply have to find it from other sources. Indeed, since we'd be removing a major source of protein from the human diet, we'd need to increase alternative protein crops in order to meet that global demand, which would, in turn, require further nitrogen. "In short," Fairlie explains, "many of these nitrous

consumers (and perhaps, as some believe, to create market opportunities for more nefarious industrial practices), the USDA came up with the definition of "grassfed" explained on the previous page. Most of us think it's pretty lousy. It fails to forbid the use of antibiotics or hormones. It potentially permits a number of practices that we traditional graziers wouldn't condone.

In the USDA's defense, they could never adopt a definition that will please all of us small, locally-based farmers. We are independent, free-thinkers. If we wanted to live by rules and definitions, we'd have chosen a different line of work. Formal definitions, whether it is the simple USDA definition, or a more rigorous definition offered by an independent certification agency, introduce a cumbersome layer of bureaucracy to our lives. They imply certification, and that implies more sophisticated record-keeping (at considerable cost), inspections (at considerable cost), and membership fees to certifying associations (again, at considerable cost).

If you personally know your farmer, you can ask him or her how the food is grown. You can visit

the farm and see the animals for yourself. Those official stickers, stamps, certificates and definitions mean very little. Stickers, stamps, certificates and definitions enable the industrialized food model to prevail, because they are a substitute for a direct relationship with a farmer or small growers' cooperative.

Many of us who founded this movement want to be connected to our consumers. And, as a result, we do not participate in the certification debates. So, if you mail order your grassfed meat from a broker rather than a farm or farmer-run cooperative, or if you buy it from a big-chain grocery store, certifications will have some meaning for you. But, if you show up at your farmers' market and notice that a local producer has some grassfed meat in his or her cooler without a certification sticker, be proud to do business with them. That farm is rebuilding a community where relationships, conversation and trust matter more than a technocrat's label.

oxide emissions are a consequence not of livestock, but of an agricultural ecology in which livestock plays an incidental role, *transmitting* rather than *creating* nitrogen" (p.169).

The final greenhouse gas to consider in the livestock and climate debate has garnered the most popular discussion: the gastric emissions, that is to say, the belches and farts from ruminant animals (cows, goats, sheep) that generate methane. Enteric fermentation, the conversion of forage in the rumen, is a natural part of the digestion process for ruminant animals. Because their diet is naturally high in roughage, grassfed animals will belch more than their factory-farmed counterparts (the process is unnaturally suppressed in factory farming due to a coating of slime that grain-feeding causes in the rumen). This belching has generated some negative publicity for ruminants, which is unfortunate (and incredible!), since they and their ancestors have been roaming the earth for eons, long before there was a methane problem. Moreover, there are undoubtedly other sources of methane that merit more serious discussion: oil, coal and gas consumption and landfills being among the most salient.

Nevertheless, the FAO study reports that livestock flatulence is largely responsible for 5.4 percent of global greenhouse gas emissions. If we were to make eliminating methane emissions our new eco-goal, we would need to eliminate all ruminant livestock. Simon Fairlie points out that we would also need to remove horses from the global population, since they produce their fair share of methane as well. That's not a popular idea among folks who are counting on horses as part of the back-up plan for transportation when fossil fuel supplies run out.

Similar to the discussion above about nitrous oxide, eliminating ruminants would require that we consume even more grains, legumes and vegetables to compensate for our nutrient deficit. As it stands now, Fairlie reports that *plant crops* are responsible for 17 percent of current man-made methane emissions, a number which would surely climb once we'd removed cows, sheep and goats from the surface of the planet. Even then, the methane numbers still won't be wiped out, because the wild ruminants, such as deer and bison, would remain and perhaps increase in population.

The discussion of methane and livestock is a case of reductionist thinking at its worst: "There is methane in the atmosphere; methane causes global warming, therefore methane is bad. Livestock produce methane, therefore livestock farming is bad." In fact, methane is essential to life, and it comes from lots of things. Any of us who burp or discreetly pass gas and then divert blame to the family dog as he digests some table scraps is aware of this. Trees and insects also release methane. Wetlands, those bastions of ecological wealth, emit even more methane than livestock. At the same time, they purify our water supply, help to mitigate both floods and droughts, rejuvenate their surrounding ecosystems, provide critical habitat and important support for life on earth. Responsible grass-based livestock farming, as we'll see in the coming pages, offers similar benefits. Finger wagging about cattle belches and sheep farts simply will not resolve our planet crisis. Indeed, by misdirecting critical debate, it could even make matters worse.

Apparently, there are other researchers at the FAO who concur. Not everyone who works at the UN Food and Agriculture Organization is of the same mind as the authors of *Livestock's Long Shadow*. Unfortunately, their research didn't get the same amount of press. Notably, however, in 2008, another FAO study was released titled *Belching Ruminants, a Minor Player in Atmospheric Methane*. A subsequent study released in 2010, *Livestock in the Balance,* refutes the questionable 2006 report and also reexamines the important contributions of small-scale livestock farming.

Perhaps one of the most interesting twists in the livestock-methane debate is the role ruminants can play in *reversing* climate change. In 2009, *Scientific American* released a story about a biogeochemist, Katey Walter, who has been studying methane emissions from Alaska's thawing permafrost. Methane is emitted wherever organic matter ferments, which is exactly what happens when arctic permafrost, packed with dead plant and animal matter, begins to thaw as a result of climate change. In other cases, permafrost has frozen above deep pockets of gas called methane hydrates, which can be released into the atmosphere when the permafrost melts. Walter is concerned about the cyclical threat she is studying. Climate change, caused by increased greenhouse gas emissions, is causing the permafrost to melt. The melting of the permafrost causes dramatic increases in the release of methane into the atmosphere, further exacerbating the climate change.

Not surprisingly to us grass farmers, one solution mentioned in the story is to *increase* the number of herbivores in the Arctic landscape. But wait! Don't they burp and fart? "Snow is like a down jacket that keeps the ground warm," explains Walter in the *Scientific American* story. "As the activity of animals compresses the snow or removes it through their foraging, the cold winter temperatures can penetrate deeper into the ground and keep the permafrost frozen." Katey Walter is not the only person considering this option. In Siberia, a 625-square-mile tract of land has been fenced off and stocked with moose and Yakutian horses with this idea in mind. This brings us to a very important point in our discussion: the role of grazing livestock in healing the earth.

Farm Animals as Eco-Heroes

Around the same time that *Livestock's Long Shadow* cast aspersions on all livestock farmers, Michael Pollan's *Omnivore's Dilemma*, supported by the earlier research of one particularly devoted journalist, Jo Robinson (creator of the online panacea of grassfed research, eatwild.com), balanced out the harsh accusations, highlighting how small-scale, locally-based pasture farming truly was the exception to the negativity surrounding meat production in an industrialized food system.

Whereas factory-farming production methods rely on monoculture cropping for feed, graziers have discovered that diversity is their key to success. Properly managed grazing restores wildlife habitat and increases diversification of plant species. It has been shown to restore native plant populations, stimulate vegetative cover of stream banks, expand wetlands and extend the seasonal productivity of the pastures. Further, locally produced grassfed and pastured meats require a mere fraction of the fossil fuels needed to produce and distribute factory-farmed meat. In contrast, the average piece of conventionally produced food travels 1,300 miles before it reaches a plate, a figure that does not include additional fossil fuels required to grow the grain that is shipped to the livestock, much less the fossil fuels required to operate a factory farm at an efficient economy of scale.

Ollie came on to our farm as a feeder calf destined for beef. Dad liked him so much, he lived with us for 10 years as our lead steer (he helped us load and herd cattle).

Improving soil fertility, replenishing our planet's rapidly dwindling topsoil and providing nutritious food with the minimum of polluting inputs and fossil fuels are justification enough for grass-based farming. But there is something else that happens each time pasture is grazed—*carbon sequestration*. This is a process whereby grazing animals partner with the planet to help pull excess carbon dioxide from the atmosphere and fix, or bind, it into the soil. When the animals munch on the pasture grasses, the roots of the plants are stimulated to rapidly grow more leaves. Once they do their job, the old roots are shed into the soil, nourishing the soil microbes. In turn, this process restores elemental nutrients into the soil. This cycle repeats throughout the grazing season. Each time these shed roots feed the microbes, organic matter, which is 58 percent carbon, is generated. The total amount of carbon in our planet's ecosystem is actually finite. Thus, each time the amount of carbon bound into the earth's soil increases, the balance of carbon in the atmosphere is reduced. That's a pretty decent bonus package for eating meat that tastes better and is better for you.

But Isn't Meat an Inefficient Use of Farmland?

For many, carbon sequestration, habitat and soil fertility are all sound justifications for enjoying a juicy grassfed burger. But there are still a lot of folks who contend that raising livestock is an overly intensive use of land and resources. More people could be fed, they postulate, with grains and vegetables than could be fed with meat.

Not in West Fulton, New York, where my family farm lies. Of our 160 acres, less than 40 of them are on flat land. The rest of the land has an estimated 30 percent grade, rendering crop production not only difficult, but ecologically irresponsible owing to the increased likelihood of soil erosion. Add to that the extremely short growing season (temperatures can dip below freezing eleven months out of the year), and it is easy to understand why farmers in our neck of the woods have sustained themselves on a meat-based diet for hundreds of years. Grass doesn't require cultivation, and the animals do all the harvesting for us.

Assumptions about the most efficient use of farmland must consider the topography, the climate, and the soils of the farmland in question. Some land is ideally suited to crop production, but for other land, livestock grazing is clearly the best option for food production.

The argument that using farmland for meat animals is inefficient is based on something that we aggies call *the conversion factor*, that is, the ratio of grain required to generate a pound of gain on an animal. When you feed grain to fish, for instance, the conversion factor is about 1.25 to 1; that means that for every 1.25 pounds of grain product you feed to a fish, the fish will gain one pound of growth. The conversion for chicken is 2 pounds of feed per pound of gain, or 2:1. Pork is 4:1. When you get to the red meats, the ratio skyrockets. Figures on this vary, but lamb is estimated to require roughly 8 pounds of feed per pound of gain, and beef 9 pounds of feed.

Sounds inefficient, all right—but there's a gap in this analysis. *Ruminants are specifically designed to eat grass, not grain.* Consequently, the grain to gain ratio for a pastured ruminant is 0:1. Ruminants, the red meats animals, thrive on what our fields naturally produce—they harvest perennial grasses that reseed themselves every year, and their manure returns nutrients to the soil. In a pinch, they also eat things like straw and corn stalks—which means they have the magical capacity to convert wastes from vegetable crop production back into food.

Okay, maybe I've got you willing to concur that the herbivores aren't so hard on our ecosystem. Indeed, when living on grass alone, improving soils, aiding in carbon sequestration and converting crop waste into food, they are probably even beneficial. But what about those non-ruminants—pigs and chickens?

Omnivores and Sustainability

Human beings aren't the only omnivores. When it comes to farm animals, pigs and chickens, like people, lack the digestive capacity to live solely on grass (though both pigs and chickens eat quite a lot of it). That is why you will typically see beef and lamb labeled as *grassfed*, while pork, poultry and eggs are labeled as *pastured*.

Anyone who has raised children and dogs simultaneously can attest to the value of having an unfussy omnivore living in the household ecosystem. While the ultra-fastidious may stand aghast, dogs are handy beasts when it comes to cleaning up beneath highchairs and prewashing the dinner dishes. They happily eat what we eat. They reduce our overall waste (or at least reclaim it), degrease the kids' fingers and faces, verify that our couches and beds are suitably comfy for human use, and offer us never-ending love and devotion.

Now imagine replacing your dog with a meat-producing omnivore. Okay, maybe you won't let the pig or laying hens up on the couch. But they're still good to have around. They (like dogs) eat the scraps that your family discards, and then convert it into future meat (unlike dogs, at least in our culture!) Amazing! That is why, in the good ol' days, families often raised a pig out in the backyard, and flocks of chickens were regular features even in urban neighborhoods.

In today's modern farming system, pigs and chickens require grain. If they are pastured, they will also eat grass, which significantly diminishes their grain requirements and makes them a far more sustainable alternative to factory-farmed pork and poultry. Given the opportunity, however, they will also root through whatever you discard in your compost, clean up all your kitchen and table scraps and, in the case of a voracious sow, maybe even eye pocketbook dogs or small children with thoughts about dinner.

In all honesty, I believe that pastured animal products are not entirely sustainable in the current pasture-based farming system. Yes, I am admitting that, even on my beloved family farm, I see a sustainability shortfall. Buying feed for these critters is not a practice we will be able to continue indefinitely as grain prices rise and petroleum becomes more scarce. Each year it gets more and more costly for us to produce pork and chicken for our customers. Ironically, they are the most expensive

What about the "Meat is Murder" issue?

Aaah. That's a great question. I've spent most of my life involved with animal agriculture, and there is one thing I have learned for certain: No matter how many explanations I put forward regarding the importance of livestock production in the ecosystem, no matter how many claims I advance about the nutritional importance of grassfed and pastured meats, everything I say will ring hollow to those who are averse to the killing of animals for meat—period.

Any vegetarian who has ever challenged face-to-face the morality of a livestock farmer (especially one in the sustainability movement) can probably report receiving a touchy and defensive retort. This is because—contradictory as it might seem—we choose this vocation because we *like* animals, not because we enjoy killing them or see slaughter as a means to a profitable end.

Sadly, those of us who make our lives farming have become a national cultural anomaly. From my own view from my family's land, it seems that mainstream American culture harbors incongruous ideas about life and death. The culture has a quirky tendency toward adulation of life and abhorrence of death. When daily life is directly tied to the ebbs and flows of nature, as they are in agriculture, one cannot help but observe that life and death are forever in service to one another. We cannot have one without the other. We nurture the newborn livestock, and we process the ones that are ready for market. We harvest one crop, we plant seeds for another.

All beings, whether human or other-than-human, have an inherent right to a natural existence in the world, and each has a way to contribute to the welfare of the greater whole. Inevitably, a time will come when every life must give way to sustain balance on the earth. On the farm, there is an understanding that nothing we eat to sustain ourselves comes without the sacrifice from another living being, be it animal, plant or microorganism.

As farmers with mosquito bites up and down our arms will attest, not even we are exempt from the on-farm food chain. Thus, we take all food, whether it is a hamburger, a pork chop, a carrot, a spoonful of yogurt or a slice of an apple, in moderation and gratitude. Nothing is eaten without an understanding of the sacred life and spirit that created the nourishment, and the ecosystem that was required to sustain it.

I understand that no amount of explanation of the hows and whys of grassfed livestock production will convince the person who is opposed to killing animals that eating meat is okay. Unless they or someone they love manifests a nutritional need that can only be met by animal proteins, they may never cross that philosophical divide. Life on my family's farm and in my own household is informed by and is reflective of the concerns of such folks. I remain thankful that those perspectives and questions come forward, and will continue to learn from them; I will also continue to take nourishment from the livestock we raise on the farm.

meats for us to grow, but owing to government policies that subsidize grain-based factory farming, the average American consumer expects these meats to be the cheapest. Sooner or later there will have to be a reconciliation of costs, and pork and poultry are going to become cost-prohibitive for everyone.

But that doesn't mean folks won't continue to enjoy pork and chicken. It just means that, rather than delegate the raising of pork and poultry to farmers, more non-farm families will have to pick up some of the task. Households all around the country are discovering the ease and delight involved in this transition as backyard chickens enjoy a comeback in these hard economic times. Kitchen scraps are fed to laying hens in the country, the suburbs and the city. In exchange they offer daily eggs and nitrogen-rich droppings for the garden. At the end of their lives, they offer up themselves for the soup pot. They are generous and beautiful creatures.

So are the pigs. While scraps from one family alone may not be enough to sustain a feeder pig, multiple families can team up for some backyard hog-rearing. If these families wanted to expand production, they could cooperate with nearby schools or restaurants and ask for food scraps. A few years ago, my suggestion of this idea seemed preposterous. As folks watch their food prices climb and their savings dwindle, suddenly these ideas seem more reasonable.

What bears mention here (and will be discussed later in the pork chapter) is that raising these animals on food scraps means they are not vegetarian. In order to get their protein fix on the farm, pigs and chickens eat bugs in the grass and are fed grain that typically contains soy or fish meal. They are not given meat or other animal products. Recent fears about bovine spongiform encephalopathy in cattle (also known as BSE or mad cow disease) have resulted in government mandates that all livestock, whether herbivore or omnivore, become vegetarian. While farmers must currently adhere to that (highly problematic) regulation in order to grow food for retail consumers, the pigs and chickens have not read up on the laws. They will take whatever scraps are offered, grow fat on them, and produce delicious, safe meat for the family that keeps them.

Thus, it is true that not everything about today's grassfed livestock operations is absolutely perfect for future production. What makes us sustainable is our ability and willingness to analyze these issues, and our commitment to modify our practices to meet the demands of the present day and to amend them further as the future requires. As our landfills reach capacity and our ability to transport food across the country (or the world) diminishes, and as our need to rebuild fertile soils increases, even in urban settings, pigs and chickens are going to become ever more important to our sustainability. There will always be a few pigs and chickens running around pasture-based farms. But, hopefully, we'll start seeing them in schoolyards, backyards and city parks as well.

But Will There Be Enough Grassfed Meat to Feed the World?

That is an excellent question that many researchers and analysts, myself included, have devoted their energies to resolving. Here's my answer:

I don't know. But it doesn't matter.

Sound callous? I don't mean it that way. I just think that it is not the question we need to be asking. Instead, we should be asking, *how can we empower each community to feed itself,* and *how many more people could we be feeding in each of our communities?*

If we change the patterns of meat production by enabling small diversified farms and homesteads to grow food on a widespread sustainable scale, we enable more communities to feed themselves. When communities are locally food-secure, they are better able to sustain themselves in the event of fossil fuel shortages or natural disasters.

If we can change the current patterns of meat consumption in the United States, we can feed *a whole lot* more people with sustainable community-based resources, helping to achieve that all-important community food security.

I spend a lot of time working in the cutting room at Sap Bush Hollow Farm preparing meats for our thrifty, socially responsible, environmentally aware customers. But, even in that setting, I am deeply troubled by the tremendous waste I observe. Mountains of bones, rich in nutrients, are sent to the compost pile because customers will not take them. Fat, the concentrated source of those wondrous omega-3 fatty acids and conjugated linoleic acids and fat-soluble vitamins, goes unclaimed as well, as do the organ meats, the feet, the heads, the tails. The offal (viscera) and trim are wasted as well, as government regulations forbid us from recycling these nutrients through our omnivorous farm animals, who would be delighted to eat them.

Once I recognized the waste in the slaughterhouse, I began to see it everywhere around me: in customers who confessed to throwing out their leftovers; in the amount of food I find growing mold in my own refrigerator; or in the accumulation of off-prime cuts overlooked in our retail inventory. A sustainable meat-based diet must reach beyond burgers and sirloins to include a rich broth as a base for some fresh vegetables, rendered fat that replaces costly olive oil for cooking, a head boiled down to make head cheese for cold lunches, and scraps of meat that can be paired with vegetables to generate another new feast.

Those who ponder about whether there is "enough food" are missing the bigger picture. Corporate America can generate lots and lots of calories, as the American obesity epidemic has shown. Anyone can walk the streets of our country and understand that it is possible to overeat and nutritionally starve. But if we address the *quality* of our food, I believe we'll quickly discover that we need considerably less *quantity* of food. If we need less, there will be more to go around. Further, rather than fixating on generating more calories to feed the world, I worry about how much we waste of the animals that are giving their lives up for our nourishment. If we focus on that issue—how to make each animal fully count—the theoretical concerns become practical.

By changing the way we work with our food, and empowering more people to grow it, we can gain a whole lot more nourishment than most realize is possible. We can lower our food costs and still pay a fair wage to the farmer. We can simultaneously feed more people and push the factory farming system toward the obsolescence it deserves. Best of all, we can learn to use the treasures we have been overlooking to generate new abundance.

FOR FURTHER READING:

S. Fairlie, *Meat: A Benign Extravagance*, Chelsea Green Publishers, 2010.

H. Steinfeld *et al*, "Livestock's Long Shadow," FAO, 2006.

FAO/IAEA, "Belching Ruminants, a Minor Player in Atmospheric Methane," joint FAO/IAEA Programme: Nuclear Techniques in Food and Agriculture, 2008.

FAO, "Livestock in the Balance," *State of Food and Agriculture Report, 2009.*

S. Simpson, "The Peril below the Ice," *Scientific American,* Summer 2009.

CHAPTER TWO

Getting Good Meat

To celebrate my mom's birthday four years ago, we drove ninety minutes to the best restaurant in our region, one of the first to put exclusively local foods on their menu. I was excited to turn the cooking over to someone else for a change, and we promised to allow ourselves anything we wanted off the menu.

I chose the grassfed, locally-raised rib eye steak.

It came to the table beautifully presented—perfectly seared on the outside, and thinly sliced across the grain to show off the rosy pink inside. The chef evidently understood the importance of *never* overcooking a steak.

Relishing my moment of indulgence, I picked up knife and fork and dove in … only to discover that it had the texture of shoe leather. The worst part—the steak came from *our* family farm.

Needless to say, the whole meal was ruined for Mom and me as we puzzled over which beef had been sold to the restaurant. Realizing that they had only purchased half the animal, we quickly finished our meal and headed home so I could seize a rib eye from the half that still remained in our inventory, and cook it up. To our relief, the steak was delicious and tender.

Therein lies the riddle. If the steak in the restaurant was from the same animal and went through the same processing, and it wasn't overcooked, why should it have been so tough?

The answer, in this case, has to do with the cooking method. While it is important never to overcook a piece of grassfed meat (we'll discuss that further), it is also important not to cook it too *fast*, which causes the muscle fibers to contract too quickly and become chewy. The restaurant steak had been prepared by running it through a super-hot restaurant-grade broiler. The steak I cooked had been prepared by searing it directly over the coals on my home grill, and then finishing it with indirect heat. Both steaks were seared on the outside, both were rosy pink on the inside, but only one of them was tender.

In this particular story, the crime of the chewy meat was committed by the cook. But there are actually three phases in the grassfed food production chain where quality and flavor can be impacted: **on the farm, during processing,** and **in the kitchen**. When we better understand the production of grassfed meat and what ensures its quality, the easier it will be to find a farmer and/or butcher who can reliably provide top-notch meat and, hence, the more success we'll have in the kitchen.

On the Farm

Arguably, the single most important on-farm factor that will contribute to meat flavor and quality is the contentment of the livestock. When animals are able to live a calm and happy life, they do not release excess stress hormones (such as adrenaline) that negatively impact the flavor and quality of the meat. Thus, if you visit a farm and see the sheep grazing or lying down and dreamily chewing their cud, the cattle are calm, the pigs are occupied rooting around rather than biting each other's tails, and the chickens are busy scratching the ground and hunting for bugs, you can be pretty certain the animals are happy.

Once you have ascertained the animals' contentment, the next thing to explore is pasture management. Even if you don't know the first thing about grazing management, it is relatively easy to see if a pasture is managed properly. Look at the grass; if it looks like a golf course, with blades cropped close to the ground, perhaps with a few bare patches, even if it is green, it is not a suitable pasture for properly feeding ruminant livestock. It may be a fine playground to allow cattle and sheep to roam about in the sunshine, and it may look lovely, but if that is the state of the pasture, chances are that the meat you are getting isn't truly grassfed. When the grass isn't long enough for a ruminant to get a mouthful with every bite, it cannot provide enough food for the animals to gain weight properly. If the animals you are seeing on those barren pastures appear well-fed and fattened, then it is likely that the farmer is grain-feeding them once you go home. An ideal pasture should be lush, with thick grasses that are so dense it is impossible to see the soil. You shouldn't be able to pad lightly through the field as though you were traversing a lawn at a croquet tournament; you should have to lift your feet high enough to step clear of the thick forage.

Good pasture management is critical to ensuring beef tenderness. For beef to be tender, cattle need to gain one to two pounds per day for every day of their life. In order to do this on grass, they need to be on well-managed pastures when grass is available, and on high-energy hay, haylage, grass silage, or stockpiled forage (long, nutrient-rich grasses left growing that can be grazed through the snow) throughout the winter. Beefers that have gained one-half pound or less per day will be less tender. Thus, if you see cattle out grazing on something that (were it not for the cow

Delicious dairy cows, magnificent mutton and succulent sow

To ensure optimum tenderness, grassfed and pastured animals are typically processed at a relatively young age. But if flavor and marbling is more your bailiwick, then the older the animal, the better. The best pot roast I ever tasted came from a ten-year-old dairy cow, the best pork chop from a three-year-old sow, and the best "lamb" chop from a two-year-old ewe.

In this country, the conventional meat industry has conditioned us to believe that tenderness is the single most important factor when evaluating meat quality. It is easy to understand why: tenderness is the easiest factor for the industrial food system to control. Flavor in meat comes from careful stewardship (something that doesn't happen in the factory-farm setting), and juiciness comes from successful cooking at home. Thus, if our only expectation of our meat be that it is easy to chew, the factory-farm system won't disappoint.

But once you've gotten hooked on grassfed meat and learned to anticipate that your meat should have discernible texture and genuine rich flavor, some of the finest cuts of meat will come from older farm animals.

I'm not the only person who thinks meat from older animals is delicious. While doing research for *The Farmer and the Grill*, we spent a considerable

amount of time feasting on beef and analyzing flavor with a number of grill aficionados around the Argentine countryside, famous for its grilling traditions. The best grilled short ribs I ate came from a four-year-old steer, and the asador who served it assured me that the older the animal, the tastier.

When we taste meat, very often we confuse texture with flavor and juiciness. If a piece of meat is tender, we might swallow it barely masticated and assume it is good, without fully sensing the flavor and detecting each element separately (tenderness, flavor, juiciness). The beef connoisseurs in Argentina who favored older meat were recognizing the spectacular flavor that comes only with age, and they expected to chew their food in order to savor it.

If you still have an aversion to less tender meat, but wish to experience a more intensely rewarding meat flavor, seek out a dairy farmer and persuade him or her to part with one of the chuck roasts from his own private stock of dairy cow beef. Find a sheep farmer who will sell you a cut of shoulder from an older ewe, or a pig farmer who will willingly part with a picnic roast from a sow. (All dairy and breeding livestock eventually reach an unproductive age and must be culled from the herd.) Each of these cuts can be braised slowly, which breaks down the connective tissue, making the meat tender. While these cuts may require a little extra cooking time, the abundant flavor is worth the wait.

pies) might be confused for a golf course, chances are the meat is either not grassfed, or it will not be as tender as you are hoping.

Ruminants aren't the only critters who appreciate good-quality lush grass for grazing. Chickens benefit from it, too. As omnivores, they cannot get all their nutrition from grass, but thick, lush pasture provides a bountiful buffet of insects, which are critical to their health, happiness and continued weight gain with as little grain as possible.

Because pigs tend to root up any ground they are on, farmers may not always offer them their best pastures. Hogs' gift for rooting makes them ideal cultivators, however, and they do impressive work when turned out on brushy areas that the farmer may want to convert to grazing land. They may also occupy a designated "pig pasture," which the farmer allows them to root up and turn over to their hearts' content. On Sap Bush Hollow Farm, my dad stores the farm compost in the pig pasture, giving them the added pleasure of putting their rooting behavior to good use by turning the compost pile for us. They may also be turned out to harvest wild apples, acorns or other fodder in the fall. Thus, a pig pasture, adorned with its inevitable (and critical) mud wallow, needn't be as lush and green as a cattle or sheep pasture.

Shelter and shade at different times of the year are also important for animal welfare and, therefore, meat quality. To minimize their stress levels, cattle, sheep, chickens and pigs all need access to shade in the summer months. In the case of chickens, this is typically a portable man-made shelter that enables them to escape both the heat and predators. For cattle and sheep, who have thick hair coats to protect them from the elements, adequate summer shelter can be a patch of forest edge where they can get out of the noonday sun. Pigs can make use of forested hedgerows as well, but often benefit from a more formal structure, such as a sturdy hut. In the winter, access to protection from the elements is important for keeping stress levels down and maximizing weight gain, ensuring top-quality flavor and tenderness.

The final on-farm tenderness factor is the age of livestock at processing. Typical age of grassfed cattle at harvest is eighteen to twenty-four months. Lambs are generally between eight and thirteen months old, and yearling lamb is between thirteen and twenty months of age. Pigs are usually around five to eight months, turkeys are around four or five months, and meat chickens are eight weeks. That is not to say that fabulous meat cannot be had if the animals are processed outside of these time frames (see sidebar 2-1). These are simply typical ages where the optimal balance of flavor, tenderness, meat and fat are generally achieved. Older animals may have more fat and higher flavor, but less tenderness; younger animals may have less fat, less meat, and milder flavor, but more tenderness.

Transport, Harvest and Processing

Once the farmer has spent weeks, months or years giving these animals a good life on excellent-quality pastures, it is important to protect the quality of this investment through conscientious transport, harvest and processing.

No matter how inured we may have become, harvest time is always sad for us livestock farmers. While slaughtering livestock is the means by which we are able to feed ourselves and generate enough money to live, generally it is not the reason we choose this business. Livestock farmers select their vocation because we like animals, not because we like killing them. But the farmer who assiduously attends to the various elements of livestock slaughter will help minimize stress to the livestock, and hence to himself/herself during the hardest part of this business.

Farmers generally agree that the least stressful way to process an animal is to "field dress" it. One minute the animal is grazing peacefully in its pasture, and the next a sharpshooter instantly kills it with a well-placed bullet. The animal has no awareness of what is happening, and therefore no opportunity to be traumatized. Unfortunately, any meat processed this way is illegal to sell (we just keep it for ourselves). With the exception of limited numbers of poultry, the meat that is made available for retail sale must usually be transported to an off-site federally inspected facility for slaughter and processing.

To do this successfully, the farmer must have a dedicated loading area with a system of gates and/or chutes that enables the livestock to find their way onto the truck as easily as possible. Loading must be calm and quiet, with no arm flailing, poking or shouting to coerce a reticent critter onto the truck. The drive on the livestock trailer should be calm and steady, as should the unloading and the actual slaughter.

Once the animal has been slaughtered and eviscerated, the carcass needs time to age in order for naturally occurring enzymes to break down the meat and make it tender. For chickens and turkeys, a few hours in a cold chill tank and overnight in a cooler prior to freezing or cooking is adequate aging time. Pigs and lambs require about a week of hang time in the butcher's cooler, and beef requires about two weeks.

There are two primary methods for aging meat: wet aging, and dry aging. In the **wet aging** process, the predominant industrial meat practice, slaughtered animals are immediately cut into primals (the major body sections), then vacuum-packed in plastic bags and immediately shipped out to their retail sales destinations. This method is extremely convenient, because the big meat packers do not have to store the meat in order to age it. There is less shrinkage loss to air-drying; this enables

True/False:
"Grassfed is leaner. Therefore it is chewier."

False. Grassfed is *variable*. It is *not* leaner. I have seen meat go across our cutting room table at Sap Bush Hollow that graded standard (devoid of marbling), select, choice and prime (highly marbled). Grassfed animals can fall into any of these categories owing to natural variability in the seasons, farming ecosystems, management practices and genetics. It can all turn out tender if we've seen to the tenderness factors on the farm, during transport and processing, and in the kitchen.

To clarify (and repeat myself), grassfed meat is *variable*, but factory-farmed meat is *consistent*. Consistency and homogeneity are values of the industrial food system, where it is presumed that unskilled cooks need to generate large quantities of foods that are always identical in taste and appearance. This reliance on standardization has become a substitute for time and skill, and this paradigm has come at a cost to our environment, our biodiversity, and to the animals that are moved through the process.

We must learn to embrace variability in grassfed meat. If the grassfed movement strives to capitulate to the "consistency" so lauded by the conventional food system, our harvest season for grassfed animals becomes limited, we run the danger of mechanically supplanting natural pastures to monoculture species in order to standardize marbling and flavor, and we risk diminishing the diversity of our genetic stock, which jeopardizes the security of our food system. A goal of "consistent" grassfed beef in terms of flavor and marbling is a bad idea. We'd be jeopardizing the natural environment to suit unnatural demands, rather than cultivating the very best of what nature has to offer us.

a maximum yield. It is easy to ship the product long distances. And it is a faster and cheaper process. Just about all meat available through conventional grocery stores is wet-aged.

By contrast, most grass farmers elect to have their meat **dry aged.** In this process, whole carcasses are hung in a temperature- and humidity-controlled cooler for about one week for lamb and pork, and for ten to twenty-eight days for beef. As it hangs, moisture evaporates from the carcass, concentrating the flavor. The longer the meat hangs, the more concentrated the flavor will be. Within the first two weeks, natural enzymes also tenderize the meat.

Dry aging makes meat more expensive. A small-scale butcher's cooler space is very limited, and care must be taken to not over-pack it. Without proper air circulation, spoilage can occur. Thus, the butcher's "through-put," or productivity, is limited. This incurs cost that is passed along to the farmer. The farmer takes another loss with the meat because of reduced yields: during dry aging, a beef typically loses 10–15 percent of its carcass weight, which means there is less product for the farmer to sell. The benefit of higher-quality meat and superior flavor, however, is a tradeoff most of us happily accept.

Quality in the Kitchen

The final phase where we must safeguard meat quality is in the kitchen. To handle the meat successfully, it is helpful to understand the criteria by which most of us unknowingly evaluate meat palatability: **juiciness**, **flavor**, and **tenderness**.

Juiciness. On occasion, I've had customers approach me at my market after buying a piece of meat, complaining that it was dry. Rather than reimbursing their money, I give them a copy of one of my cookbooks. The juiciness of a piece of meat is completely in control of the cook; the farmer and the butcher have no control over whether your chops or roasts are dry. Prolonged exposure to high heat causes the muscle fibers to contract and squeeze the juice out of meat. Lower the flame if you are worried about losing juice. Also, be aware that once meat crosses 145 degrees Fahrenheit as an internal temperature, the muscle fibers are going to contract at an accelerated rate, drying the meat out super fast. If you are working with meat that might be lean (grassfed meat may be lean or fatty, depending on myriad variables), lower the heat.

Flavor: Okay, prepare yourself for a bit of a rant . . . Flavor sensitivity has by and large been obliterated from the American palate. Most Americans, accustomed almost exclusively to eating processed foods, are limited to discerning little more than sweet, sour or salty. Often they are simply unable to detect genuine flavor or, if they do, they may find its presence alienating. Hence, most Americans seem more fixated on the texture and tenderness of a cut of meat, rather than the overall taste.

Grassfed beef flavors are more assertive. The beefiness comes through as a result of the dry-aging, and it has the added dimension of a mineral flavor profile and a sweet herbaceousness that can only come from animals who've feasted on nutrient-rich pastures. Grain-fed beef tends to have a flatter, indistinct, almost nonexistent taste. When we ran blind taste tests with factory-farmed meat in our home kitchen, we discovered that we couldn't differentiate between factory-farmed beef, lamb and pork. The wet-aging probably has a lot to do with this, because there was no concentration of the inherent species-specific flavor. Moreover, the added dimension that would have come from the pastures was also missing from the flavor profile.

Quite often, when a person does have a well-developed palate, he or she will find that grassfed meat is the *only* acceptable meat. Factory-farmed meat simply tastes repugnant to them. This is important to think about as we seek to create a more sustainable world for our children. If we help them cultivate an acute sense of taste, I believe that they will instinctively make food choices that are ideal for our planet.

Tenderness: Contrary to my frequent diatribes about flavor, tenderness is probably the single most important factor in determining meat palatability among most Americans. In the meat industry, tenderness is evaluated using a Warner-Bratzler scale, which calculates a tenderness score based on a shear force value. Basically, the amount of force required to shear a half-inch core of a meat sample, reported either in pounds or kilograms, is the tenderness score. The lower the score, the more tender the meat.

Researchers at Texas A & M University found that if beef loin samples (one of the most tender primals) had shear values of seven pounds, they could be 95 percent confident that consumers would find their steaks to be "slightly tender." At Cornell University, I ran some tenderness tests with meat scientist Denny Shaw, using top round roasts, cuts that came from one of the *less* tender primals on the beef. We ran shear tests on wet-aged certified factory-farmed angus rounds, and on dry-aged grassfed rounds.

Why does grassfed cost more?

I have said unequivocally that grassfed meat is better. It is lower in calories, it is a source of omega-3 fatty acids and conjugated linoleic acids, and it is higher in vitamins. We've learned that, because of the way it is grown and the way it is aged, it will have significantly better flavor. We know the ecological benefits: increased biodiversity, soil fertility, carbon sequestration, greater food system security. It is also better for our local communities. Responsibly managed pasture-based farms help to ensure that our waters are clean and pure, our lands are productive and therefore protected, our viewsheds are kept beautiful, and our food economy is built around a regenerative agricultural practice. But, however clear the advantages of what you are buying may be, many still question the higher cost of grassfed meats. In truth, the price the farmer asks for providing all these benefits allows his or her family to garner a modest living wage. The real question to ask is, "Why is the factory-farmed meat so cheap?"

Faster growth rates. Raised naturally on top-quality seasonal grass, a steer will have a rate of weight gain of about 1–2 pounds per day. With the use of grain, growth hormone implants and antibiotics, CAFOs (Confined Animal Feeding Operations, a.k.a. "factory farms") are able to achieve a rate of gain on their cattle of 3 or more pounds per day. At this artificially accelerated rate, a grain-fed animal can be ready for market in almost half the time and at any time of year.

Economies of scale. Industrial agriculture relies upon economies of scale that simply aren't workable on a grass-based farm. Fattening a steer on corn is relatively easy. I'm no nutritionist, but by comparison it seems that fattening a child on corn chips is pretty easy, too, but we all know that this is not a nutritious option. Industrialized cattle operations often use computer programs to automate the grain feeding until the steers are trucked to meat packing houses that slaughter thousands of cattle daily from all over the country. By contrast, grass-based agriculture is more of an artisan craft. Farmers need to vigilantly monitor their animals' health and the condition

The average score for the factory-farmed beef was 6.27 pounds. The average score for the grassfed beef was 5.20 pounds. The grassfed was more tender every time.

How could this be, when grassfed has the reputation of being tougher? The answer is simple: all of the tenderness and quality factors discussed above were properly addressed. On the farm, the animals and pastures were well handled. The harvest was gentle and quiet; the carcasses were dry-aged. And, finally, the cook handled the meat properly (yes, I cooked it).

And what is "proper" when it comes to grassfed meat cooking, you ask? Excellent question. Indeed, you have an entire volume before you on just the subject, plus my two previous cookbooks! However, despite the hundreds of recipes covering that content, there are really only three rules you need to remember:

1. Use lower flames. Lower flames (or oven temperatures) help to hold juice in a piece of meat, and they slow the contraction of the muscle fibers, preserving

of their pastures to ensure optimum nutrition and weight gain. The livestock will be ready for market at all different times, and the grazier needs to be able to assess their market-readiness through daily observation. Further, they will be processed by small-scale, local, independent butchers, one animal at a time.

Ecological havoc. Factory farms pollute community water supplies, wreak havoc on rural economies, expose employees and livestock to abusive working and living conditions, and generate excessive greenhouse gas emissions owing to their long-distance transport and their reliance on petrochemical-intensive monoculture feed cropping. These costs are passed along to society ("externalized"), and therefore aren't reflected in the price of the cheap meat in the grocery store.

You pay for the factory meat twice. Through the Farm Bill, U.S. taxpayers pay approximately $20 billion per year in direct payments to industrial farm operations, over one-third of which goes for the production of feed grain. Much of this subsidy is paid out to vertically-integrated industrialized meat

production companies who, as a result, are able to feed their livestock grain for less than the price of growing it. There are no such subsidies or price supports for small-scale farmers raising animals on sunlight, water and grass, and who are raising animals that take longer to bring to market, require more care and skill, and demand none of the grain subsidy support. Those pasture farms raising pigs and poultry do use grain, but they are typically too small to vertically integrate their grain production. Thus, they cannot gain the same advantage from these grain subsidies.

Grassfed meat costs more, not only because it is better, but because you are directly paying the true cost of its production rather than an artificially low price supported by tax-funded subsidies. However, as you'll learn in the coming chapters, you don't have to go broke to afford it. When we pay the authentic price for wholesome food, we must learn how to use it prudently. If we minimize our kitchen waste and make use of the animal products that are most often overlooked, we'll discover that it is relatively easy to afford good-quality meat when we make a little go a long way.

the meat's inherent tenderness. Lower cooking temperatures also reduce the risk of overcooking meat.

2. Monitor internal temperatures. Reliably-sourced grassfed meats needn't be cooked to the high "doneness" temperatures recommended by the USDA. Experts at the USDA reflexively direct us to make sure our meat is well-done, fearing exposure to food-borne pathogens. Of particular concern is *E.coli*, a potentially harmful, even deadly, bacteria. But empirical evidence suggests this hazard is greatly reduced in grassfed meats. Not only is *E.coli* found in much lower numbers in grassfed meat, it is also a strain that is still susceptible to our bodies' natural defenses; even when *E.coli* is found on grassfed meats, it rarely survives our own digestive acids. Further, it is unlikely to be the virulent strain of *E.coli* 0157:H7, because that strain evolved in the unnaturally acidic stomachs of factory-farmed beef, owing to the artificial practice of grain-feeding.

That said, how rare you eat your meat is a personal choice. As much as I might like to, I cannot dictate how you run your kitchen. However, I do advocate for internal doneness temperatures that are significantly lower than the USDA guidelines. The end results are tastier and easier to digest. The chart below contains two different internal temperature ranges: one lists USDA recommendations, and the other shows my own preferences. If the internal temperatures I suggest are too low for your comfort, feel free to use the USDA guidelines, unless I'm coming to dinner!

Meat	Suggested Internal Temperatures for Grassfed and Pastured Meats	USDA Recommended Internal Temperatures
Beef, Bison	120–140° F	145–170°F
Ground Meat	160°F	160°F
Veal	125–155°F	145–170°F
Lamb and Goat	120–145°F	145–170°F
Pork	145–160°F	145–170°F
Chicken (unstuffed)	165°F	165°F
Turkey (unstuffed)	165°F	165°F

3. Understand which cuts require which cooking methods. The appropriate cooking method will depend on where a piece of meat comes from on the animal. If it comes from a muscle that works hard, such as the shoulder, the neck or the shanks, it will contain more connective tissue, which can make meat tough. Connective tissue typically requires liquid in order to break down. Thus, the hard-working cuts require moist-heat cooking methods, such as braising, barbecuing (which is different from grilling), smoking, slow-cooking or stewing. The exception to this is a cooking method I'll discuss again in Chapter four, called Super Slow Roasting, where a normally tough cut of meat is tenderized by low temperature cooking that "braises" the meat in its own contained juices.

By contrast, the muscles that do the least amount of work produce meat that is the most tender, such as the tenderloin and most steaks and chops. These cuts actually need exposure to heat to firm the muscle fibers enough for you to enjoy them. Thus, steaks, chops and most roasts from the loin or legs of grassfed and pastured animals require dry-heat methods, such as grilling, pan-frying or roasting. Recalling the story from the opening of this chapter (and cooking rule number one, above), remember not to make that flame too intense!

Finally, I'd like to suggest minimizing the use of intense seasonings and heavy sauces. As a cookbook author, I always feel a bit strange offering this advice when my job is to generate over a hundred different ways for cooking meat. Obviously, the way to do that is through the seasonings. However, if you'll leaf through the coming pages, you'll notice that the basic cuts—the chops and the roasts—are almost always presented with minimal seasonings: salt, pepper, perhaps some garlic and herbs. Minimizing seasoning will highlight that inherent flavor I talked about earlier, which is truly delightful to experience. If you are new to grassfed meat, I encourage you to make use of the simpler recipes first so that you can experience that taste. Then, as you progress to the more sophisticated recipes, your palate will be able to detect the flavor of the good meat you are working with and pair seasonings that enhance, rather than obscure it.

CHAPTER THREE

Bones and Fat

In writing this chapter, I am asking you to change your life. Admittedly, that statement may seem a tad ambitious for a cookbook. After all, this volume was marketed to you as a collection of recipes, not a self-help book. But as far as I'm concerned a cookbook, done well, is the ultimate self-help book. It presents a theory for engaging with the most fundamental need in life, *food*, and then offers pages and pages of pragmatic techniques to implement the theory in the form of recipes.

One of the core theories behind this book is the incorporation of bones and animal fats into your family's diet on a daily basis. That's right, *daily basis*. My hope is that, upon your reading this, your kitchen will no longer be a room that sees action only prior to mealtimes. I hope it becomes a place where a pot of broth is nearly always simmering on the stove, where rendering fat becomes a normal activity. I want you to think nothing of grabbing a pat of lard to grease your pan when sautéing vegetables; of heating cups of bone broth to give your family extra stamina and nourishment with their breakfast (truly, a mug of bone broth pairs much better with a plate of eggs than a cup of coffee); of grabbing a jar of demi-glace from the refrigerator and, in less than twenty minutes, turning a few spoonfuls of it into a satisfying pot of soup for supper; or of turning your kitchen into a craft center, making long-lasting soaps, healing salves, even candles, for family and friends.

Sustainable livestock farming cannot happen without sustainable livestock consumption. We must make use of *all* the gifts an animal provides when we take its life. Quite often, when we think of using the whole animal, thoughts turn to the organ meats—scrambled eggs and brains, stuffed hearts, fried liver. These are certainly good attention-getters, but the American public long ago spurned these nutrient-rich foods, branding them as distasteful, even horrifying. Thus, when an earth-conscious chef places them on the menu, he or she becomes something of a superhero for reintroducing them to our culture. While it is important to our nutrition to incorporate organ meats into our diet, the choice to eat a little heart or liver, while admirable, is not the ecological panacea that some epicureans may claim. Truth be told, organ meats make up only 3–5 percent of an animal's carcass. The bones and fat, however, which are usually discarded in the cutting room and off the dinner plate, make up a whopping 20 percent of a beef carcass, 24 percent of a hog carcass, and 30 percent of a lamb carcass. That's serious waste of the animals, and serious waste of a valuable resource.

In their landmark book *Nourishing Traditions*, authors Sally Fallon and Mary Enig explain that broth contains the minerals of bone, cartilage, marrow and vegetables in the form of electrolytes, ionic solutions that are easily assimilated into the body. It also contains proteinaceous gelatin, which supplies the diet with hydrophilic colloids, a property that attracts your stomach's digestive juices to the surface of cooked food particles. This is especially beneficial for folks suffering from intestinal disorders such as hyperacidity, colitis and Crohn's disease. Moreover, when meat seems too expensive to serve daily, the gelatin in bone broth helps the body fully utilize any other proteins that are ingested. And, of course, there are the time-tested remedies of good broth for relieving the symptoms of colds, flu, myriad forms of gastroenteritis, and even bone injuries.

Good, clean animal fats are equally vital to our health. They are our source for the all-important fat-soluble vitamins A, D, E and K, which enable us to absorb minerals from our food. They make our food nutrient-rich, enabling us to go longer periods of time without getting hungry and, write Fallon and Enig, they provide the building blocks for cell membranes and hormones. Knowing this, one can't help but wonder why these fats were mistakenly vilified through "anti-fat" campaigns. In 1950, prior to our national fat phobia, lard consumption in this country was 12.6 pounds per person per year. By 1997, the figure was down to 2.3 pounds per person. And, guess what: obesity rates have *increased* dramatically in that time. Further, I can only assume there must be a connection between this extreme dietary change and emerging vitamin D deficiency illnesses in America.

Beyond their nutritional value, bones and fat are flavorful. The world's greatest cuisines are not founded on prime cuts of filet mignon or porterhouse steaks, but on the prudent use of the 20–30 percent of the animal that is frequently discarded in this country. Incorporating bones into our diet through meat broth and demi-glace immeasurably improves the flavor of our soups, stews and braised dishes. Potatoes fried in tallow have an unmistakable, delicious flavor, pie crusts made with lard are flakier, cookies made with a combination of lard and butter are softer. Better still, there is a cost savings. At a few dollars per pound, bones are one of the cheapest ways to incorporate the health benefits of grassfed meats into your family's diet. As for the fat, grassfed butter in our area ranges from $7 to $12 per pound. Olive oil can run anywhere from $8–$16 per pound. Yet the fats from our grassfed beef, lambs and pastured pigs sell for less than the price of a tin of Crisco. If our farm inventory of bones and fats gets out of hand, we've even been known to give them away for free. When it comes to stretching your food dollars and eating in harmony with the earth, I cannot think of a more important dietary change than working these two ingredients into your diet.

Meat Broth

MAKES 5 QUARTS

4–6 pounds bones (Beef, lamb, pork or poultry bones will all work. Ideally, some will be raw and some will be precooked from previous meals, which will add a rich color and flavor dimension.)

2 large carrots, scrubbed and unpeeled, cut into large chunks

3 ribs celery, cut into large chunks, leafy tops included

2 medium onions, halved (if onions are clean, feel free to leave the skins on)

8 quarts water

3–4 sprigs fresh thyme

3–4 sprigs oregano

3 cloves garlic, crushed but not peeled (optional)

1 medium tomato, coarsely chopped (optional)

Any other leftover vegetables you might have lying around (except maybe for lettuce)

2 teaspoons coarse salt

3 tablespoons red wine vinegar or cider vinegar (or 1–2 cups wine)

ESTIMATED CARBOHYDRATES:
Carrots: 13.8 g
Celery: 3.57 g
Onions: 20.54 g
Thyme: 0.59 g
Oregano: 0.69 g
Garlic: 2.97 g
Tomato: 4.78 g
Red wine vinegar: 0.12 g
Total carbohydrates per recipe: 47.06 g
Total carbohydrates per 1 cup broth: 2.35 g

Here is a classic broth recipe that diligently makes use of the standard repertoire of ingredients. Remember: the list of ingredients in this case is really only a suggestion. Improvise with what you have on hand!

Add all the above ingredients to a very large stockpot. Allow all the ingredients to rest for 30 minutes to one hour before turning the flame under the pot to medium. This step will enable the acids in the vinegar or wine to draw the minerals from the bones.

Bring the mixture to a boil slowly, skimming off any froth that rises to the surface. Reduce the heat to low, and slowly simmer the broth for a minimum of 12 hours. The longer you cook it, the richer it will be. If your cooktop will allow a slow, steady simmer and you will be nearby, consider allowing the mixture to slowly bubble, with the lid in place, for about three days straight, adding water as necessary.

If you don't feel secure leaving the pot untended overnight, simmer the stock all day, or while you are home. Turn it off before going to bed or leaving, then resume simmering it when you are around once more. Be vigilant about adding additional water if the fluid level gets too low. (Personally, if the cooking is interrupted for less than 12 hours, I leave the stock unrefrigerated on the stove, as I know it will be returned to a high enough temperature to kill food-borne pathogens. If this practice makes you uncomfortable, simply refrigerate your stock between simmer sessions.)

When the final simmering is complete, pour the broth through a sieve to strain out all the bones, vegetables and herbs.

Pour the broth into jars, or return it to the stove top and simmer once more, uncovered, until the volume is reduced to about 5 quarts for a more concentrated broth. Chill for several hours. Ideally, once it is cold it should be mildly gelatinous. A layer of fat will have solidified on the surface.

Remove the fat layer prior to using. If you like, it can be saved and used to sauté vegetables and meat. Once you have skimmed the fat off your broth, store the broth in the refrigerator or freezer.

The elements of broth

The Italians have an expression, *"Tutto fa brodo"*—"Everything is broth." Nearly anything you can find in your kitchen can be added to a broth to enrich its flavor and nutritional value. The five basic elements are bones, vegetables, herbs, acid and water.

Bones. Naturally, this is the most essential ingredient. Many mistakenly believe that only the marrow bones make good stock. While marrow does add lots of flavor and minerals, a variety of different bones is ideal. "Knuckle" bones (leg joints) and oxtails are a great source of gelatin; neck, rib and other meaty bones add color and flavor, as does that leftover bone from Friday night's rib eye steak, or the remains from Sunday's leg of lamb. For an extra calcium boost, I often save my egg shells and add them to the pot, as well. All the meat, bones, shells and vegetables that have simmered in the pot for hours will be strained and discarded from the complete broth; virtually all of their nutritive value is in the liquid.

Be creative with your broth. A pure beef or chicken stock is lovely, but some of the most exciting dishes result from mixing varieties of bones, using anything that is on hand—a few lamb bones, perhaps a chicken carcass, mixed in with some pork chop leftovers, all create a dynamic broth flavor. Long ago in France, cooks had *la bouilloire éternelle*—the "eternal kettle," a large pot that never left the fire. If a piece of chicken was taken out, then new chicken was added; the same with a piece of beef or a slab of pork. Whenever broth was removed from the kettle, water was added, yielding a steady supply of delicious stock and a ready boiling medium for cooking meats for feasts. Incorporating all different kinds of meats when making stock eases your work (you don't need to sort your leftover bones according to species), reduces waste and creates complex flavor. Most of the recipes in this book call for "meat broth." Only on rare occasion does a dish explicitly require chicken broth. I've discovered that all the different mixes of bones will taste equally delicious, so there is no need to make extra work for yourself.

Vegetables. Leftover cooked vegetables can go into the pot, along with fresh veggies, and even those errant odds and ends that might be on the cusp of spoiling. Open your produce drawer and be generous to your stock—broccoli about to flower, carrots gone floppy; peppers, tomatoes and onions growing soft on the kitchen counter. Set aside carrot tops and tips for the broth, as well as the woody ends of broccoli stalks, or the outer leaves of cabbage that may be a bit marred from the garden. Don't be fussy, as they will all be discarded (hopefully composted) once their flavors and minerals have been captured by the broth.

Herbs. Herbs, whether fresh or dried, add both flavor and nutrients to your broth. However, if you don't have any on hand, don't let that stop you!

Acid and water. Once the vegetables, herbs and bones have been added to the stock pot, fill it with water, then pour in an acid, such as vinegar or wine. Use as little as a tablespoon of vinegar, or as much as a few cups of wine, depending on your taste. Allow the stock to rest for 30 minutes to an hour prior to cooking, so the acid can draw minerals out of the bones and into the broth. It will also enhance the flavor.

Bring the stock to a medium boil, then turn it down to a simmer, keeping it covered at all times. The longer you can simmer your stock, the better. Twelve hours will be sufficient, but seventy-two hours will be even better. If the pot gets too low on liquid, add more water. Once it is complete, you have a wonderful base for cooking soups, for cooking rice, grains and legumes, for a hot drink, or for braising those other luscious (and inexpensive) bone-in cuts of meat so often overlooked: shanks, necks, oxtails, bone-in shoulders, or ribs. To magnify the intensity of the flavors and save storage space, you can take the broth to the next level by reducing it down to a demi-glace (see sidebar).

Shannon's Meat Broth

6–8 pounds pre-roasted bones

1 large onion

1 large carrot

4 cups mixed greens

½ cup cider vinegar

8 quarts water

ESTIMATED CARBOHYDRATES:

Onion: 14 g

Carrot: 6.90 g

Mixed greens: 6 g

Cider vinegar: 1.11 g

Total carbohydrates per recipe: 28.01 g

Total carbohydrates per 1 cup of broth: 1.4 g

The above broth recipe is perfect if you are the type of person who likes to do things right. I'm the type of person who likes to do things simply. In my family we drink almost two gallons of broth per week, in addition to what we use for soups, stews, braises and sauces. That means I'm making broth year-round, a couple times per week, and I don't always have all the necessary ingredients on hand. In the interest of working with what's almost always in my fridge, here's a shortened version.

I prepare it using the same instructions as *Basic Meat Broth*.

A note to the frugal: To help my vegetables dollars go farther, I don't always use first-quality produce in my broth. I save the onion skins and ends from other dishes I've cooked, as well as the carrot tops and tips, and the woody stems and ribs of the greens. I collect them in a bag all week, and by the time I'm ready to start a new batch of broth, there's usually plenty of vegetable scraps to make this recipe.

Demi-Glace, Shannon-style

If asked to select the single most important ingredient in my kitchen, in the absence of broth, it would have to be the little glass tub of demi-glace that jiggles in the back corner of my refrigerator. Admittedly, I use the term casually. A French chef would likely have me strung up by my toes for awarding this wondrous gelatinous blob such a name. By definition, a true demi-glace is a brown sauce made by first concocting an *espagnole* sauce, then blending it with an *estouffade*, or clear soup, then making a reduction. My version of a demi-glace (if you will allow me the privilege of the term) is simply done by making a huge vat of broth, straining it, then bringing it to a rolling boil and reducing it down to just a few cups, monitoring often to make sure it doesn't scorch.

Ordinarily, with broth I chill the liquid, then skim off the fat that settles on the top. I do *not* do this with demi-glace. Since it will be kept for a long time in the refrigerator, I allow the fat to solidify over the surface, which seals it for longer storage in the manner of a *confit*. If I discover a little mold growing on the surface, I spoon it off, add it to the compost, then bravely move forward with dinner preparations. I don't let gastronomic rules, pretensions and regulations interfere with my quest for a good repast.

While a jury of French chefs may convict me of gastronomic heresy, I have every faith that an army of French housewives would scurry to my defense, brandishing their stockpots and wooden spoons with intimidating valor. Most French chefs aren't trying to get a preschooler to stop playing with the kitchen knives, another daughter to learn her addition and subtraction, fixing lunch, scheduling meat-processing dates on the telephone, *and* turning

out a serviceable demi-glace all at the same time. I daresay that, if faced with those daily challenges, most French chefs would probably choose the Shannon Hayes "semi-demi-glace" technique as well.

Demi-glace, made in my slovenly way, is an amazing ingredient. It concentrates all the benefits of a rich, nourishing broth down to a small, easy-to-store volume that can then be reconstituted to add flavor and nutrients to nearly all my dishes. When the kids are swapping winter flu germs, I add 3–6 tablespoons of my demi-glace to 2–3 cups of water to make them a lovely clear stock to sip (taste and add more demi-glace or water until the strength is to your liking). I toss a few tablespoons into the water when preparing beans, rice and legumes. I use it to make gravies and pan sauces even richer. Reconstituted in water, the demi-glace performs just like meat broth, and spares a lot of space in your refrigerator and freezer.

A little pot of demi-glace, preserved beneath a layer of fat, can come to the rescue of nearly any meal.

Roasted Marrow Bone Gremolata

SERVES 8

6–10 pieces of beef or veal
    marrowbones, about 1 pound

1 cup minced fresh parsley

1 cup finely crushed walnuts

2 cloves minced garlic

2 tablespoons lemon zest

Coarse salt, to taste

Carrot sticks, endive leaves,
    Parmesan Parsley Almond
    Crackers (Chapter 8) or toast
    points, for serving, optional

ESTIMATED CARBOHYDRATES:
Parsley: 3.8 g
Walnuts: 16.04 g
Garlic: 1.98 g
Lemon zest: 1.92 g
Total carbohydrates per recipe:
    23.74 g
Total carbohydrates per ¼ recipe:
    2.97 g

Marrow bones have long been regarded as a rich indulgence by epicureans-in-the-know. While they were spurned in recent years for their high fat content, grassfed enthusiasts eager to find sources of those healthful grassfed fats are rediscovering them. According to Ramiel Nagel, author of Cure Tooth Decay, *bone marrow from grassfed animals can also be very helpful in re-mineralizing teeth, reversing tooth decay. Nagel explains the marrow contains stem cells that help to rejuvenate the body and promote bone growth. Whether true or not, roasted bone marrow is delicious, especially when served as part of this fresh parsley and walnut gremolata.*

Preheat the oven to 375°F. Set the marrow bones in a cast-iron skillet and roast 20–25 minutes, until the marrow starts to bubble. Some bones might take longer to roast than others, depending on their size. If necessary, remove the smaller bones earlier. Otherwise, the fat will render out and the remaining marrow will get chewy.

Remove the bones from the oven. Allow them to cool while you combine the parsley, walnuts, garlic and lemon zest. Using a butter knife or a small spoon, scrape out the bone marrow and add it to the gremolata. Mix well. Season to taste with the coarse salt. Serve as a dip with carrot sticks, spooned onto endive leaves, or spread on the Parmesan Parsley Almond Crackers (Chapter 8) or on toast points.

Leftovers: Save these bones, as well as any bones from roasts and steaks, and add them to your next batch of broth. We keep a large plastic bag in the freezer for collecting whatever bone treasures remain after meals.

What happens after the bones are cooked?

If we want American culture to become truly sustainable, then we need to do more than reinstate our local farmers. We need local craftspeople, too, who can create useful things from our locally-derived resources. Our ancestors let nothing on an animal go to waste. The skin was used for clothing and shelter, the bone and horn were used for tools, and tendons and intestines were used for weapons and tools and bindings. Teeth, claws, hair and feathers served as ornaments; stomachs, bladders and skins were containers. Not all of these materials would be used in the same way today, of course, but the skilled craftsperson can find many uses for our animal resources besides taking up space in a landfill or compost pile. The bones, once they've been boiled, can be used for myriad things: buttons, crochet and knitting needles, sewing needles, pipe stems, dice, game pieces, electrical bushings and washers, buttons, napkin rings, goblets, and handles on silverware, tools, and even umbrellas.

Basic Lard Pie Crust

MAKES 1 (9-INCH) PIE CRUST

1 cup flour

½ teaspoon fine salt

3 tablespoons cold butter

3 tablespoons cold lard

2–4 tablespoons cold water

ESTIMATED CARBOHYDRATES:
Flour: 92.27 g
Butter: 0.03 g
Total carbohydrates per recipe:
92.3 g
Total carbohydrates per ⅛ recipe:
11.54 g

This handy recipe is worth committing to memory. It works for pies, tarts and quiches alike, enabling you to prepare a number of dishes without having to crack open a cookbook.

Sift together the flour and salt. Using a pastry blender, cut in the butter and lard to make a crumbly mixture. Add just enough water to make the dough just hold together, and mix. Wrap the pastry dough in plastic or place it in a glass container with a lid and chill 1 hour before using.

Choosing the right fat

Pork fat isn't the only source of cooking fat. Suitable fat can be rendered from beef and lambs, too. Each of the animal fats has different properties that make them better suited to different kitchen activities. Lard, which is less saturated, is much softer, making it easier to work into pie crusts, corn bread and biscuits. French cooking has long instructed us to pair our shell bean dishes with lard. Examples include Potée Alsacienne, a dish of red kidney beans cooked with fresh pork and sausages, or cassoulets, which require a bounty of duck, goose or pork fat. A country paté is dry and crumbly without a generous coating of lard spread thick on top, like a buttercream frosting. Although its smoke point (see sidebar) is lower than tallow or lamb fat, lard is a better choice for frying any foods that you might want to serve cold, such as fried chicken or homemade potato chips. When frying foods in tallow or lamb fat, you will want to enjoy them hot, as the highly saturated fat may leave a coating on your tongue if you eat them cold. Lard, on the other hand, will not do this. So if you plan on taking cold fried chicken on a picnic, opt to fry in the lard. If you want fresh hot doughnuts that don't smoke up your kitchen and cause grease to cling to your hanging pots, use tallow or lamb fat. (But if you're going to enjoy them cold, lower the cooking temperature and work with lard). Tallow and rendered lamb fat are also good for suet cakes for your birds, for searing steaks at high temperatures, as well as some traditional British treats like Christmas puddings and mincemeat.

Mexican Cracklings

SERVES 4

1 pound pork skin, cut into 1-by-4-inch strips

Water

4 teaspoons baking soda

1 teaspoon coarse salt, plus more for finishing

Tabasco or Mexican bottled hot sauce (optional)

ESTIMATED CARBOHYDRATES:
Tabasco: 0.04 g per 1 teaspoon

This recipe comes directly from my all-time favorite meat writer, Bruce Aidells, from his cookbook, Bruce Aidells' Complete Book of Pork *(Ten Speed Press). It is the best recipe I've found for working with straight pig skin and fat. Bruce convincingly argues that these cracklings taste best with a few cold beers. I'm inclined to have them with a martini and some sour cream dip.*

Put the pork skin in a large saucepan, cover with the water, and add the baking soda and salt. Bring to a boil over high heat, then reduce the heat to maintain a simmer and cook until the skin is soft, about 1 hour.

Preheat the oven to 425°F. Remove the skin and discard the water. Pat the skin dry and put fat-side down on a rimmed baking sheet. Bake for 20–30 minutes, or until the skin is bubbling and crisp.

Remove the skin from the oven and let cool slightly. Serve warm with a sprinkling of salt and hot sauce to taste. Store in an airtight container in the refrigerator for up to 1 week.

Leftovers: Cracklings can be diced up and used in cornbread, or they can simply be reheated. Place them fat-side down on a baking sheet and put them in a 350-degree oven for 5–10 minutes.

Fats and smoke points

One of the wonders of cooking with animal fats is that they have high smoke points. The smoke point is the temperature at which a cooking fat starts to break down and give off smoke. Smoke points are important considerations when frying, because super-hot fat can make a kitchen stinky, suffocating, and deeply annoying to spouses and children, causing a considerable strain in family relationships (I've learned this from experience). Also, once fats exceed their smoke points, they contain so-called "free radicals," molecules that have been linked to increased risks of cancer. Whereas the smoke points for extra-virgin olive oil and butter are 320 and 350 degrees respectively, the smoke point for lard is 370 degrees, and tallow is a whopping 420 degrees. Because of their higher smoke points, lard, tallow and lamb fat are ideal choices, superior even to butter, for searing your meats on the stove top.

There's more fat than what's on the kidneys

The over-selective breeding of certain farm animals to meet industrial agriculture production requirements has resulted in modern livestock breeds that have practical-minded grass farmers rolling their eyes: the large-frame Angus that simply cannot finish on a season's worth of grass, the Holstein dairy cow with extreme milk production and an impractically short lifespan, enormous turkeys incapable of natural breeding. Among the most senseless to me, however, is the lean pig. Once prized for their ability to produce bountiful quantities of fat, old-style pig breeds were largely forgotten when Americans decided that animal fats needed to be removed from their diets. Today's small-farm renaissance has restored our interest in the older, more thrifty, heritage breeds, and locavore customers are enjoying some extra trim on their pork chops and a little more marbling in their hams. Still, I hear of too many butchers discarding copious amounts of back fat, and of too many farmers cursing the waste of feed if the fat-to-muscle ratio on the pig is too high. While some folks are beginning to reclaim the leaf fat, that layer of pure white fat surrounding the kidneys, too many people are allowing the bounty of back fat to go to waste.

In my opinion, the reputation of back fat has been unfairly tainted by food snobs. Admittedly, epicureans can be thanked for being the truth-keepers over the last 50 years when America neglected the fatty pig. In the face of rampant fat-phobia, they bravely maintained that lard made the best biscuits and the best pie dough. But too many of those who presumed to be "in the know" spurned the farmers' offering of back fat for the production of lard, claiming that it had more impurities and that it did not render as efficiently. That is all true. However, when I package up the leaf lard on one of our pigs, it amounts to about 1–4 pounds, depending on the leanness of the pig. When I bag up the fat closest to the meat, the back fat, even after leaving a full half-inch of trim on the pork chops, I often find myself with another 10 pounds of bounty. (Note: The fat closest to the skin does not render easily, and is best used for barding lean meats or in sausage-making.)

Some have argued that rendering back fat results in a porkier-smelling lard than the leaf fat, which makes it useless for cooking anything other than savory dishes. However, after some experimentation, I've discovered that much of the pork scent is eliminated as long as the fat is not rendered for too long.

I've used back fat lard to sauté vegetables and make biscuits and cornbread, all of which will tolerate a little savory pork flavor. However, in an effort to see if I could extend the use further, I experimented with it for more delicate operations, where a hint of pork flavor would be most unwelcome. In a carb-and-refined-sugar frenzy (I know, we're not supposed to eat this way . . . but if I don't provide occasional treats at home, my husband will start running around to bakeries behind my back), I used the lard to fry my Halloween doughnuts, melted it for my daughter's birthday cupcake batter, cut it into my Thanksgiving pie crusts, and even baked ginger snaps and chocolate chip cookies for my girls on a few rainy nights. The doughnuts were splendid. The cupcakes were moist and deeply chocolaty, without revealing a trace of their porcine origins. The pie crusts, made with a combination of butter and lard, held up to manipulation and were flaky, tender and flavorful.

And then there were the cookies. I tried them first with pure lard. Not so good. But then, I changed the recipe to use half butter and half lard. They were positively transformative, the best cookies I've ever made. Lard keeps the cookies soft and chewy; butter gives them deep flavor. With pride, I presented them to my most discerning cookie-loving friends and family. They have been awarded the distinction (among my biased fans) of "the best chocolate chip cookies ever." And the secret lies in the lard.

How to render fat

Once you've acquired a nice bag of fat (I like to work in volumes of 5–9 pound batches), settle into your kitchen and cut it into small pieces, ideally less than one inch long, taking care to discard any fleshy or fibrous spots. Toss the good bits into your pot until it is no more than ⅔ full. It has been said that heavy pots (such as cast iron) are best for rendering, but I've come to favor a lighter, good-quality stainless-steel pot. It is easier and safer to carry, and clean-up is a breeze.

Many books instruct you to layer your fat on top of water to prevent it from burning, but I've found this step unnecessary. Most modern stoves have a simmer burner that will cook the fat at a low enough temperature to prevent scorching. If your stove doesn't have this, then use a slow-cooker. To help ensure a nice color, sprinkle a half-teaspoon of baking soda over the fat. There is no need to stir it in. Turn the heat on to the lowest possible setting and put the lid on the pot, leaving it slightly ajar so that the water escapes. Simmer for several hours, returning every 90 minutes or so to stir it carefully with a wooden spoon. After about 4 hours (more, if you have a really large batch, less if you're working with a smaller amount), you will notice that the cracklings—browned bits of crisped fat—will be floating on the surface. This is your cue to turn off the heat. Allow the fat to partially cool while you set a colander over a large stainless-steel, porcelain, or glass bowl (not plastic!). Line the colander with cheese cloth, then pour the fat through, straining out all the cracklings and leaving a clear, golden liquid in the bowl. Let the fat cool 5–10 minutes longer before pouring it into wide-mouthed containers to be stored in the refrigerator or freezer. To keep your fat from souring, store it in a cool, dark place. Rendered fat will keep up to *two years* in a refrigerator, or indefinitely in the freezer. As for the cracklings, if working with pork, serious fat fans can drain the remaining cracklings over brown paper. Salt them for a snack, or add some to your biscuits or cornbread. My old copy of *Stocking Up* suggests making a spread by chopping them finely with onion, salt, pepper and herbs, then simmering them with ½ cup of white wine or broth until the mixture is thick and bubbly. The spread can be packed into a container and refrigerated . . . and sounds like a heavenly complement to cocktail hour.

Fat is rendered and ready to strain when the cracklings are floating

Holiday Pudding with Rum Sauce

ADVANCED PREPARATION REQUIRED.

SERVES 16

½ cup golden raisins

½ pound dried apricots or prunes, cut into pieces

½ pound dried cranberries

½ pound pitted dates, cut into pieces

¾ cup grated raw carrots

Grated zest of ½ orange

Grated zest of ½ lemon

½ cup sherry

2 cups finely chopped pecans or walnuts

8 ounces minced tallow

3 eggs

¼ cup milk or heavy cream

1 teaspoon cinnamon

⅛ teaspoon allspice

1 teaspoon fine salt

1 cup cooked mashed potatoes or sweet potatoes

Rum Sauce (recipe follows)

RUM SAUCE

1 cup heavy cream

3 egg yolks

2 tablespoons honey

½ teaspoon fine salt

⅓ cup rum

This is one of our Christmas favorites, a twist on the traditional Christmas pudding. It has been adapted to our family's dietary needs: there is no flour or added sugar, but the fat—tallow in this case—happily, has stayed put.

Preheat the oven to 350°F. Combine the fruits, carrot, and orange and lemon zests in a large bowl. Add the sherry and let stand for at least 1 hour. Meanwhile, mix the nuts and tallow together, then mix them into the sherry-soaked fruit. Beat the eggs, milk, cinnamon, allspice and salt together, then gradually blend them into the mashed potatoes. Using your hands or a wooden spoon, thoroughly combine the potatoes with the fruit.

Divide the mixture into 2 well-greased 1-quart pudding molds (coffee cans or stainless steel bowls will suffice). Fill them ¾ full. Cover tightly with aluminum foil. Place the pudding molds on a rack in a large pot. Add enough boiling water to the pot to come halfway up the sides of the molds. Cover the pot and steam pudding over medium-low heat until tester inserted into center comes out clean, about 2 hours, adding more boiling water to pot if necessary.

Remove foil, transfer mold to rack, and cool 5 minutes. Turn out the puddings onto ovenproof platters or baking pans. Cool completely, then cover and refrigerate, allowing the flavors to ripen, for 2 days, or up to one week. Before serving, reheat in a 200-degree oven for about 45 minutes, or until heated through. Serve with Rum Sauce. Unused portions can be stored up to 6 months in the freezer.

RUM SAUCE

Prepare the bottom half of a double boiler with 1 inch of water and bring it to a simmer. Add all the ingredients to the top part of a double boiler and whisk well. Put the top boiler over the bottom half and whisk continuously until the sauce thickens. Serve immediately.

ESTIMATED CARBOHYDRATES:		
Holiday Pudding	Sherry: 6 g	**Rum Sauce**
Raisins: 65.60 g	Pecans: 30.21 g	Heavy cream: 6.64 g
Apricots: 142.19 g	Eggs: 1.08 g	Egg yolks: 1.83 g
Cranberries: 186.96 g	Milk: 2.93 g	Honey: 34.61 g
Dates: 170.18 g	Cinnamon: 2.10 g	Total carbohydrates per recipe: 43.08 g
Carrots: 7.90 g	Allspice: 0.17 g	Total carbohydrates per ¹⁄₁₆ recipe: 2.69 g
Orange zest: 1.50 g	Mashed potatoes: 36.90 g	
Lemon Zest: 0.96 g	Total carbohydrates per recipe: 654.68 g	
	Total carbohydrates per ¹⁄₁₆ recipe: 40.92 g	

Honey-Oatmeal Farmers' Soap

11.5 ounces lye

32 ounces cold water

5 pounds rendered beef fat
(tallow), or tallow mixed with
a combination of lard and/or
rendered lamb fat

2 ounces essential oil of your choice
(for scent)

½ cup ground oats

½ cup raw honey, slightly warmed

EQUIPMENT:

1 40-ounce heat-resistant glass jar (a
clean glass juice jar is perfect)

Safety glasses

1 old wooden spoon

2 thermometers

1 large shoebox

1 garbage bag

1 bench knife

Kitchen scale

No, you can't eat it, but this basic thrifty recipe for tallow soap helped Bob and me pay off our mortgage while maintaining terrific complexions. We saved money by not having to buy soap, and we sold the surplus to our customers. Soaps made from super-saturated beef fat last a long time and are great for the skin. If you don't have enough beef fat for a full batch, you can mix in lard or rendered lamb fat.

Two hours before you plan to make the soap, select a well-ventilated work surface where you won't be troubled if there is a potential lye spill (perhaps an old cutting board or outdoor picnic table). Ideally, choose a location and work time when children and pets will not be around to distract you or potentially get burned from the lye.

An hour or two before you make the soap, set the jar on a scale and pour in the lye granules until you have 11.5 ounces. Wearing your safety glasses, slowly add the cold water, taking care to protect your eyes and not breathe in the fumes. Stir rapidly with the handle of an old wooden spoon (it will become scarred and burned, so don't use your best spoon), until the lye is completely in solution. Set it aside and allow it to cool. Keep the solution and any leftover lye granules far away from children. Using rubber gloves to prevent burning your hands, wash the spoon thoroughly.

Meanwhile, melt the tallow in a large stainless steel pot over a low flame until it is about 80 percent liquefied. Turn off the flame and allow the remaining fat to melt in the ambient heat. Once the fat is liquefied, begin monitoring the temperature as it cools. When it is around 110 degrees, set the glass jar of lye in a basin of hot water.

Monitor the temperature of the melted fat as it falls, and the lye solution as it rises. Once both are between 102 and 105 degrees, you are ready to use the lye to saponify the fat.

Using your wooden spoon (right-side-up this time), begin stirring the fat in a steady circular motion, adding the lye in a slow stream. Continue the circular stirring after all the lye is added to make sure the lye makes contact with all the fat in the pot. The mixture will turn opaque. Once the fat is opaque, continue stirring constantly for about 30 minutes, until the mixture thickens to the consistency of thick pea soup and it "traces," or leaves a trail across the surface, when you lift the spoon out of the pot. Stir in the essential oil, oats and honey.

Line the shoebox with the garbage bag. The bag should come up and over the sides. Pour the soap into your new "soap mold" and fold the plastic bag gently over the top of the liquid. Cover your soap mold with a piece of cardboard or Styrofoam, then with some blankets and towels. The idea is to insulate the mold so that the heat escapes very slowly.

After 24 hours, remove the blankets, turn the soap out on a cutting board, and use a bench knife to cut it into bars. Leave the bars some-place where the air can circulate around them freely for a minimum of two weeks (longer is even better). Use a sharp paring knife to shave off the powdery layer of soda ash that may settle on the outside of the bars before you take it into the bath.

Ula hones her marketing skills at one of our on-farm sales.

World's Best Bay Rum Shaving Soap

6¾ ounces lye

17 ounces water

4 ounces castor oil

4 ounces tallow

4 ounces coconut oil

27 ounces lard

12 ounces olive oil

1 ounce bay essential oil

¼ ounce lime essential oil

3 tablespoons bentonite clay

EQUIPMENT:

1 40-ounce heat-resistant glass jar (a clean glass juice jar is perfect)

Safety glasses

1 old wooden spoon

2 thermometers

Soap molds (enough for 18 [3-ounce] bars)

Several pieces of cardboard cut large enough to cover each soap mold

Kitchen scale

My dad grows a thick beard and has long struggled to find a good shaving soap or cream that allows for a clean shave without irritating his skin. As it turns out, he didn't need to look any farther than the barnyard. This shaving soap makes use of rendered tallow and lard, making it cheap to produce, but far superior to any product available conventionally. And it lasts a very long time, too! It takes my dad about one year of shaves to go through a single 3-ounce bar. This recipe will yield 18 (3-ounce) bars. Milky Way Molds out of Portland, Oregon, sells beautiful 3-ounce round soap molds that fit perfectly into any shaving cup. This recipe calls for bentonite clay, which helps give the soap the extra slip it needs to get over a set of whiskers. Bentonite can be found at most health food stores, or online from Frontier Natural Products Co-op.

To prep the lye, select a work surface where you won't be troubled if there is a potential lye spill (perhaps an old cutting board or outdoor picnic table). Ideally, choose a location and work time when children and pets will not be around to distract you or potentially get burned from the lye.

An hour or two before you make the soap, set the jar on the kitchen scale and pour in the lye granules until you have 6¾ ounces. Wearing your safety glasses, slowly add the water, taking care to protect your eyes and not breathe in the fumes. Stir rapidly with the handle of an old wooden spoon (it will become scarred and burned, so don't use your best spoon), until the lye is completely in solution. Set it aside and allow it to cool. Keep the solution and any leftover lye granules far away from children. Using rubber gloves to prevent burning your hands, wash the spoon thoroughly.

Meanwhile, melt the fat and oils in a large stainless-steel pot over a low flame until it is about 80 percent liquefied. Turn off the flame and allow the remaining fat to melt in the ambient heat. Once the fat is liquefied, begin monitoring the temperature as it cools. When the fat is around 105 degrees, set the glass jar of lye in a basin of hot water.

Monitor the temperature of the melted fat as it falls, and the lye solution as it rises. Once both are between 96 and 100 degrees, you are ready to use the lye to saponify the fat.

Using your wooden spoon (right-side-up this time), begin stirring the fat in a steady circular motion, adding the lye in a slow stream. Continue the circular stirring after all the lye is added to make sure the lye makes contact with all the fat in the pot. The mixture will turn opaque. Once the fat is opaque, continue stirring constantly for about 30–60 minutes until the mixture thickens to the consistency of thick pea soup and it "traces," or leaves a trail across the surface, when you lift the spoon out of the pot. Stir in the essential oils and bentonite clay.

Spoon the soap batter into the molds. Once you have filled an entire mold tray, cover it with a sheet of cardboard, set the next mold on top, and continue filling. In the end you will have a tower of about 6 filled trays sandwiched with layers of cardboard. Wrap the tray tower in a blanket. The idea is to insulate the soaps so that the heat escapes very slowly.

After 24 hours, remove the blanket and turn the soap out of the molds. Leave the bars someplace where the air can circulate around them freely for a minimum of two weeks before using.

BuzzOINKment Lip Balm

3 ounces lard

1 ounce clean, filtered beeswax

½ ounce essential oil of your choice (orange, peppermint with tea tree, lavender or jojoba are all terrific)

Hardly a Northeastern winter used to go by without my lips falling prey to incessant cracking, drying and peeling. I used to buy so much lip balm, Bob argued we needed to create an expense line for it in our budget. I began making my own, using beeswax from our hives and purchased avocado oil, and vitamin E oil . . . until I realized that my vitamin E was generated from genetically modified soy. Looking around for a more natural (and locally available) source, I had to look no farther than my counter, where a pot of pure white lard sits next to my cooktop. I experimented blending the lard with beeswax, and presto! Amazing lip balm that can be made in less than a few minutes. Truly, this is the best lip balm I've ever used, and my customers agree. One batch will yield about 25 tubes (easily found online), or about 4.5 ounces if you simply want to pour it into a small jar to keep for yourself.

Melt the lard and beeswax in a small saucepan over medium heat. Turn off the flame and stir in the essential oil. Make sure there are no open flames near the pot as you pour the mixture into tubes or jars. The mixture would be highly flammable. The lip balm will harden to the proper consistency when it cools.

Be sure not to dump any excess pan drippings down your drain, as the hardening wax can accumulate over time and eventually generate a plumbing nightmare. Instead, return the empty soiled saucepan to the cooktop and turn on the heat until all the lip balm residue is melted. Wipe the pot out thoroughly with a paper towel. Discard the towel in your compost, and wash out your pan normally.

BuzzOINKment Herbal Salve

1½ tablespoons dried comfrey leaf

1½ tablespoons dried comfrey root

1½ tablespoons dried calendula petals

1½ tablespoons dried lavender blossoms

1½ tablespoons dried nettle leaves

1 pound lard

3 ounces cleaned, filtered beeswax

2–3 disposable tea filters (1-cup size)

Once I realized how wonderful lard-based lip balms were, it was easy to take the next step to make skin salve. This is one of my best-selling products at the farm, a useful remedy for cuts, cracks, scrapes, and irritated or chapped skin. If you don't have these herbs in your backyard or home medicine chest, they are usually available in the bulk section of most health food stores, or online through Frontier Natural Products Co-op. This recipe makes 15 ounces of salve.

Place the herbs in the tea filters and add them to a slow cooker, along with the lard and beeswax. Cook on the lowest setting for a minimum of 6 hours, or for as long as 24 hours. Remove the herbs and tea filters and add them to your compost. Pour the salve into wide-mouthed jars.

Be sure not to dump any excess drippings down your drain, as the hardening wax can accumulate over time and eventually generate a plumbing nightmare. Instead, wipe the crock out thoroughly with a paper towel. Discard the towel in your compost, and wash out your crock normally.

Tallow candles

Growing up in one of the former original thirteen colonies, I often heard stories about how the early Americans made their way in the new world. Tallow candles were a common source of light among those who could not afford beeswax or bayberry. On school field trips, we'd visit living history museums where some of these candles would be on display. Their creamy surface called out to my fingers. I longed to touch them. I wanted to see them lit. "Don't bother," costumed museum guides would tell me, "tallow candles melt too easily, they break easily, they're smoky, and they stink."

Each time I rendered a pot of tallow, I remembered those candles and longed to challenge the conventional wisdom. In 2011, while exploring new value-added enterprises for our farm, I decided to give it a try. But rather than using pure tallow, I blended it with beeswax. The first attempt, made with two parts tallow and one part beeswax, left me with droopy candles that broke at the slightest touch. But with further experimenting, I discovered that by using equal parts beeswax and tallow, I could make fantastic candles. They were hard, durable, long-lasting, smokeless, and odorless (unless I chose to add a scent). I had the finest properties of both fats—durability and sweet scent from beeswax, and thrifty ingredients from the tallow. Best of all, the candles had the beautiful creamy finish of the old-fashioned tallow candles, making them a sensuous pleasure for the eyes as well as the hands.

Making your own homemade hand-dipped candles is easy. I recommend getting a copy of the Storey Country Wisdom Bulletin, *Making Hand-Dipped Candles* by Betty Oppenheimer for simple easy-to-follow instructions to get started. Instead of using her beeswax/paraffin/stearic acid formulas, use the simple 50 percent beeswax/50 percent tallow formula I've outlined here, and follow the rest of her instructions. You'll love the results.

CHAPTER FOUR

Beef

The world of sustainable meat production is populated by a motley cross-section of America. Attendees at grassfed beef conferences will include ultraconservative Christians, Amish, Mennonites, libertarians, nose-pierced twenty-somethings with dreadlocks, white-collared politicians and academic activists, community organizers, former corporate employees seeking refuge and healing in a new vocation, precocious homeschooled children starting their own on-farm enterprises, retirees embarking on a new farm dream, mothers with infants and small children bound to their chests, and long-time cattlemen and dairy farmers seeking a way to improve the viability of their family farms and ranches.

When it comes to their beef, they might have some disagreements about what breeds are most superior: a heritage breed specially suited to thrive on pasture; a thick-coated breed that is particularly thrifty to keep in the winter; or a motley genetic mix of breeds, bred locally to do well in the specific climate of the region. These folks might harbor opinions that their particular home breed is superior—perhaps they prefer the texture better on one breed, or the overall flavor. Maybe they prefer certain cattle because they are docile, or because they are beautiful to look at, or because they've been on a particular farm or ranch for several generations.

While opinions will be widely diverse about which cattle are superior, when it comes to beef, they'll all agree on two points:

1. Beef needn't grade prime in order to be tender or delicious. If the animals have had a good life, if they were out on well-managed pasture, were processed responsibly, were dry-aged and were cooked appropriately, they'll be delicious.

Marbling across the breeds and across the seasons will vary from animal to animal. Natural variation will occur on every farm, and that variation is natural and healthy. The only way to get consistent marbling is to resort to industrial farming practices, and that is not an acceptable path; and

2. For goodness' sake, never overcook it! With the exception of stews and pot roasts, these folks will tell you the meat should be served pink. Heck, some of them will tell you it should be served raw. Eating the more tender cuts of red meat raw or rare will keep the enzymes intact, facilitating digestion. It also improves the flavor and tenderness by preventing the muscle fibers from contracting too tightly, squeezing out the tasty juices and toughening the meat.

Learning to work with every cut on a beef can be daunting. The variety of cuts seems endless, and the names of the cuts will vary from region to region. Sadly, customers' insecurities about working with everything on the beef results in a lot of meat going unsold. Farmers may find that they quickly run out of rib eye steaks and porterhouses, but that they have a surplus of London broils and chuck roasts. In my experience, it isn't that these cuts aren't delicious. Rather, customers are simply unsure of how to prepare them.

There is an easy way to get over this insecurity. Get down on all fours on your living room floor. Or, if you want to feel more authentic and the weather is nice, head out to your yard. Crawl around and pretend to eat the grass. As you do so, pay attention to which muscles move the most and which muscles move the least. Those muscles that move the most—the cuts from the **chuck** (as you crawl around, that would be your shoulders), the **foreleg** and **brisket** (those would be your arms and chest), and the **plate** and **flank** (your belly area)—are all doing the most work. They are propelling your body forward, lifting your neck up and down, enabling you to be a happy, active, grazing cow (or steer, as the case may be). All of these cuts are commonly referred to as the "tougher cuts," which is a very unfair designation. If they are slapped across the grate of a flaming grill, they may be tough. But, if they are slow-cooked in a little wine or broth, they become some of the most tender meat you will ever eat. This is because these cuts, in order to do their job in helping the beef move about, contain connective tissue interwoven among the muscles. Connective tissue requires moist heat in order to break down. Thus, these cuts are ideal for slow cooking, pot roasting, braising, or stewing. They will also be suitable candidates for **super-slow roasting**, which is explained in a sidebar later in this chapter. If intense beef flavor is your goal, these are the ideal cuts. Cuts from these primal areas include **stew beef, brisket, short ribs, chuck roasts, arm pots, ground beef,** and **shanks**. They also include **skirt** and **flank** steaks, which are very thin steaks that are often marinated and cooked rare using a dry heat method, and are prized for their flavor and chewy texture.

Okay, stay down on the ground. Don't get up yet. Graze a little more. As you do, pay attention to what other muscles are working. While the shoulders and forelegs do most of the work, the hind legs and rump must move along with them. Muscles from the round (that would be your rump and the top of your thighs) are active, but they don't do the bulk of the beef's grazing work. They just follow from behind. They are not the most tender parts of the beef, but they are not the chewiest, either. These cuts can be roasted using conventional methods, but I find them perfect for **super-slow roasting**. They can also be marinated and grilled,

Some of the best cuts for braising come from retired dairy cows who've had a long life on pasture to intensify the flavor of their meat.

or sliced super-thin into **sandwich steaks** (also called **minute steaks** or **skillet steaks**—thin slices of beef that can be fried in under a minute). Cuts from this primal area include **top, bottom** and **eye round roasts; sandwich steaks, stew beef, ground beef,** and **London broils**. While it is technically not part of the same primal, I include the **sirloin tip** in this area as well. The sirloin tip is located right next to the round. It is not as tender as the actual sirloin primal, and is cooked using the same methods as for the round. Sirloin tips can be done in roasts or steaks, or as **kebabs**, perfect for marinating and grilling.

Are you still grazing out on your lawn? Good. Now let's focus on what muscles *aren't* moving much as you browse the pasture. The middle part of your body, all along your back, doesn't have to do much work. On the beef, the primal just behind the shoulders would be the rib primal (where **rib eye** or **Delmonico steaks** and **rib roasts** originate), followed by the **short loin** (home of the most tender cuts—**filet mignon steaks, tenderloin roasts, top loin** or **NY strip steaks,** porterhouses, and **t–bones**). Behind the short loin is the **sirloin**, the primal where **sirloin steaks** and **roasts** are cut. All the cuts from these primals are the most tender parts of the animal. Cuts from the short loin will be the most tender with the least amount of flavor, and cuts from the rib eye and sirloin will be slightly less tender, but with more marbling and flavor. All of them are suited well to dry-heat cooking methods, like pan frying, roasting, or grilling.

Now that you know how the body of a grazing beef works, it should be relatively easy to select a cut at your farmers' market. If the name of the cut is not the same as what I mentioned here (again, there is tremendous regional variability regarding cut names), simply ask the farmer or butcher where it came from on the animal. As soon as you have that information, picture yourself crawling around again, vision where that muscle would be on the animal, and you'll know whether to select a dry heat, moist heat, or super-slow cooking method.

The Simplest Pot Roast Ever

SERVES 4–10

1 (3–5 pound) beef pot roast, bone-in or boneless (chuck roasts or brisket are ideal)

2 tablespoons coarse salt

1 tablespoon ground black pepper

2 tablespoons lard, butter or tallow

1 cup meat broth, such as Shannon's Meat Broth, Chapter 3

1 large yellow or white onion, sliced in rings

ESTIMATED CARBOHYDRATES

Black pepper: 4.41 g

Meat broth: 1.4 g*

Onion: 14.01 g

Total number of carbohydrates per recipe: 19.82 g

Total number of carbohydrates per ⅙ recipe: 3.3 g

* Number of carbohydrates in home-made broth will vary. This figure is calculated using the recipe for Shannon's Meat Broth (Chapter 3).

The secret to this recipe is a good sear, followed by time in the slow cooker with very little liquid, resulting in concentrated beef flavor and an intense sauce.

Wipe the roast well with paper towels and rub the salt and pepper into all sides of the meat. Heat a skillet over a medium-high flame, add the fat and swirl to coat. Sear the meat 3–4 minutes per side. Put it in the bottom of a slow cooker. Add the broth to the pan and simmer about 5 minutes, scraping up any browned bits and incorporating them into the juices. When the broth is reduced by about one-third, add it to the slow cooker. Layer the onion on top of the meat, cover and cook on low 6–8 hours, until tender. Serve the meat with the juice spooned over the top.

Leftovers: The seasoning on this beef is so simple, it will be compatible with all of the leftover recipes that allow for beef in Chapter 8, including Moussaka, Black Bean Chili with Dark Roast Coffee, Summer Harvest Casserole, or the Mulligatawny. Better still, simply re-warm the leftovers in the slow cooker to make another rich, beefy meal out of them.

What size roast do I need?

If there is one single question that Bob and I need to answer for nearly every customer who visits our farmers' market stall, it is "how much meat do I need?" The simple rule is that if your roast contains a bone, figure on one pound of meat per person. If the roast is boneless, calculate for ½ pound per person. Once you've done that basic calculation, consider how many of your dinner companions actually eat meat, whether their appetites are hearty or light, whether there are any small children at the table who won't eat a full helping, and how many extra side dishes will be accompanying the meal. Round up or down based on these factors.

Buttermilk Marinated Pot Roast in a Ginger Garlic Chili Sauce

ADVANCE PREPARATION REQUIRED.

SERVES 6–8

1 tablespoon coarse salt

2 cups buttermilk, thin yogurt or thick whey*

3–4-pound beef chuck roast (bone in or boneless), short ribs, brisket or bottom round

3 tablespoons lard, butter or tallow

2 medium yellow or white onions, sliced thin

2 teaspoons ground cardamom

1 teaspoon ground coriander

1 teaspoon ground cumin

1 teaspoon chili powder

3 cloves garlic, peeled and crushed

1 tablespoon grated fresh ginger

½ teaspoon ground turmeric

1–2 whole red chipotle peppers, dried

1 tomato, diced

ESTIMATED CARBOHYDRATES:

Buttermilk: 25.97 g, Yogurt (whole, plain): 22.83 g, Whey: 25.19 g, Average: 24.66 g

Onions (average): 17.10 g

Spices: 15.71 g

Tomato: 4.78 g

Number of carbohydrates for entire recipe: 62.25 g

Number of carbohydrates per ⅙ of recipe: 10.38 g

Number of carbohydrates per ⅛ of recipe: 7.78 g

Tired of boring ol' pot roast? Try this fun dish, where Eastern Europe meets India. Eastern Europeans have long marinated their pot roasts in buttermilk, and Indian cuisine often makes use of yogurt marinades and exotic spices. This recipe draws from both traditions and results in a lightly perfumed beef dish with distinctive yet subtle flavors. We loved this.

Whisk together the salt and buttermilk. Place the beef in a deep-sided glass, stainless-steel, earthenware or other nonreactive dish. Cover with the buttermilk and allow it to marinate overnight in the refrigerator in a covered dish.

Remove the meat from the marinade and pat dry. Reserve the marinade.

Heat 2 tablespoons of the fat in a skillet over a medium-high flame. Add the meat and sear 5 minutes per side. Remove from the pan and place in a slow cooker. If needed, add 1 more tablespoon of fat to the skillet. Add the onions and sauté until clear. Turn the heat down low. Add the cardamom, coriander, cumin, chili powder, garlic, ginger and turmeric. Mix well.

Spread the seasoned onions over the top of the beef in the slow cooker. Add the dried chilies (left whole), diced tomato, and the leftover marinade. Cook on low 6–8 hours until the beef is tender. Remove and discard chilies. Serve the beef with the onions and sauce spooned over the top.

Leftovers: As this is a braised dish, the leftovers will taste even better than the original feast. Simply re-warm them in the slow cooker or in a covered dish in a 200-degree oven, or over low heat on the stove top. They can also be added to the Coconut Soup in Chapter 8.

* We make our own yogurt and strain it through cheesecloth so that it is extra-thick. The resulting creamy whey is perfect for this recipe.

Braised Beef in a Cinnamon-Orange Coffee Sauce

ADVANCED PREPARATION REQUIRED.

SERVES 6

1 (3–4-pound) bone-in or boneless chuck roast, bottom round roast, short ribs or brisket

2 tablespoons coarse salt

1 tablespoon ground black pepper

3 tablespoons lard, tallow or butter

2 large yellow or white onions, sliced into thin wedges

2 cups strong black coffee

1 cinnamon stick

1 tablespoon honey or maple syrup

2 tablespoons grated orange zest

ESTIMATED CARBOHYDRATES:

Honey: 34.6 g, Maple Syrup: 26.82 g

Onions: 13.68 g

Orange peel 3.0 g

Number of carbohydrates for entire recipe: 51.28 g (with honey), 43.5 g (with maple syrup)

Total carbohydrates per ⅙ of recipe: 8.54 g (with honey), 7.25 g (with maple syrup)

Here is a mildly sweet and deeply fragrant twist on plain ol' pot roast.

Wipe the meat dry, then rub it all over with salt and pepper. Heat a nonreactive skillet over a medium-high flame, add 2 tablespoons of the fat and swirl to coat. Add the beef and brown it on all sides, about 4 minutes per side. Remove it from the pan and place it on the bottom of a slow cooker.

Lower the heat under the skillet slightly, then add the remaining fat. Once it melts, add the onions. They should sizzle as they hit the pan. If they sputter or splatter, lower the flame. Stir well, coating the onions in the cooking fat and scraping up any browned bits from the bottom of the pan. Continue to cook 2–3 minutes longer until the onions have given up two-thirds of their volume in water. Once they start to brown, lower the flame and allow them to caramelize by cooking 15–20 minutes longer, stirring often. Lower the heat if they start to burn.

Pour the onions over the top of the beef in the slow cooker. Return the pan to the flame and add the coffee, cinnamon stick, and honey or maple syrup. Whisk to blend, scraping up any browned bits and incorporating them into the sauce. Bring it to a boil and cook until it is reduced by half. Pour it over the meat, adding the cinnamon stick to the slow cooker as well. Add the orange zest, cover, and cook on low for 6–8 hours until tender. Serve the meat with the onions and sauce spooned over the top.

Leftovers: A braised dish such as this builds flavor the second day. Thus, leftovers can simply be re-warmed and served again. If you need to get a few more meals out of it, dice the meat into small pieces, stir it into the sauce, then spoon it over rice or another preferred grain cooked in broth. It can also be added to the Onion Soup in Chapter 8 to give it an exotic twist.

Slow-Cooker Japanese-Style Curried Beef

SERVES 6–8

4 medium yellow or white onions, thinly sliced

1 clove garlic, minced

2 medium potatoes, unpeeled, cut into 1-inch chunks

5 carrots, unpeeled, cut into 1-inch chunks

¾ cup all-purpose flour, divided

1 tablespoon coarse salt

1 tablespoon freshly ground black pepper

3 tablespoons curry powder, divided use (reduce the amount if you like your food less spicy)

3 pounds stew beef, cubed

7 tablespoons unsalted butter, divided, plus extra, if needed

4 cups canned tomatoes, diced, undrained

2 cups beef broth

2 teaspoons garam masala, lightly toasted, then ground, see Appendix 1 (optional)

When I worked as a schoolteacher in Japan, the cafeteria women prepared enormous stew pots filled with beef curry for our lunches every day throughout the winter. I grew fond of this warming dish, even though Japanese curry is nothing like traditional Thai or Indian curries (I prefer the hot Indian muchi curry from my local co-op). Many folks craving a Japanese-style curry will purchase the ready-made roux mixes from Japanese grocery stores or Asian food markets. I've yet to find this product in the hinterlands of Upstate New York, so the following recipe includes a homemade curry roux that is much better: It is free from the added sugar, colorings, MSG and other mysterious ingredients of questionable origin found in store-bought mixes. If you are shy of spices, reduce the amount of curry powder or serve it with a generous splash of yogurt. This dish is traditionally served with kimchi, which is a fermented cabbage pickle popular in Eastern Asia.

Layer the onions, garlic, potatoes, and carrots in the bottom of a large slow cooker. Combine ½ cup of the flour, the salt, pepper, and 1 tablespoon of the curry powder in a shallow bowl. Add the beef and toss to coat thoroughly. Heat 3 tablespoons of the butter in a large skillet over medium-high heat. Add the beef and brown on all sides, working in batches and adding more butter if necessary. As it is browned, put the beef on top of the vegetables in the slow cooker. Pour in the tomatoes and beef broth.

Cook on low for 6½ hours (4 hours on high), or until the meat is tender. Stir in the garam masala and allow the stew to continue cooking while you prepare the curry roux.

FOR THE CURRY ROUX:
Melt 4 tablespoons butter in a 1-quart saucepan over medium heat. Stir in the remaining ¼ cup flour and 1 to 2 tablespoons of the curry powder (depending on how spicy you like it). Spoon 2 cups liquid from the slow cooker and slowly stir it into the roux. Stir well. Continue to cook and stir until the mixture has thickened, about 2 to 3 minutes. Return the thickened sauce to the cooker and mix well with a wooden spoon.

If you like your sauce thicker, put the slow cooker setting on high and cook 20 to 30 minutes longer with the cover off, stirring often, until the sauce reaches your desired consistency. Serve with rice and a nice helping of kimchi, if you've got it.

ESTIMATED CARBOHYDRATES:
Onions: 10.27 g
Garlic: 0.99 g
Potatoes: 67.73 g
Carrots: 29.20 g
Flour (all-purpose): 69.20 g
Black pepper: 4.41 g
Curry powder: 10.99 g
Butter: 0.07 g
Tomatoes: 38.40 g
Meat broth: 1.40 g*
Garam Masala: 2 g
Total carbohydrates per recipe: 266.87 g
Total carbohydrates per ⅙ recipe:
    44.48 g
* Number of carbohydrates in homemade
broth will vary. This figure is calculated
using the recipe for Shannon's Meat Broth
(Chapter 3).

Leftovers: Curried beef develops more flavor on the second day. Reheat it in your slow cooker or over low heat on your stove top.

Note: Garam Masala is an Indian spice blend made up of cinnamon, cardamom, cloves, cumin, peppercorns, fennel and bay leaves. It is available whole or already ground in most well-stocked grocery stores, through Indian groceries, or online. To make your own blend, see Appendix 1. The recipe will also be successful if you opt to leave it out of the mix.

We moved to Sap Bush Hollow when I was five. From that time on, I never wanted to be far from home.

Slow-Cooked Brisket Hash with Sweet Peppers and Caramelized Onions

SERVES 7–8

1 flat-cut brisket, about 3 ½ pounds

2 tablespoons coarse salt

1 tablespoon plus 1 teaspoon ground black pepper, divided

6 tablespoons lard, tallow, or butter

1 cup meat broth, such as Shannon's Meat Broth, Chapter 3

4 medium potatoes, unpeeled, diced

1½ cups diced roasted red peppers packed in vinegar

3 medium onions, sliced into wedges

1 teaspoon fine salt, or to taste

For topping: 7–16 poached eggs (depending on your company's appetite) and Hollandaise (Chapter 7)

ESTIMATED CARBOHYDRATES:

Black pepper: 5.88 g

Meat broth: 1.4 g*

Potatoes: 33.87 g

Roasted red peppers: 8.19 g

Onions: 30.81 g

Total carbohydrates per recipe: 80.15 g

Total carbohydrates per ⅟₇ recipe: 11.45 g

* Number of carbohydrates in homemade broth will vary. This figure is calculated using the recipe for Shannon's Meat Broth (Chapter 3).

Try this recipe for a show-stopping Christmas brunch. Top it with poached eggs and the Hollandaise in Chapter 7, and you'll have an unforgettable feast. I guarantee your guests won't be hungry for a good 12 hours or so!

DAY BEFORE:

Rub the brisket on all sides with salt and 1 tablespoon of the black pepper. Heat a large cast-iron skillet over a medium flame until you can see a little steam coming off it, then add 2 tablespoons of the fat to the pan and swirl to coat. Sear the brisket well, about 2 minutes per side.

Put meat broth into the slow cooker and set the brisket on top. Pour in any remaining pan juices. Cook on low for 5 hours or until meat pulls apart easily. Allow the meat to cool, then use your fingers to shred it into bite-sized pieces. Add it back to the broth and refrigerate.

DAY OF:

Preheat the oven to 250°F. Remove the meat from the refrigerator and allow it to come to room temperature. Meanwhile, heat a large Dutch oven over a medium flame. Add 2 tablespoons of the fat to the pan and swirl to coat. Add the diced potatoes and sauté until browned. Season with the fine ground salt and remaining pepper, and continue sautéing until tender, about 15 minutes longer. Remove the potatoes and return the Dutch oven to the heat.

Add 2 more tablespoons of the fat to the Dutch oven and swirl to coat. Once it is hot, add the onions. They should sizzle when they hit the pan, but the heat should not be so high that they make a loud sputter. Stir thoroughly, coating the onions with the fat. Continue stirring for 1 minute longer until the onions begin to brown and have lost over half of their volume to water. Lower the flame and cook, stirring often, until they are a deep brown color, about 15 minutes longer.

Add the onions, potatoes, meat and juices, and the roasted red peppers to a large bowl. Mix well and transfer it to a roasting pan. Cover and cook 40 minutes, then remove the cover and cook 20 minutes longer. Serve topped with poached eggs and hollandaise.

Leftovers: Re-warm leftovers in a covered baking dish in a 250-degree oven and feast again. Leftovers will taste even better a day or two later, as the flavors will have had time to meld. Better still, repurpose the hash into an elegant leftover by serving a small spoonful on top of a Potato-Parsnip Blini (Chapter 7), garnished with a little crème fresh or sour cream.

Slow-Cooked Brisket in Beer and Onions

ADVANCE PREPARATION
REQUIRED.

SERVES 6–8

1 3–4-pound flat-cut brisket

1 tablespoon coarse salt

1 teaspoon ground black pepper

2 tablespoons lard, butter or tallow

4 medium onions, sliced thin

3 tablespoons demi-glace
 (Chapter 3)

1 tablespoon tomato ketchup

12 ounces beer

ESTIMATED CARBOHYDRATES:
Onions: 41.10 g
Demi-Glace: 1.4 g*
Ketchup: 3.77 g
Beer: 12.64 g
Number of carbohydrates for entire
 recipe: 59.91 g
Estimated number of carbohydrates per
 ⅙ recipe: 9.82 g
* Carbohydrate values on homemade
 demi-glace will vary.

Here is a recipe for those truly harried days when you can't spend time in the kitchen. Ten minutes of prep time in the morning will have a delicious payoff at suppertime.

Wipe the meat dry with a cloth or paper towels and rub the salt and pepper into it. Heat the skillet over a medium–high flame until you see steam coming off of it. Add the fat and swirl to coat. Sear the meat 3–4 minutes per side, then place it on the bottom of a slow cooker. Top with the onions, demi-glace, ketchup, and beer and cook on low, 6–8 hours, until tender.

Leftovers: Leftover meat, broth and onions can be re-warmed as a meal, or used in Onion Soup (Chapter 8).

Short Ribs (or Brisket or Shanks) Slow-Cooked with Bacon and Tomatoes

SERVES 6

1 large yellow or white onion, chopped

2 medium carrots, chopped

2 stalks celery, chopped

3–4 pounds beef short ribs, brisket or shanks

1 batch Coriander-Herb Paste, Appendix 1

1 tablespoon butter, lard or tallow

3 ounces diced bacon (about 4 thick-cut slices)

2 tablespoons grated lemon zest

½ teaspoon dried thyme (or 1½ teaspoons fresh)

4 cups diced fresh or canned tomatoes

GREMOLATA TOPPING:

3 tablespoons fresh parsley (1 tablespoon dried)

1 tablespoon grated lemon zest

½ cup walnut halves

ESTIMATED CARBOHYDRATES:
Coriander-Herb Paste: 7.86 g
Onion: 14.01 g
Carrots: 11.68 g
Celery: 2.38 g
Lemon zest: 2.88 g
Thyme: 0.32 g
Tomatoes: 28.01 g
Parsley: 0.72 g
Walnuts: 8.23 g
Total carbohydrates per recipe: 76.09 g
Total carbohydrates per ⅙ recipe: 12.68 g

This is hearty fare that tastes great as a one-dish feast, or stretches farther if poured over a buttery heap of mashed potatoes. The leftovers, when turned into a stew (read on for details), make for a bunch of great meals, too. There will be a rich, meaty broth when you are finished cooking. If you prefer that your broth have as little grease as possible, use a flat-cut brisket or beef shanks. Leave the short ribs for folks like me, who love the fatty meat!

Place the onions, carrots and celery on the bottom of a large slow cooker. Rub the beef all over with the coriander-herb paste. Heat a skillet over a medium flame and brown the beef, about 4 minutes per side. Set the meat on top of the vegetables in the slow cooker. Add the bacon to the skillet and sauté until lightly browned. Add it to the slow cooker.

Pour ½ cup water into the skillet. Bring it to a simmer, using a wooden spoon to scrape up any browned bits and incorporate them into the pan juices. Pour the pan juices around (not on) the meat in the slow cooker. Add the lemon zest, thyme and tomatoes. Cover and cook on low for 6–8 hours, until tender.

Meanwhile, make the gremolata: combine the parsley, lemon zest and walnuts in the small bowl of a food processor. Process until the nuts are ground. Carve the cooked beef into slices or chunks and serve in shallow bowls, topped with the vegetables, tomatoes and a sprinkling of gremolata.

Leftovers: Re-warm leftovers in the slow cooker or in a covered dish in a 250-degree oven. Leftovers can also be incorporated into the Black Bean Chili with Dark Roast Coffee, or the Onion Soup (both in Chapter 8).

To convert the leftovers to a stew: chill the leftovers overnight. 2½ hours before you are ready to eat, take them out of the refrigerator and remove any solidified fat from the top of the broth (this can be discarded, composted, or used in place of butter for sautéing and searing savory foods). Remove all bones and meat from the pot (yes, your hands will get messy; it's fun).

Discard or compost the bones, then dice all remaining meat into bite-sized pieces and return them (along with all the leftover sauce and vegetables) to the slow cooker. Add 2–3 cups diced cabbage or green beans (or a combination thereof), along with 1–2 cups of meat stock. Cook on low for 2 hours and serve.

Choosing your best steak

One of our favorite jobs at our farmers' market is helping customers choose the perfect steak to take home for supper. **Porterhouse** and **filet mignon** steaks may have the reputation for being "the best," but that is not necessarily the case. The reason they are considered "the best" is because they are tender, and because there are relatively few of them on a beef animal. Other steaks may be a better fit for your taste. If you like lean, tender meat, **porterhouse**, **NY strips** (aka **top loin**), and **filet mignon** may be your best bet. If you like tenderness, but don't mind cutting your meat with a steak knife if it means a little more marbling and flavor, go for the **rib eyes** (or **Delmonicos**) and **sirloins**. If you are on a budget or need to feed a crowd, **London broils** and **sirloin tip**

steaks have very little waste and can go a long way. They are also cheaper, have nice beefy flavor and lend themselves well to marinating. They are best served rare to medium-rare, and should be sliced thinly across the grain when served. **Skirt**, **hanger** and **flank steaks** are the ideal choices for folks who love to really chew their meat. Unfortunately, there are only two skirts and two flanks per animal. **Hanger steak**, which is a piece of meat that hangs off the diaphragm, is even more uncommon, as it often disintegrates during the dry-age process, and thus the farmer only occasionally has it in stock. If high-flavor, high-texture meats are your top choice, look toward the chuck for some great alternatives. The **flat-iron** and **chuck eye** steaks, both cut from the shoulder, are great bargain cuts with fantastic marbling and lots of flavor.

The Best Steak, Cooked Outdoors

1–2 tablespoons coarse salt

2–3 teaspoons ground black pepper

1–2 cloves garlic, minced

1 sirloin, sirloin tip, tri-tip, top round or London broil steak; OR 2 shoulder top blade, shoulder petite tender, rib, porterhouse, t-bone, top loin (NY strip), or tenderloin (filet mignon) steaks, cut 1¼ to 1½ inches thick.

ESTIMATED CARBOHYDRATES:

2 teaspoons ground black pepper: 2.94 g

1 clove garlic: 0.99 g

Number of carbohydrates for entire recipe: 3.93 g

The more experience I gain cooking steak, the more opinionated I've become about limiting seasonings to salt, pepper and garlic. There is too much glorious flavor in beef to justify corrupting it with excessive seasonings. However, if you would prefer to do something more glamorous, select any of the spice rubs, pastes or marinades from the back of the book that are suitable for beef. If you choose a marinade, do not let the meat sit in it for more than 2 hours.

Combine the salt, pepper and garlic in a small bowl. Rub the mixture into both sides of the meat, then allow it to come to room temperature. Start the grill and warm it until it is hot. If you are using a gas grill, turn off all but one of the burners once it has come up to temperature. If you are using charcoal, be sure all the coals have been raked to one side. Use the hand test: the grate will be hot enough when you can hold your palm 3–4 inches above the metal grate for no more than three or four seconds.

Sear the steaks, covered, for 2 minutes on each side over direct heat. Move the steaks off direct heat, close the lid, and allow the steaks to cook over indirect heat, without turning, until they reach 120–135 degrees, about 5–7 minutes per pound.

Once they are cooked, remove the steaks to a platter and allow them to rest 5 minutes before serving.

Leftovers: Slice cold steak thinly and serve over a salad with Parmesan-Peppercorn Dressing (Chapter 7); serve cold with sharp cheddar cheese on crackers, accompanied by Horseradish Cream (explained in the recipe for Garlic-Rubbed Chuck Eye Roast with Horseradish Cream), or a dollop of spicy mustard. Tidbits of steak can also be diced up and tossed into Refrigerator Soup (Chapter 8).

The Best Steak, Cooked Indoors

1–2 tablespoons coarse salt

2–3 teaspoons ground black pepper

1–2 cloves garlic, minced

2 tablespoons butter, tallow or rendered lamb fat

1 sirloin, sirloin tip, tri-tip, top round or London broil steak; OR 2 shoulder top blade, shoulder petite tender, rib, porterhouse, t-bone, top loin (NY strip), or tenderloin (filet mignon) steaks, cut 1¼ to 1½ inches thick

---

ESTIMATED CARBOHYDRATES:

2 teaspoons ground black pepper: 2.94 g

1 clove garlic: 0.99 g

Number of carbohydrates for entire recipe: 3.93 g

Steak doesn't have to be a luxury enjoyed only by those folks with enough backyard space to hold a grill. It can be just as delicious cooked indoors (especially if the outdoor grill is under 4 feet of snow).

Combine the salt, pepper and garlic in a small bowl. Rub the mixture into both sides of the steak, then allow the meat to come to room temperature. Preheat the oven to 200°F., then heat a large cast-iron or other ovenproof skillet over a high flame. Once the skillet is so hot that you can see a little smoke rising off it, add the butter and/or fat and sear the steak for 2 minutes on each side.

Turn off the flame and insert an ovenproof meat thermometer into a boneless side of the steak (do not insert it into the top, as there is not enough depth for the thermometer to take an accurate reading). Leaving the steaks in the skillet, place them in the oven and allow them to finish cooking, about 10–20 minutes, until the internal temperature reads 115–135 degrees. Remove the steaks and allow them to rest 5 minutes before carving and serving. The temperature will rise a few more degrees during this time.

Leftovers: See the suggestions for The Best Steak, Cooked Outdoors, previous page.

Meat in cubes

I've seen a number of customers get confused when purchasing stew beef and kebabs. The packages look very similar—cubes of beef wrapped in tight little one- or two-pound packs. While they may look similar, they are not interchangeable. Kebabs are most often cut from the sirloin tip, and occasionally from the sirloin. They are cut into 2-inch cubes, and their intended use is for marinating and grilling. To keep them from drying out, they are best served rare or medium rare.

Stew is typically cut into 1-inch cubes, taken from the chuck, the brisket, shanks or bottom round.

Stew meat will be very chewy if it is grilled. It is meant to be slow-cooked in liquid.

A further distinction that some farmers make is between bottom round stew and chuck, brisket and shank stew meat. Bottom round stew is leaner and contains less connective tissue. Thus, if you need to get a stew made in 90 minutes or less, or if you are fat-averse, bottom round may be your preferred choice. Cooking bottom round for too long can cause it to dry out. If you are slow-cooking a stew all day, and you prefer a silkier (fattier) texture in your stew meat, the meat cut from the chuck, brisket or shanks will work best.

Beef Kebabs

ADVANCE PREPARATION
REQUIRED.

SERVES 4–6

1 recipe Garlic Lime Marinade,
   Appendix 1, OR
   Dad's Tamari-Balsamic Marinade,
   Appendix 1

2 pounds beef cut for kebabs
   (alternatively, use a London broil,
   sirloin tip, or sirloin steak cut into
   1½-inch cubes)

Metal skewers, or bamboo skewers
   soaked in water for 30 minutes

ESTIMATED CARBOHYDRATES:

Garlic Lime Marinade: 11.99 g

Dad's Tamari-Balsamic Marinade: 66.32 g

Total amount of carbohydrate per
serving will depend on how much of the
marinade is absorbed by the meat, and
how much is brushed on during cooking.
To gauge an estimate, weigh the
amount of marinade before you begin
cooking, and divide the carbohydrates
by the number of ounces (which will tell
you roughly how many carbohydrates
per ounce). Weigh the leftover marinade
once you've finished. Subtract it from
the original. The difference will be
the number of ounces used on your
meat. Multiply that by the number of
carbohydrates per ounce, and you'll
have an estimate for the total number of
carbohydrates for the recipe.

Kebabs, when marinated in advance, are a terrific way to create a fast, tasty meal. I find that the secret to enjoying them lies in appreciating the fact that they come from slightly chewier cuts of meat—not so chewy as to warrant stewing, but just chewy enough to enjoy a lusty pull with your teeth as the rare meat releases juices on your tongue. If a few extra hungry souls show up at your table, expand the food available by skewering up and grilling some onions, peppers, tomatoes or summer squash to go with it.

Pour the marinade into a large, stainless-steel, porcelain, glass, or other nonreactive bowl. Add the beef and mix well to coat. Cover and refrigerate overnight or for a minimum of 2 hours. Stir them periodically to ensure all parts of the meat have an opportunity to absorb the marinade.

When you are ready to grill, remove the meat from the marinade, blot dry with a paper towel, thread it on skewers, and allow it to come to room temperature while you prepare the grill.

Heat one side of the grill until the flame is medium-hot. You should be able to hold your hand five inches beyond the flame for no more than 4 seconds. Scrape the grate clean with a wire brush, then brush it lightly with oil.

Grill over direct heat, covered, for 2 minutes. Turn the skewers, and grill 2 minutes longer, still covered. Move them off the heat, cover, and cook over indirect heat for 5 minutes longer for medium-rare meat. Serve immediately.

Leftovers: Leftover beef kebabs taste great served cold with a salad, stirred into Onion Soup or Refrigerator Soup, or diced up for Meat Canapés with Goat Cheese and Roasted Red Pepper (all in Chapter 8).

Peanut-Crusted London Broil or Sirloin Tip Steak

ADVANCE PREPARATION REQUIRED.

SERVES 4

1 recipe Green Pepper and Garlic Marinade, Appendix 1

2 pounds sirloin tip or London broil steak

1 cup chopped unsalted oil-roasted peanuts

ESTIMATED CARBOHYDRATES:
Green Pepper and Garlic Marinade: 22.55 g
Chopped peanuts: 21.97 g
Total number of carbohydrates per recipe: 44.52 g
Total number of carbohydrates per serving will vary based on the amount of marinade not absorbed and the amount of peanut crust that does not adhere to the meat.

London broils and sirloin tip steaks are great "family" steaks. They are less expensive and, because they contain a bit more connective tissue, they'll stand up well to marinades and fun seasonings, such as this twist on West African culinary tradition. If these particular seasonings aren't your thing, the technique described below will work with any of the beef marinades listed in the back.

Pour the marinade into a glass baking dish, large zipper-locking plastic bag, or a nonreactive bowl. Add the steak and turn thoroughly to coat. Cover, refrigerate, and allow it to marinate several hours or overnight, turning occasionally. Before cooking, remove it from the refrigerator, blot the steak dry, then roll it in the chopped peanuts. Allow the meat to come to room temperature before you start your grill.

Start the grill and warm one side only until it is medium-hot. Using the hand test, the grate will be hot enough when you can hold your palm 5 inches above it on the hot side for no more than 4 seconds.

Sear the steaks for 2 minutes per side over direct heat, then move them off the heat, close the lid, and cook, without turning, until they reach 120–140 degrees, about 5–7 minutes per pound (rarer meat will be more tender and juicy). Remove the meat to a platter and let rest 5 minutes before carving into thin slices along the diagonal (across the grain).

Leftovers: Serve leftover thin-sliced steak cold over field greens dressed with lemon juice and olive oil.

Spiced Chuck Steak with Caramelized Onions

SERVES 4

1 (2–3-pound) bone-in chuck steak

1 batch Coriander-Cinnamon Spice Rub, Appendix 1

2 tablespoons lard, tallow, butter or olive oil

4 medium onions, sliced

ESTIMATED CARBOHYDRATES:
Coriander-Cinnamon Spice Rub: 13.63 g
Onions: 41.08 g
Total carbohydrates per recipe: 54.71 g
Total carbohydrates per ¼ recipe: 13.68 g

The chuck steak, ever affordable, is often overlooked by everyone except we farmers, who build up a back-stock of them in our freezers. That's not necessarily a bad thing, because cooked using this super-slow method, it is tender and flavorful. Top it with the caramelized onions, and it is luscious.

Rub the steak all over with the spice rub. Cover and refrigerate at least two hours or, preferably, overnight. Allow it to come to room temperature before you cook it.

Preheat the oven to 170°F. Place the steak in a roasting pan and cook, uncovered, for 30–35 minutes per pound, or until the meat reaches an internal temperature of 120 to 140 degrees.

Turn the oven off and allow the meat to rest and keep warm there while you prepare the onions (because you are working with a super-slow roasting temperature, you needn't worry about overcooking the steak).

Heat a large skillet over a medium flame, add the fat, and swirl to coat. Let it melt and add the onions. They should sizzle as they hit the pan. If they sputter or splatter, lower the flame. Stir well, coating the onions in the fat. Continue to cook 2–3 minutes longer, until the onions have given up two-thirds of their volume in water. Once they start to brown, lower the heat and allow them to caramelize by cooking slowly for 15–20 minutes longer, stirring often. Lower the heat further if they start to burn.

Remove the bone and gristle from the steak, then slice the meat thinly across the grain. Top with the caramelized onions and serve.

Leftovers: This leftover steak would taste delicious in the Vegetable, Meat and Potato Salad with Warm Bacon Dressing, added to Onion Soup, or in Moussaka (all recipes appear in Chapter 8).

Carpaccio

SERVES 4

1½–2 pounds filet mignon or sirloin
  steak, frozen for a minimum of 2
  weeks, then thawed

Fine salt and fresh ground pepper,
  to taste

1 recipe Mayonnaise, Chapter 7

1 teaspoon Worcestershire sauce

1 teaspoon lemon juice

¼ cup milk

4 teaspoons capers

ESTIMATED CARBOHYDRATES:
Mayonnaise: 1.28 g
Worcestershire sauce: 1.09 g
Lemon juice: 0.32 g
Milk: 2.92 g
Capers: 0.56 g
Total carbohydrates per recipe: 6.17 g
Total carbohydrates per ¼ recipe: 1.54 g

Over the years as I've cooked filet mignon and sirloin steak, I found myself perpetually feeling the meat was overdone. I was forever craving rarer and rarer meat. Apparently I'm not the first one to feel this way. The Italians have long enjoyed carpaccio, paper-thin strips of raw filet mignon or sirloin steak drizzled with a mayonnaise sauce. Now that I've discovered it, I finally have a suitably rare way to enjoy my filet and sirloin! Since carpaccio is essentially raw beef, this recipe calls for meat that has been frozen for a minimum of two weeks to ensure any potential pathogens are killed off.

Trim any fat or gristle from the beef, then allow it to chill in the refrigerator for an hour. Use a sharp knife to cut it into extremely thin (paper thin) slices. Arrange the slices on the plates. Sprinkle lightly with the salt and pepper.

Mix together the mayonnaise, Worcestershire sauce, and lemon juice in a small bowl, and thin it with the milk to your preferred consistency. Drizzle the dressing over the steak, then garnish each plate with capers. Chill until ready to serve.

We don't use purebred stock on our farm. Rather, our livestock are a mix of breeds that have been bred for several generations to thrive on grass in our climate.

Steak Fajita Salad

SERVES 4

½ cup lime juice

½ cup tequila

4 tablespoons olive oil

2 pounds skirt, flank or flat-iron steak

3 medium yellow or white onions, peeled and sliced lengthwise, with root left intact

2 teaspoons balsamic vinegar

2 teaspoons coarse salt

2 teaspoons ground black pepper

4 cups field greens

1 cup chopped fresh cilantro

3 avocados, peeled and sliced

2 medium sweet red peppers, sliced into julienned strips

4 medium tomatoes

Special equipment: grill basket

ESTIMATED CARBOHYDRATES:

Lime juice: 4.11 g

Onions: 30.81 g

Balsamic vinegar: 1.81 g

Black pepper: 2.94 g

Field greens: 6 g (this figure will vary based on the composition of the greens)

Cilantro: 0.29 g

Avocados: 51.45 g

Red sweet peppers: 14.35 g

Tomatoes: 19.14 g

Total carbohydrates per recipe: 130.90 g

Total carbohydrates per ¼ recipe: 32.73 g

Here's a cool dish for a hot summer night that would pair well with a margarita or just a glass of chilled kombucha.

Whisk together the lime juice, tequila, and 3 tablespoons of oil. Pour the marinade into a nonreactive dish, then add the steaks. Marinate 1–2 hours, turning periodically to keep evenly coated.

Heat one side of the grill until you can hold your hand 5 inches above the grate for no more than 3 seconds.

Brush the onions with olive oil, then place them in the grill basket. Grill over direct heat until tender, about 5 minutes per side. Remove the onions to a cutting board. Once they are cool enough to handle, remove the root ends and toss the slices with balsamic vinegar, salt and pepper.

Remove the steaks from the marinade and pat dry. Lay them directly over the flames. Sear the steaks over direct heat for 2 minutes per side. Move them off the heat, cover, and cook 4 minutes longer, or until it is done to your liking, remembering that skirt, flank and flat-iron steaks are best served rare.

Remove the steaks to a cutting board and let rest 5 minutes before carving. Slice ¼ inch thick diagonally across the grain. Arrange them on top of the field greens, along with the onions, cilantro, avocados, peppers and tomatoes. Dress with some olive oil and lemon or lime juice and a sprinkling of fine salt.

Leftovers: While the dressed field greens might not taste so great on a second day, the meat and vegetables can be stored in an airtight container to be served atop fresh greens on a subsequent day. The steak can also be gently re-warmed and served along with the vegetables in a tortilla.

Coriander–Cinnamon Spiced Steak

SERVES 4

1 batch Coriander-Cinnamon Spice
   Rub, Appendix 1

2 pounds skirt, flank or flat-iron steak

ESTIMATED CARBOHYDRATES:
Coriander-Cinnamon Spice Rub: 13.63 g
Total carbohydrates per recipe: 13.63 g
Total carbohydrates per ¼ recipe: 3.41 g

Skirt and flank steaks are some of our most popular cuts for the serious beef eaters who like a little extra flavor and texture to their meat. Unfortunately, there are only 2 small steaks per beef animal. Thus, the lesser-known flat-iron, cut from the chuck primal, is a fantastic alternative for folks who like to exercise their canines on a high-flavor cut of meat.

Rub the spice rub all over the surface of the meat. Cover and refrigerate overnight. When you are ready to cook them, remove the steaks from the refrigerator and allow them to come to room temperature while you heat one side of the grill until you can hold your hand 5 inches above the grate for no more than 3 seconds.

Sear the steaks over direct heat for 2 minutes per side. Move them off direct heat, cover, and cook 4–8 minutes longer, or until it is done to your liking, remembering that skirt, flank and flat-iron steaks are best served rare. *Skirt steaks will take less indirect cooking time, as they are thinner (usually less than 1 inch thick). Flat-irons, which are typically thicker (usually thicker than 1 inch), will take more time.*

Leftovers: Thin slices of this leftover steak taste great served over field greens with a lemon vinaigrette and shaved slices of a nutty-flavored hard cheese (I like Piave from Italy or Abbaye de Beloc from the Pyrenees but, admittedly, those aren't exactly local).

Tamari-Ginger Shaved Steaks

SERVES 6

½ cup tamari

2 tablespoons grated fresh ginger

4 tablespoons toasted sesame oil

1 tablespoon honey or maple syrup

2 tablespoons diced shallot, chives, leeks or green onion

4 cloves garlic, peeled

2 tablespoons Mirin (sweet Japanese cooking wine) or sherry

1 tablespoon crushed red pepper (reduce this amount or eliminate it completely if you are serving spice-averse children)

2 pounds shaved steak (thinly sliced round steak)

2 tablespoons peanut oil

ESTIMATED CARBOHYDRATES:

Tamari: 4.01 g

Ginger: 2.14 g

Honey: 17.30 g

Shallot: 3.36 g

Garlic: 2.97 g

Mirin: 1.5 g

Crushed red pepper: 3 g

Total carbohydrates per recipe: 34.28 g*

Total carbohydrates per ⅙ recipe: 5.71 g*

* The actual number of carbohydrates per recipe will be less than this amount, because the meat will not fully absorb all the contents of the marinade. For a truly accurate measure, weigh the marinade before the meat is added, then weigh it after the meat is removed. The difference will be the amount of marinade that actually penetrated the meat.

Shaved steaks, also called "sandwich steaks," are extremely thin slices of meat that your butcher cuts from the top, bottom and eye round with a rotary meat slicer. They are often used for Philly cheese steak sandwiches, but here they take a fabulous Asian twist that is one of my kids' favorite dishes. Once marinated, they are very quick to cook up. I serve them with stir-fried vegetables and kimchi, a fermented cabbage pickle popular in Eastern Asia.

Add the tamari, ginger, sesame oil, honey, shallot, garlic, mirin and crushed red pepper to the small bowl of a food processor. Puree. Place the marinade in a glass bowl and add the beef. Turn to coat. Marinate for 1–2 hours or overnight (covered) in the refrigerator.

When you are ready to cook the steaks, remove them from the marinade and blot dry. Heat a skillet over a medium flame. Add just enough oil to lubricate the pan, then add the steaks, laying them flat. Take care to cook only a few at a time so that there is ample space around each piece of meat, otherwise it will not brown. Fry 30 seconds per side, or until browned. Repeat with remaining steak, using additional fat if needed. Serve immediately.

Leftovers: If it looks like there are more steaks on hand than we can eat in one sitting, I'll store the uncooked steaks in a glass container and use them for another meal. If the steaks are already cooked, serve them with the Asian-Style Cold Meat Salad in Chapter 8.

Thai Shaved Steaks

SERVES 4

1 recipe Thai Marinade, Appendix 1

2 pounds shaved steaks (thinly sliced round steak)

2 tablespoons lard, tallow or butter

Thai Dipping Sauce (see recipe in Thai-Style Country Ribs with a Dipping Sauce, Chapter 6)

ESTIMATED CARBOHYDRATES:
Thai Marinade: 32.77 g
Thai Dipping sauce: 22.65 g
Total carbohydrates per recipe: 55.42†
Total carbohydrates per ¼ recipe: 13.86*

* Actual number of carbohydrates will vary based on how much of the marinade is absorbed by the meat.

Here's an exciting way to turn an inexpensive cut of meat into a flashy dinner.

Place the marinade in a glass bowl and add the beef. Turn to coat. Marinate for 1–2 hours or overnight (covered) in the refrigerator.

When you are ready to cook the steaks, remove them from the marinade and blot dry. Heat a skillet over a medium flame. Add just enough fat to lubricate the pan, then add the steaks, laying them flat. Take care to cook only a few at a time so that there is ample space around each piece of meat, otherwise it will not brown. Fry 30 seconds per side or until browned. Repeat with remaining steak, using additional fat if needed. Serve with the Thai Dipping Sauce from Thai-Style Country Ribs with a Dipping Sauce in Chapter 6.

Leftovers: These steaks cook very fast, so I recommend cooking a few less than you think you will need, then cooking the rest as your dinner companions require them. That way, leftovers can be kept in the marinade and fried up for a later meal. If you have extra cooked steak on hand, consider adding it to the Asian-Style Cold Meat Salad (Chapter 8).

Paprika Lime Skillet Steaks

SERVES 4

1 recipe Paprika-Lime Marinade,
    Appendix 1

1 pound shaved steak (thinly sliced
    round steak)

2 tablespoons lard or butter

ESTIMATED CARBOHYDRATES:

Paprika-Lime Marinade 27.92 g

Total amount of carbohydrate per serving will depend on how much of the marinade is absorbed by the meat. To gauge an estimate, weigh the amount of marinade before you begin cooking, and divide the carbohydrates by the number of ounces (which will tell you roughly how many carbohydrates per ounce). Weigh the leftover marinade once you've finished. Subtract it from the original. The difference will be the number of ounces used on your meat. Multiply that by the number of carbohydrates per ounce, and you'll have an estimate for the total number of carbohydrates for the recipe.

These brightly flavored steaks fry up fast once they've been marinated. Paired with a side of coleslaw, they make a terrific quick lunch.

Place the marinade in a glass bowl and add the beef. Turn to coat. Marinate for 1–2 hours or overnight (covered) in the refrigerator.

When you are ready to cook the steaks, remove them from the marinade and blot dry. Heat a skillet over a medium flame. Add just enough fat to lubricate the pan, then add the steaks, laying them flat. Take care to cook only a few at a time so that there is ample space around each piece of meat, otherwise it will not brown. Fry 30 seconds per side or until browned. Repeat with remaining steak, using additional fat if needed. Serve immediately.

Leftovers: If it looks like there are more steaks on hand than we can eat in one sitting, I'll store the uncooked steaks in a glass container and fry them fresh for another meal. They are terrific if they are fried fresh or re-warmed and served with the Cuban Black Beans and Rice (Chapter 8). If the steaks are already cooked, toss them in with the with the Asian-Style Cold Meat Salad (Chapter 8).

Super-slow roasting

Learning how to properly cook lean meat was one of my biggest challenges when I started writing grassfed cookbooks. Conventional cookbooks recommended roasting lean cuts like London broils and eye rounds in a 350-degree oven, and the results were often gray and chewy. There had to be a better way to prepare grassfed meat than the recipes I was finding in most of my current cookbooks. But to do it, I couldn't look forward. I had to look backward, to a time when not all meat was grain-fed. That's when I discovered Adelle Davis's 1947 cookbook, *Let's Cook It Right*. Once I had her volume in hand, I was truly able to learn how to cook meat.

Adelle Davis argued that the tougher cuts from the round and the chuck would be tender and delicious if cooked in a very cool oven, ideally at a temperature no greater than 150–160 degrees. Most modern ovens don't go below 170 degrees, but I went ahead and experimented with her technique, choosing to take it out when the internal temperature was 125 degrees, long before I reached the USDA recommended internal temperature for "rare" meat (145 degrees). It was fantastic.

What had happened?

The meat wasn't overdone. During the cooking process, myofibrillar proteins begin to harden once meat approaches higher internal temperatures. Furthermore, once meat crosses the internal temperature of 145 degrees, the muscle fibers contract at an accelerated rate, drying the roast out. While the USDA recommends that beef be cooked to a minimum temperature of 145 degrees for food safety concerns, it is important to remember that they assume you are eating beef from factory-farmed animals, processed in large batches in industrial slaughterhouses where there is a much greater chance that your dinner could be harboring food-borne pathogens. Since anyone reading this sidebar is likely using reliably-sourced local beef that was raised on grass (which greatly reduces the risk of disease transmission), I advocate enjoying beef cooked to lower internal temperatures.

The oven temperature was super-low. During this super-slow roasting process, the external surface of the meat dries out, but moisture is locked in. The oven temperature is so low that the muscles fibers do not contract and force the juice out of the meat and into the pan. Thus, the connective tissue in the meat is broken down by the meat's own juices, resulting in a wonderfully tender roast.

The best part of this method is that it is the absolutely easiest way to cook a roast that I know of. It will work on a London broil, a sirloin tip, an eye round, top round, bottom round, or any chuck roast. It is no-fail. Here's how to do it:

Super-Slow Roasted Beef

Preheat the oven to 170°F. Rub any of the above-mentioned roasts with a little salt and pepper, or any dry-rub seasoning blend of your choice. Place the meat in a cast-iron skillet or roasting pan, and roast, uncovered, for 30–40 minutes per pound (leaner roasts will cook closer to 30 minutes per pound; fattier cuts will cook closer to 40 minutes per pound). Use an internal meat thermometer to determine when the meat is done to your liking

Super-Slow Roasted Beef

1 beef roast: bone-in chuck, top round, bottom round, eye round, sirloin tip or London broil are all ideal candidates.

Garlic Spice Rub, Appendix 1 (or any of the dry rubs listed in the back that appeals to you, or sea salt and freshly ground black pepper)

ESTIMATED CARBOHYDRATES:

Garlic Spice Rub: 11.46 g

Total number of carbohydrates per recipe: 11.46 g

Total number of carbohydrates per serving will vary based on the size of the roast and the number of servings.

When I wrote The Grassfed Gourmet Cookbook, *the super-slow roasting method had people talking. Recipe editors from magazines called to verify the food safety (I reviewed it with a meat scientist prior to publishing), and farmers called to offer their thanks. It is the one foolproof method for cooking any cut of beef.*

As there is little shrinkage, allow ¼–½ pound meat per serving if you are working with a boneless roast. Allow ¾ pound of meat per serving if you have a bone-in roast.

Preheat the oven to 170°F. Rub any of the above-mentioned roasts with the Garlic Spice Rub or any dry-rub seasoning blend of your choice, or just or a little salt and pepper. Place the meat in a cast-iron skillet or roasting pan, and roast, uncovered, for 30–40 minutes per pound (leaner roasts and bone-in roasts will cook closer to 30 minutes per pound; fattier cuts will cook closer to 40 minutes per pound). Use an internal meat thermometer to determine when the meat is done to your liking. The internal temperature should be 120–140 degrees.

Since the juices will not have been disturbed when cooking at such low temperatures, there is no need to rest the meat prior to carving. Slice thin to serve.

Leftovers: Slice leftover roast thin for sandwiches, or combine ½ cup softened cream cheese with ½ cup sour cream and 4 teaspoons prepared horseradish. Place a dollop on each slice of leftover beef, roll it, and chill until firm. These make elegant little appetizers.

Garlic-Rubbed Chuck Eye Roast with Horseradish Cream

MINIMAL PREPARATION

SERVES 8

1 batch Garlic Spice Rub, Appendix 1

1 4-pound boneless chuck eye roast

HORSERADISH CREAM

1 cup sour cream

2–4 teaspoons grated horseradish

ESTIMATED CARBOHYDRATES:
Garlic Spice Rub: 11.46 g
Sour cream: 6.62 g
Horseradish (3 teaspoons): 1.69 g
Total carbohydrates per recipe: 19.77 g
Total carbohydrates per ⅛ recipe: 2.47 g

The chuck eye is an extraordinary cut of beef. It is a piece of rib eye muscle that extends forward into the chuck primal, giving it great marbling and flavor, with a surprising degree of tenderness for a chuck cut. Since one is often able to buy this piece of the rib eye muscle at chuck roast prices, we call it the "poor man's prime rib."

Rub the Garlic Spice Rub all over the meat. If there is any extra, reserve it for another use. Allow the roast to come to room temperature on the kitchen counter while you preheat the oven to 300°F.

Place the meat in a pan and roast, uncovered, for about 24 minutes per pound or until the internal temperature is between 120 and 140 degrees.

To make the horseradish cream sauce, combine the sour cream with 2 teaspoons grated horseradish. Add additional horseradish until it is seasoned to your liking.

Leftovers: My favorite way to use chuck eye roast leftovers is in the Parmesan-Cheddar One-Crust Meat Pie, the Summer Harvest Casserole, or the Black Bean Chili with Dark Roast Coffee (all recipes appear in Chapter 8).

Roast Tenderloin of Beef with Goat Cheese

2 tablespoons coarse salt

1 tablespoon ground black pepper

2 tablespoons tallow (preferred), or lard or butter

1 tenderloin roast

1 batch Garlic-Chive Goat Cheese (see Oven Roasted Burgers with Garlic-Chive Goat Cheese)

ESTIMATED CARBOHYDRATES:
Ground black pepper: 4.41 g
Garlic-Chive goat cheese: 5.39 g
Number of carbohydrates for entire recipe: 9.8 g
Number of carbohydrates for ⅙ recipe: 1.63 g

The filet is the tenderest cut on the animal and, as a whole roast, can make for a very elegant meal, especially when paired with Garlic-Chive Goat Cheese (see Oven-Roasted Burgers with Garlic-Chive Goat Cheese for recipe). To figure serving size, allow for ½ pound of meat per person.

Preheat the oven to 200°F. Blot the roast dry, then sprinkle with salt and pepper. Heat a cast-iron skillet or other ovenproof frying pan over high heat. When you see smoke rising off the pan, grease it with the tallow, then add the tenderloin and sear it over high heat 4 minutes per side (total searing time will be 8 minutes).

Place the pan in the oven and roast for approximately 4 minutes per pound, or until a meat thermometer registers about 115 degrees. While some may prefer their beef more well-done, I feel that the delicate flavors of the tenderloin will be significantly more pronounced if the meat is kept *very* rare. Slice the roast and serve with the goat cheese sprinkled on top.

Leftovers: Try slicing the meat thin and serving it over field greens with any leftover goat cheese, paired with the Buttermilk Mustard Dressing in Chapter 7. Like the other higher-end steak cuts, this is also terrific served cold with cheese, mustard, or horseradish.

Hillside farms like ours were once considered non-viable because the steep hills couldn't be tilled. Today, with grazing, they are an important part of the local food system.

Prime Rib Roast with Yorkshire Pudding

1 recipe Rosemary Herb Rub,
    Appendix 1

1 standing rib roast

Yorkshire Pudding (recipe follows)

Horseradish Cream (see Garlic-
    Rubbed Chuck-Eye Roast with
    Horseradish Cream)

ESTIMATED CARBOHYDRATES:
Rosemary Herb Rub: 14.68 g
Yorkshire Pudding: 128.61 g
Horseradish Cream: 8.31 g
Total carbohydrates per recipe: 151.6 g
Total carbohydrates per serving:
    25.27 g

Christmas in our family begins in the fall, when my dad and I examine the rib primal of every beef that we process, searching out the perfect standing rib roast. When we make our choice, I write NOT FOR SALE, SHANNY'S MEAT all across the packaging, and we go into the dark months reassured that our favorite holiday feast is already in the freezer. When estimating the size roast you will need, figure that a standing rib roast typically serves two people per rib. Thus, a four-bone rib roast will serve 8, a 5-bone will serve 10, etc. If the roast seems small to you (perhaps it came from a smaller-framed animal), simply round up what you'll need. You'll always find a use for the leftovers.

Rub the Rosemary Herb rub all over the meat, including the bones. Set it aside at room temperature for about 2 hours.

Preheat the oven to 300°F.

Place the beef, bone-side down, in a roasting pan. Insert a meat thermometer into the rib eye muscle. Roast about 20 minutes per pound, or until the internal temperature is between 120 and 140 degrees.

Remove the meat from the oven and allow it to rest while you prepare the Yorkshire Pudding (recipe follows), and Horseradish Cream.

Yorkshire Pudding

SERVES 6

¼ cup roast beef pan drippings,
    melted tallow, or butter

3 eggs, beaten

1 cup whole milk

1 cup flour

1 teaspoon fine salt

ESTIMATED CARBOHYDRATES:
Eggs: 1.08 g
Milk: 11.71 g
Flour: 92.26 g
Number of carbohydrates for entire
    recipe: 116.12 g
Number of carbohydrates per ⅙ recipe:
    19.35 g

Closely related to the popover, Yorkshire Pudding, puffed gloriously high, paired with prime rib and some horseradish cream sauce, is how we define Christmas dinner. It is simple, easy to prepare, and delicious.

Preheat the oven to 450°F. Pour the pan drippings into a 9-by-9-inch pan, and put it into the oven to keep hot while you prepare the batter. If you don't have enough pan drippings for a full ¼ cup, use tallow or butter to make up the difference.

Whisk together the eggs, milk, flour and salt. Pour the batter into the hot pan and bake 25 minutes or until puffed and golden.

Leftovers: We love to slice our leftover roast beef very thin and serve it cold with extra sharp cheddar cheese, either over salad greens or on top of crackers. We garnish it with a dollop of spicy mustard or horseradish cream. It would also taste delicious with Croquettes with Black Pepper and Onion Sauce, Meat Canapés with Goat Cheese and Roasted Red Pepper, or Onion Soup (all recipes appear in Chapter 8).

We don't have a store front at the farm. Rather, we sell right from the kitchen counter.

Shepherd's Pie

SERVES 6

FOR THE MASHED-POTATO TOPPING:

2 pounds coarsely chopped potatoes

4 tablespoons unsalted butter

½ cup whole milk or cream

1 clove garlic, minced

½ teaspoon coarse salt

½ teaspoon ground pepper

FOR THE FILLING:

2 tablespoons unsalted butter, lard, or olive oil, plus more if needed

2 medium onions, diced

4 medium carrots, diced

2 cups green beans, coarsely chopped

1 cup corn (or peas, or a combination of both)

2 pounds ground beef

1½ teaspoons coarse salt, plus more to taste

1 teaspoon freshly ground pepper, plus more to taste

⅓ cup all-purpose flour (or 3 tablespoons arrowroot whisked into 3 tablespoons ice water)

1 quart meat broth, such as Shannon's Meat Broth, Chapter 3

4 ounces freshly grated Parmesan cheese

This one is a favorite in our house. It is simple, comforting, nourishing, flavorful, and we all clamor for the leftovers.

Put the potatoes in a pot of water to cover and bring to a boil. Cook until tender and drain off all the water. Alternatively, put the potatoes in a pressure cooker with 8 ounces of water and cook for 7 minutes at 15 psi. Allow the pressure to subside using the natural release method, following the manufacturer's directions. Strain off the water.

Put the potatoes in a large bowl. Add the butter, milk, garlic, salt, pepper, and smash thoroughly until smooth. Set aside.

Preheat the oven to 350° F.

Place a large ovenproof casserole over medium heat. Add the butter and onions, carrots, green beans and any other vegetables you choose. Sauté until the onions are clear and the vegetables crisp-tender, about 7 minutes. Remove all to a separate bowl.

Crumble the ground beef and add to the casserole, season with the salt and pepper (add more fat to the pot if needed), and sauté until browned. Sprinkle in the flour and slowly stir in the broth. (If using arrowroot and water, add it now.) Bring the mixture to a boil, stirring often, and then reduce it to a simmer and cook until thickened. Return the vegetables to the casserole, stir well, and taste for salt and pepper.

Remove the casserole from the heat. Spread the mashed potatoes over the top, sprinkle with the Parmesan cheese and bake until the surface of the potato topping is lightly browned, about 30 to 45 minutes.

Leftovers: Reheat leftovers in a covered dish in a 250-degree oven until warmed through. If you get to a point where only a tiny bit remains, hardly enough to make a meal, add it to the Refrigerator Soup (Chapter 8), where the mashed potatoes will help to thicken it.

ESTIMATED CARBOHYDRATES:	
Potatoes: 144.21 g	Corn: 27.11 g
Butter: 0.06 g	Black pepper: 1.47 g
Milk: 5.86 g	Flour: 30.76 g
Garlic: 0.99 g	Meat broth: 5.6 g*
Pepper: 0.74 g	Total carbohydrates per recipe: 273.64 g
Parmesan: 4.60 g	Total carbohydrates per ⅙ recipe: 45.61 g
Onions: 20.54 g	* Number of carbohydrates in homemade broth will vary. This figure is calculated using the recipe for Shannon's Meat Broth (Chapter 3).
Carrots: 23.36 g	
Green beans: 13.94 g	

Simple Meat Loaf

SERVES 6

4 tablespoons unsalted butter or lard

1 medium onion, diced

1 pound ground beef

1 pound bulk pork sausage (sweet Italian, hot Italian, bratwurst, or kielbasa all work well), or one pound ground veal, or one more pound of ground beef

1 teaspoon coarse salt

1 teaspoon ground black pepper

ESTIMATED CARBOHYDRATES:
Butter: 0.04 g
Onion: 10.27 g
Black pepper: 1.47 g
Total carbohydrates per recipe: 11.78 g
Total carbohydrates per ⅙ recipe: 1.96 g

Meat loaf has noble, albeit humble, origins back to the days of meat scarcity, when bread crumbs or oatmeal made a little ground beef go a long way. Were I to be faithful to this tradition, I'd have written a recipe that included the extra starch . . . but I just never liked it cooked that way. I want my meat loaf to be made of meat, and to be so simple that I never have to look up a recipe for it. With only four ingredients plus salt and pepper, I think this is the best version you'll ever taste. It's every bit as homey as what your grandmother fixed, but not as mealy.

Preheat the oven to 350° F.

Melt the butter in a sauté pan over medium heat. Add the onion and sauté until translucent. Turn off the heat and allow the onion to cool. Place the beef and sausage in a bowl. Add the salt, pepper, and butter-onion mixture. Using your hands, mix well, but lightly; press meat into a 9-inch loaf pan. Roast 1 hour. Serve immediately, spooning any pan juices on top of the meat.

Leftovers: Quite often I double this recipe and prepare two pans—one to serve for lunch, the other to hold for the next day. I cover and reheat it in a 250-degree oven until it is warmed through. Once we've had our fill of it, I cut it into pieces, toss it into some simmering broth along with some tomatoes or tomato sauce, add some vegetables, and turn it into a tasty soup. My good friend and editor, Damon Lee Fowler, assures me that meat loaf sandwiches, with caramelized onions and Dijon mustard on an English muffin, are a religious experience. He warms the sliced meatloaf in the skillet where he has just sautéed thin-sliced onion in butter until browned. He paints the muffins with mustard, fills them with warmed meatloaf and onions, then wipes out the pan and toasts the sandwiches in a little butter.

Garlic and Olive Meatballs with Braised Vegetables

SERVES 6–8

1 pound ground pork, ground veal or loose sweet Italian or hot Italian sausage

1 pound ground beef

2 hard-boiled eggs, finely diced (see Chapter 7 for instructions on preparing hard-boiled eggs)

1 cup green olives, pitted and diced

3 cloves garlic, minced

5 tablespoons dried parsley, divided use

About 1 teaspoon fine salt (to taste)

About 1 teaspoon ground black pepper (to taste)

4 tablespoons lard, tallow or butter

2 medium fennel bulbs, cut into ¼-inch-thick wedges

6 carrots, cut diagonally into ½-inch pieces

2 medium turnips, peeled and diced into ½-inch pieces

3 cups meat broth, such as Shannon's Meat Broth, Chapter 3

2 tablespoons cold water

1 tablespoon arrowroot

ESTIMATED CARBOHYDRATES:

Eggs: 0.72 g	Olives: 8 g
Garlic: 0.99 g	Black pepper: 1.47 g
Parsley: 4.05 g	Fennel bulbs: 34.12 g
Carrots: 35.04 g	Turnips: 15.69 g
Meat broth: 4.2 g*	Arrow root: 7.0 g

Total carbohydrates per recipe: 111.28 g

Total carbohydrates per ⅙ recipe: 18.55 g

* Number of carbohydrates in home-made broth will vary. This figure is calculated using the recipe for Shannon's Meat Broth (Chapter 3).

Grassfed ground beef is some of the most flavorful meat that comes off a steer or cow. While it is wonderful to enjoy it as a deeply satisfying burger, it seems a pity not to let it play a part in more sophisticated fare. Recipe test note: My kids loved these meatballs (they love anything with olives), and they liked the fennel and carrots. They weren't so keen on the turnips . . . but we grown-ups sure enjoyed them!

Place the ground meat in a large bowl. Add the diced eggs, ¾ cup of the olives, the garlic, parsley, and salt and pepper to taste. Using your hands, mix well, then shape into 1 ½-inch-diameter balls.

Position a rack 4–6 inches below the heat source and preheat the oven broiler. Rub a large cast-iron skillet or baking sheet with 1 tablespoon of the fat. Line up meatballs on the pan, allowing at least 1 inch space around each ball (you may need to do multiple batches). Broil 4–6 inches from the heat for 5 minutes, use tongs to turn them over, and broil 5 minutes longer.

While meatballs are broiling, heat 1 tablespoon of the fat over medium-high heat in a large Dutch oven or 8-quart soup pot. Working in small batches so as not to crowd your pan, brown all the vegetables, about 4 minutes per batch. Remove vegetables to a bowl after browning each batch, and add more fat as needed.

Once all the vegetables are browned, return them all to the Dutch oven. Set the meatballs on top and pour in the broth. Cover and simmer until the vegetables are tender, about 15–20 minutes. Using a slotted spoon, remove the vegetables and meatballs to a large serving bowl. Leave the broth simmering in the pot.

In a small bowl, whisk together the arrowroot and cold water. Pour the mixture into the Dutch oven and gently stir until the sauce is slightly thickened. Remove from the heat, Pour over the vegetables and meatballs and serve, garnished with the remaining parsley and olives.

Leftovers: Leftovers of this dish are easily re-warmed in a covered pan in a 250-degree oven, for about 30–45 minutes or until heated through. To stretch more meals out of this dish, add more meat stock the second time around, turning it from a braised dish to a soup. Leftovers can be used in Stuffed Peppers or Hearty Macaroni and Cheese (both recipes appear in Chapter 8). The meatballs, vegetables and leftover sauce can also be stirred into a marinara sauce and used for whatever purpose suits you.

Stuffed Chard with Lemon Cream Sauce

10–12 large Swiss chard leaves, stems removed

1 egg, beaten

1 pound ground beef, veal, pork or lamb

2 cups finely shredded cabbage

1 tablespoon chopped fresh dill leaves (or 1 teaspoon dried)

2 teaspoons grated lemon zest

½ teaspoon ground allspice

1 teaspoon fine salt

1 teaspoon ground black pepper

2 tablespoons butter

1 clove garlic, crushed

2 cups meat broth, such as Shannon's Meat Broth, Chapter 3

1 cup sour cream or heavy cream

2 tablespoons lemon juice

ESTIMATED CARBOHYDRATES:
Swiss chard: 21.68 g
Egg: 0.36 g
Cabbage: 8.12 g
Dill: 0.07 g
Lemon zest: 0.64 g
Allspice: 0.69 g
Black pepper: 1.47 g
Butter: 0.02 g
Meat broth: 2.8 g*
Garlic: 0.99 g
Lemon juice: 1.94 g
Total carbohydrates per recipe: 38.78 g
Total carbohydrates per ¼ recipe: 9.70 g
* Number of carbohydrates in home-made broth will vary. This figure is calculated using the recipe for Shannon's Meat Broth (Chapter 3).

Here is a clever (and tasty) way to convert humble ingredients like greens, cabbage and ground beef into stylish fare.

Remove the stems from the greens and discard. Place the leaves in a large heatproof bowl and cover with boiling water. After 5 minutes, strain off the water, lay the leaves out on a towel and pat dry.

Combine the egg, ground meat, cabbage, dill, lemon zest, allspice, salt and pepper in a bowl. Mix well. Scoop up meat and cabbage mixture by quarter cupfuls, shape into cylinders and set each cylinder at the stem end of each leaf. Roll up, tucking the sides as you go to form a bundle.

Heat a large, nonreactive skillet over a medium flame. Add the butter and swirl to coat. Place the stuffed greens in the skillet seam-side down. Whisk the crushed garlic into the broth, then pour it into the skillet. Bring the broth to a light simmer, reduce heat, cover, and cook 30 minutes.

Remove the greens to a serving platter using a slotted spoon. Increase the heat in the skillet and simmer the broth down until it is reduced by two-thirds. Whisk in the sour cream, then the lemon juice. Season to taste with salt and pepper. Pour over the stuffed greens and serve.

Leftovers: These are terrific served cold with a dollop of sour cream, as an appetizer or carried along on a picnic lunch.

Grilled Burgers

SERVES 4

1½ pounds ground beef

1¼ teaspoons fine salt

1¼ teaspoons ground black pepper

Cooking oil

ESTIMATED CARBOHYDRATES:

Black pepper: 1.84 g

Total carbohydrates per recipe: 1.84 g

Total carbohydrates per ¼ recipe: 0.46 g

For years I frittered around trying to make the perfect burger. I added garlic, Worcestershire sauce, any number of ingredients. Over time I discovered that, because ground beef is made from the most flavorful meat on the animal, less is more. A tiny bit of salt and a dash of pepper is all you need. Much of the flavor is built up by the sear on the grill, and then the prolonged indirect cooking time, which allows the sugars to caramelize over the surface of the meat. We like these burgers so much we eat them plain, as though they were fine steak—no ketchup, no mustard. We revel in the full, glorious, mineral-rich intense beef flavor all on its own.

Combine the ground beef with the salt and pepper. Loosely shape the meat into four balls. Gently flatten them until they are about 1 inch thick. With your fingertips, make a small well in the top of each patty to prevent the meat from getting puffy over the flames. Set the patties aside while you light one side of your grill and clean off the cooking grate with a wire brush.

When one side of the grill is medium-hot and you can hold your hand five inches above it for no more than four seconds, brush it down lightly with oil, then set the patties directly over the flame. Cover and cook 4 minutes per side. Move the burgers off the coals to indirect heat, cover, and cook 10 minutes longer.

Leftovers: If my kids leave any leftover burger on their plates, I don't let it go to waste. I toss cooked leftover burger into the Minestra Maritata Soup, or Refrigerator Soup (both recipes appear in Chapter 8).

Well-done burgers and raw meat

Okay, if you've been paying attention, you are probably aware I'm of the opinion that meat should never be cooked beyond medium-rare, unless it is a pot roast or stew. There is one other exception: burgers.

When we grind beef in the cutting room, we make it from all the little good-quality scraps of meat we can salvage, in an effort to prevent waste. Some of the meat and fat is meat from the exterior of the carcass, some of it from the interior. Exterior meat does have a greater chance of carrying potentially harmful pathogens, such as *E.coli*. Although *E.coli* is less prevalent on grassfed beef, and the strain of *E.coli* found in grassfed is usually one that our stomach acids can easily destroy, I prefer to play it safe with my burger-cooking recommendations. If *E.coli* is located on the exterior surface of a steak, it is almost always killed in the cooking process. But when the exterior meat is blended with the interior meat, which is what happens with ground beef, some of it will be inside your burger, and some of it will be on the outside. Any pathogens on the exterior will be killed upon exposure to the heat. But the inside of the burger, if left rare, can still harbor the little vectors of illness, *if the beef was tainted*. For that reason, I recommend searing burgers over high heat, then finishing them indirectly on the grill, or in the oven. This extra cooking time helps ensure that the meat is cooked through without drying it out. Better still, it gives the sugars an opportunity to caramelize over the surface of the burger, giving it a glossy finish and delicious flavor.

That said, if you like a rare burger, I think choosing local, grassfed beef is your safest bet. The same is true if you like steak carpaccio, kibbeh (raw ground lamb), or steak tartare. I've included a few raw meat recipes in the book, and my family has happily eaten them repeatedly, with no ill effects. However, it is important to be aware of the risks when choosing to eat these foods. If you are curious about what raw meat tastes like, but are not keen on taking any risks with food-borne pathogens, try the Steak Carpaccio. Instead of serving it raw, simply sear the steak briefly over high heat before chilling it and slicing it.

Oven Roasted Burgers with Garlic-Chive Goat Cheese

SERVES 4

FOR THE GARLIC-CHIVE GOAT CHEESE

4 ounces goat cheese

2 teaspoons fine salt, divided use

3 tablespoons olive oil

1 teaspoon granulated garlic

2 tablespoons minced fresh chives or green onions, or 2 teaspoons dried chives

1 pound ground beef

1 teaspoon ground black pepper

2 tablespoons tallow, lard, or butter

ESTIMATED CARBOHYDRATES:
Goat cheese: 2.88 g
Granulated garlic: 2.25 g
Chives: 0.26 g
Black pepper: 1.47 g
Number of carbohydrates for entire recipe. 6.86 g
Number of carbohydrates per ¼ recipe: 1 72 g

Here is another family-favorite, a delightful way to enjoy a rich beefy burger, even if I don't feel like trudging out to the grill midwinter.

Place the goat cheese, 1 teaspoon salt, olive oil, granulated garlic, and chives in a small dish. Use a fork to smash it all together and thoroughly mix it. Set it aside.

Preheat the oven to 200°F.

Combine the ground beef with the remaining salt and pepper. Loosely shape the meat into four balls. Gently flatten them until they are about 1 inch thick. With your fingertips, make a small well in the top of each patty to prevent them from swelling.

Place a large ovenproof skillet over a high flame. When you begin to see a little smoke rising off the skillet, add the fat, swirl to coat, then add the burgers. Make sure there is about 1 inch of space around each burger as it sears in the pan. Sear the burgers for 4 minutes on each side.

Transfer the pan to the oven. Roast 10 minutes, then serve topped with the garlic-chive goat cheese.

Leftovers: See the leftover suggestions for Grilled Burgers, above.

Oven Roasted Breakfast Burgers

SERVES 4

1 pound ground beef

1 teaspoon fine salt

1 teaspoon ground black pepper

2 teaspoons dried thyme

3 ounces finely diced uncooked bacon

2 tablespoons lard, tallow or butter

ESTIMATED CARBOHYDRATES:
Black Pepper: 1.47 g
Thyme: 1.28 g
Number of carbohydrates for entire recipe: 2.75 g
Number of carbohydrates per ¼ recipe: 0.69 g

Yup. You read the title right. Burgers for breakfast. Why not? It can't be eggs every day, you know. Meat for breakfast, beyond the typical bacon, ham and sausage routine, is actually an old farm tradition.

Preheat the oven to 200°F.

Combine the ground beef with the salt, pepper, thyme and bacon. Loosely shape the meat into four balls. Gently flatten them until they are about 1 inch thick. With your fingertips, make a small well in the top of each patty to prevent them from swelling.

Place a large ovenproof skillet over a high flame. When you begin to see a little smoke rising off the skillet, add the fat, swirl to coat, then add the burgers. Make sure there is about 1 inch of space around each burger as it sears in the pan. Sear the burgers for 4 minutes on each side.

Transfer the pan to the oven and roast 10 minutes longer.

Leftovers: See the leftover suggestions for Grilled Burgers, above.

CHAPTER FIVE

Lamb

Some of my earliest memories are of toddling in and the table of the Schoharie County Sheepmen's Association meetings. From my child's-eye view, I could watch the women's hands busily knitting in their laps, baskets of yarn at their feet, whilst they discussed the business of raising sheep with the men at the table overhead.

My mother and father participated in these meetings, as did my grandparents. But the relationships among all the members was so familial, I believe my brother and I were well into our teens before we had a keen idea of who in the group was a blood relative and who was not.

Even today, although the Sheepmen's Association stopped meeting decades ago, when a public gathering takes place where two or more shepherding families are present, we find a way to share space and time together.

Only recently do those public gatherings include a mix of shepherds with other farmers.

The range wars out west in the late 1800s spurred a great deal of animosity and violence between shepherds and cowboys. The cowboys argued that the sheep grazed the grasses of the open range down too far, leaving inadequate forage for the cattle. And while that contention spurred its share of gunfights in the Wild West, and still leaves some Western cowboys disdainful of sheep even today, the social fabric of farming in the Northeast became factionalized much later.

Shepherding was a common practice throughout the Northeastern states from the colonial period forward. Sheep could flourish on rocky New England hillsides, could produce meat, fiber and milk on limited acreage, and were an important part of the economy. Cattle were also common here, and in fact most farms were highly diversified, with a mélange of cattle, pigs, goats, sheep, poultry, vegetables and fruit. Northeastern farm families kept their expenses low by producing the fiber, food and raw materials they needed to survive, and then generated wealth by selling their surplus. The key to their success wasn't in mastering trade of any one commodity; it was in the synergy from all the diversified components working together.

All that changed following World War II, as farms came under increasing pressure to modernize and "get big or get out." The small diversified farm that once supported several generations of a family was suddenly marginalized as a "hobby" venture, and any agriculturalists that stayed in business were pushed to specialize in one particular commodity.

And the farming community fell into tribes. Anyone left in business was never simply a "farmer." He or she was a *dairy* farmer, a *pork* producer, a *beef* producer, a *vegetable* or *fruit* grower, or a *shepherd*. We came to believe that we had little in common, and rather than politically organizing and working to support each other as an agricultural industry, we began associating almost exclusively within our commodity groups and watched as, one by one, neighboring farm families went out of business.

Happily, as the local food system digs deeper into our reawakening culture of sustainability, the social fabric among farmers is being rewoven. Nationwide, grass farmers are realizing the benefits of grazing sheep and beef together. Indeed, the overgrazing of the West was not inherently a sheep problem, but a *management* problem. As the wounds begin to heal, even the hard-core cattlemen are beginning to acknowledge the important role of shepherding, not the least of which is that *lamb is delicious*.

At Sap Bush Hollow, my dad prefers to keep the sheep and the beef together as he moves them across our pastures. The large steers help deter predators, and the sheep efficiently make use of certain grasses that the cattle refuse to eat, helping to graze the fields evenly and to generate as much protein-rich food as possible from the land base.

Lamb has for decades held a reputation as an undesirable meat in this country, with per capita annual consumption being *less than one pound*. This is hardly the case among the locavores, who have discovered that the sheep industry hasn't fallen prey to the same factory-farming pressures that assaulted the beef industry. Even before the resurgence of farmers' markets, good grassfed lamb could be found just about anywhere in the country if a person was willing to search it out. I suspect that our cultural spurning of lamb has little to do with its flavor and more to do with marketing and the politics of industrial farming. On our farm, it is one of our most popular

*My dad likes to graze our sheep and
beef together. The cattle help deter predators, and
the sheep make good use of any grasses the cattle won't eat.*

meats. When a fresh harvest of lamb is available, our customers scramble to buy it up and return to regale us with stories about the magnificent feasts that ensued.

For vegetarians who are considering reclaiming an omnivorous lifestyle, lamb is a great place to start. It is rich in easy-to-digest macro and trace minerals, fat-soluble vitamins and carnitine, a substance that helps the body turn fat into energy. As with beef, there will be variation in flavor from flock to flock. Darker breed sheep are presumed to yield more-pronounced taste, while the lighter breeds are believed to be more mildly flavored. The taste of younger lamb will be more delicate, which is why most producers harvest them between eight and twelve months of age. That said, the true lamb lovers often prefer yearling lamb, which is between thirteen and twenty months of age. The flavor is more assertive in these slightly older sheep, and they are still young enough to be tender.

The methods and caveats for cooking lamb are similar to those I've outlined for beef. The muscles that work hardest will have developed collagen in them, which means they'll benefit from moist-heat cooking methods. These cuts include shoulder chops and roasts, shanks and neck pieces, and stew meat cut from these areas. The rest of the lamb is quite tender. Rib and loin chops should be grilled or broiled, and leg of lamb is best roasted. That said, because the lamb is so young at processing, deviating from this cooking scheme is allowable. I'm a big fan of flavor, and I prefer grilled shoulder chops to loin chops any day. While they are a tad chewier, they are still tender enough to cut easily with a steak knife, and the flavor intensity, in my opinion, is worth the trade-off.

Slow-Cooked Lamb Shoulder with Onions

SERVES 4

2 pounds onions, sliced into thin
  rings

6 cloves garlic, peeled and left whole

2 teaspoons dried rosemary

2 tablespoons coarse salt

2 teaspoons black pepper

¼ cup olive oil

1 lamb shoulder roast, bone-in or
  boneless, 2–3 pounds

ESTIMATED CARBOHYDRATES:
Onions: 84.71 g
Garlic: 5.94 g
Black pepper: 2.94 g
Rosemary: 1.54 g
Total carbohydrates per recipe: 95.13 g
Total carbohydrates per ¼ recipe:
  23.78 g

Lamb shoulder is one of the most overlooked cuts on the animal. That is a pity, because it is one of the most flavorful and easy to prepare pieces of meat available, as this recipe attests.

Place the onions and garlic on the bottom of a slow cooker. Combine the rosemary, salt, pepper and olive oil in a small dish. Massage the mixture into the lamb roast. Heat a skillet over a medium flame (make sure that the flame is low enough so that the olive oil on the lamb doesn't smoke) and brown the lamb roast about 5 minutes per side. Add the roast to the slow cooker and pour in any rendered fat that was left in the skillet. Cook on low for about 6 hours or until tender. Remove the lamb, loosely cover with foil, and let rest at least 15 minutes. Carve it and serve it with the onions and garlic spooned on top.

Leftovers: Leftovers can be re-warmed in the slow cooker or in a covered dish in a 300-degree oven for 30 minutes or until warmed through. Alternatively, dice the lamb and add it to Onion Soup, Moussaka, or Vegetable, Meat and Potato Salad with Warm Bacon Dressing (see Chapter 8 for recipes).

One of the best management decisions we made on the farm was to forego winter lambing in the barn. Instead, our ewes birth in harmony with their natural cycles in May, when the pastures are lush and the temperatures more comfortable.

Searing

The single greatest improvement in my meat cooking ability in recent years is learning how to properly sear a piece of meat. While searing doesn't actually modify the intrinsic flavor of a piece of meat, it does heighten the overall flavor profile of a dish. It is a case where the cooking method itself becomes an essential ingredient.

Searing has always been critical to a good steak, but it should not be overlooked when working with your slow cooker. It is possible to cook a piece of meat in your slow cooker without searing it first (this method is called *à blanc*), and when you are in a time crunch, that may be necessary. However, the sear adds color, flavor and a delightful slight crunch to the exterior of the meat that will greatly enhance your gustatory pleasure. Here are some tips to ensure a great sear:

Make sure your meat is dry. Pat it dry with a paper towel before you apply it to the grill or skillet, as the additional moisture will steam, rather than sear the surface of your meat.

Make sure the searing surface is good and hot. If you are working with a grill, when you are able to hold your hand 5 inches above the grate for no more than 4 seconds, you are ready to sear. If you are working on the stove top, I recommend using a cast-iron skillet. When you begin to see smoke rising off the surface of the skillet, you are ready to proceed. **Important**: Don't grease your skillet until you are certain it is hot enough to sear. Otherwise the fat will smoke, and you won't know whether your skillet is amply hot or whether you are just burning fat.

Give yourself the luxury of space and time. Never crowd your meat on your grill or in your skillet. Allow at least one inch of room around every piece of meat. When you are working with stew, this can seem a bothersome step. However, crowding the meat builds up moisture, and moisture results in steamed, rather than browned, meat. You can't rush the searing. If taking the extra time at the skillet tries your patience, meditate on the great flavor reward that awaits you.

Le Cassoulet de Castelnaudary

ADVANCE PREPARATION
REQUIRED.

SERVES 12

2 pounds medium-sized dried white haricot or cannellini (white kidney) beans, soaked overnight in water to cover by at least 3 inches and 3 tablespoons plain yogurt

½ pound bacon, cut into 1-inch squares

3 medium onions, coarsely chopped

5 cloves garlic, peeled

4 fresh tomatoes or 1 quart canned chopped tomatoes

2 teaspoons dried thyme (2 tablespoons fresh, chopped)

2 teaspoons dried oregano (2 tablespoons fresh, chopped)

1 quart meat broth, such as Shannon's Meat Broth, Chapter 3

2 pounds duck confit pieces (any combination of wings, legs or breast will work)—do *not* scrape the fat off! (Recipe can be found in Chapter 7.)

1 pound Fresh Garlic Sausage links or patties (see recipe in Chapter 6 if your local farmer does not sell it)

1 lamb shoulder roast (1–2 pounds), or 1–2 pounds neck slices, 1–2 pounds shoulder chops, or 1–2 pounds lamb stew meat

Coarse salt and black pepper, to taste

2 cups coarse bread crumbs

When my daughter Saoirse was eighteen months old, our little family spent a winter living in a renovated tithing barn beside a river in a small village in rural France. While there, I found an old cookbook, where I discovered this basic recipe for cassoulet (I later learned that many French people don't bother making their own cassoulet. They simply buy it in cans from the grocery store. Alors!) Since we were living in France, all the ingredients were easy to come by at the local farmers' markets, and this dish, prepared from scratch, became one of our household standbys. Our home was very cold, and this dish warmed the kitchen and our bellies.

When we returned to the United States, I was never able to replicate this dish until a neighbor started raising ducks, and I began making my own confit (for which I included the recipe in Chapter 7), and then started making my own Fresh Garlic Sausage (Chapter 6). Then, the dish tasted just as I remembered, and restored its place as one of my all-time favorite meals. It takes some advance preparation. Since I don't have a high-end grocer near me offering duck confit and garlic sausage, I have to prepare my own. Thus, it becomes a dish that I plan for weeks, or even months in advance, gathering up or preparing the ingredients as I can get my hands on them, enjoying my anticipation of the dish as much as the preparation and the moment of feasting. The final outcome is worth it.

Rinse and drain the beans. Put them in a large pressure cooker, cover with water, seal the cover and cook at 15 psi for 6 minutes. Allow the pressure to subside using the natural release method. The beans should be about three-quarters cooked. Alternatively, simmer the beans in water for about 3 hours until they are mostly cooked through. Strain and rinse them.

Add the bacon to a large pot and sauté briefly. Add the onions and continue to sauté until the onions are nearly clear, about 5 minutes.

Crush four cloves of garlic and add them to the pot, along with the tomatoes and herbs. Pour in the broth and simmer for 20 minutes. Strain the tomatoes, bacon and onion mixture out of the broth, reserving *both*.

Preheat the oven to 325°F. Find the largest earthenware pot or roasting pan you can get your hands on.★ Split the remaining clove of garlic in half, and rub the cut side all over the interior of the pot or roasting pan

---

★ If you can't find a pot or pan big enough, you may need to use two. Rub both with garlic. Place some of the duck confit in each; then put the sausages in one, and the lamb shoulder in the other. When you serve it, offer your guests a choice of lamb or pork, or give them a little of both. Once you've eaten down some of the volume, combine them into one pot, allowing their flavors to meld even more for your leftovers feasting.

Spread the duck confit, sausages and lamb shoulder out on the bottom of the pot. Top them with the tomatoes, bacon and onions. Pour the partially cooked beans on top, then pour in the reserved stock. Bake uncovered, 1 hour. Remove and season it to taste with salt and pepper, top with bread crumbs, and return it to the oven. Bake 1 hour longer, or until most of the liquid is absorbed and a crust forms on the top of the beans.

Leftovers: Many people make this dish solely for the leftovers. Some recipes recommend not eating it at all on the day you cook it, then re-warming it for day two—but I can never wait that long. Suffice to say, this dish is made for reheating. Store leftovers covered in the refrigerator. To reheat, allow the cassoulet to come to room temperature while you preheat the oven to 350°F. Add some more bread crumbs if you wish, then bake uncovered until it is heated through, 30 minutes to 1 hour depending on how much volume is in your pan.

Rack of Lamb Glazed in Balsamic Butter

SERVES 2–3

1 clove garlic, crushed

2 tablespoons butter

2 tablespoons honey

2 tablespoons Balsamic vinegar

1 1–2-pound rack of lamb

Coarse salt and black pepper, to taste

This is a kid-friendly recipe . . . if you are willing to share with them. Ula and Saoirse both enjoyed this, and demanded extra helpings.

Prepare one side of the grill, ignite it, and heat to a medium-hot flame (until you can hold your hand 5 inches above the grate for no more than 4 seconds). Melt the butter in a small saucepan. Add the garlic, honey and vinegar. Simmer, stirring often, for 2–4 minutes until the sauce is reduced to a thin syrup.

Brush the lamb with the sauce, then sprinkle it all over with salt and pepper. Sear the rack, rib-side down, over direct heat for 2 minutes. Flip it and briefly sear the top of the rack (about one minute).

Move the lamb to indirect heat, drizzle with any remaining glaze, and cover the grill. Cook 25–35 minutes to desired doneness (an internal temperature of 120–145 degrees measured in the meaty "eye" of the rack, depending on your taste).

Leftovers: Save the bones for stock. Leftovers can be re-warmed briefly in a buttered skillet for a second meal, on the off-chance that there is any left over. Bits of the meat will also taste excellent in Onion soup (Chapter 8).

Lamb Chops, Grilled or Broiled

SERVES 4

1 recipe Garlic-Parsley Herb Paste, Appendix 1

2 pounds loin or rib lamb chops, 1 ¼-inches thick

> **ESTIMATED CARBOHYDRATES:**
> Garlic: 0.99 g
> Black pepper: 3.71 g
> Parsley: 0.81 g
> Total number of carbohydrates per recipe: 5.51 g
> Total number of carbohydrates per ¼ recipe: 1.38 g

Lamb chops are such simple and elegant fare that it is hard to go wrong with them. Below are instructions for preparing them on the grill or under your broiler.

Brush the Garlic-Parsley Herb Paste on the lamb chops. Allow them to come to room temperature while you prepare the grill or preheat your broiler.

Grill Method: Prepare the grill, light it, and let it heat to a medium-hot flame (until you can hold your hand 5 inches above the grate for no more than 4 seconds). Scrape the grate clean. Grill the chops over direct heat, covered, 4–6 minutes per side, until they achieve the desired doneness (120–145 degrees).

Broiler Method: Position the rack 4 inches from the heat source and preheat the broiler at high for 15 minutes. Place the chops in a cast-iron skillet and broil about 5 minutes per side for medium-rare chops.

Leftovers: Store the leftover bones from your chops for your next pot of broth. Typically, if you allow for 2 chops per adult and 1 chop for a child, you shouldn't have leftovers. However, if you do, the Mulligatawny, Potato Cabbage Soup, or Onion Soup (all in Chapter 8) are good ways to use up a bit of leftover lamb.

Grilled Lamb Shoulder Chops

SERVES 4

1 recipe Garlic-Parsley Herb Paste,
   Appendix 1

4 lamb shoulder chops, 1¼-inches
   thick

> **ESTIMATED CARBOHYDRATES:**
> Garlic: 0.99 g
> Black pepper: 3.71 g
> Parsley: 0.81 g
> Total number of carbohydrates per
>   recipe: 5.51 g
> Total number of carbohydrates per ¼
>   recipe: 1.38 g

Most customers new to lamb seize upon the rib and loin chops as prize cuts for their grill. As they do, I quietly slip the shoulder chops back behind the counter for our own family dinner. While they are not quite as tender, they are much more flavorful, and we rather like the slightly chewier texture.

Brush the Garlic-Parsley Herb Paste on all sides of the lamb chops. Allow them to come to room temperature while you prepare the grill.

Light one side of the grill and allow it to heat up for about 5 minutes with the cover in place. Once the flames are medium-hot and you can hold your hand 5 inches above the grate for no more than 4 seconds, scrape the grate clean.

Sear the chops over direct heat 2 minutes per side, then move them to indirect heat, close the lid, and cook 7–10 minutes longer until they achieve the desired doneness (an internal temperature of 120–145 degrees).

Leftovers: Store the leftover bones from your chops for your next pot of broth. Mulligatawny, Potato Cabbage Soup, or Onion Soup (all found in Chapter 8) are good ways to use up a bit of leftover lamb.

Choosing lamb chops

When selecting their dinner at my farmers' market booth, many folks are decisive about which kind of beef steak they prefer. Some folks are die hard rib eye fans, others are only interested in the porterhouse or filet mignon.

Surprisingly, these same folks grow mystified when they have to choose their lamb chops. Often, they ask me to choose for them, as they are unsure whether they would prefer **rib chops**, **loin chops**, or **shoulder chops**.

The **rib chop** corresponds to the rib eye steak on a beef, and the **loin chop** corresponds to the porterhouse. However, on a young lamb, there is little discernible difference in tenderness and fat between the two. If the lamb is closer to one year of age or older, the difference is more pronounced. In that case, the **rib chops** are more marbled and contain a delicious layer of fat around the outside of the rib muscle that crisps up as the chop cooks. It is positively luscious to eat. The rib chops also contain more bone, a plus for those of us who are inclined to gnaw. The **loin chops** are slightly more tender and lean than the rib chops on an older lamb, and it is not uncommon if they are lacking the layer of fat surrounding the loin muscle (although larger, older and fatter lambs will have that cover). If tenderness is most important to you, then the loin chops are probably the ideal choice, but the rib chops should be okay if the loins are sold out. If you prefer more texture and flavor, the rib chops are a good bet; better still, turn to the **shoulder chops**.

Shoulder chops correspond to the chuck steaks on a beef. They are high in flavor and marbling. And, while they theoretically are chewier because the lamb is so young, even if you cook them under the broiler the chew is not insurmountable . . . and for those of us who relish the high-flavored exercise, a shoulder chop is a very rewarding pursuit.

Lamb Shoulder Chops in a Tarragon Cream Sauce

SERVES 4

3 tablespoons butter, lard or tallow

4 lamb shoulder chops, 1¼ inches thick

2 tablespoons coarse salt

1 tablespoon ground black pepper

1 medium onion, finely chopped

2 teaspoons dried tarragon

1 teaspoon dried basil

1 ½ cups meat broth, such as Shannon's Meat Broth, Chapter 3

¼ cup sherry

2 tablespoons lemon juice

1 cup heavy cream

ESTIMATED CARBOHYDRATES:

Black pepper: 4.41 g
Onion: 10.27 g
Tarragon: 0.60 g
Basil: 0.33 g
Meat broth: 2.1 g*
Sherry: 3 g
Heavy cream: 6.64 g
Lemon juice: 1.94 g
Total number of carbohydrates per recipe: 29.29 g
Total number of carbohydrates per ¼ recipe: 7.32 g
* Number of carbohydrates in homemade broth will vary. This figure is calculated using the recipe for Shannon's Meat Broth (Chapter 3).

In this recipe, the lamb shoulder chops are cooked until the meat pulls easily off the bone, and then they are topped with a silky rich sauce that will have you licking your plate and wishing for leftovers.

Place a large nonreactive (enameled iron or stainless steel) Dutch oven over a medium flame. Add 2 tablespoons of the fat and swirl to coat. Sprinkle the chops with the salt and pepper and brown them well, about 3–4 minutes per side. Make sure there is about 1 inch of space around each chop as it browns. Remove the lamb to a separate dish. Once all the chops are browned, lower the heat slightly and add the final tablespoon of fat. Add the onion and sauté until clear. Sprinkle the herbs over the onion and mix well. Pour in the meat broth and simmer 3 minutes, stirring often with a wooden spoon, scraping the browned bits off the bottom of the pan and incorporating them into the sauce. Stir in the sherry, then add the chops back to the pot, cover, and simmer 45 minutes or until the lamb is fork-tender.

Remove the chops to a serving platter. Raise the heat and allow the sauce to simmer 10 minutes uncovered, or until the volume is reduced by half. Stir in the lemon juice, then the cream. Pour the sauce over the lamb and serve at once.

Leftovers: To re-warm, heat the lamb in a covered pan in a 200-degree oven for 45 minutes. Reheat the sauce separately. Alternatively, pull any remaining meat off the bones and stir it into the sauce to be served over rice or noodles. It can also be mixed into Mulligatawny (Chapter 8), adding it right at the end, just before you serve the soup, and letting it cook just long enough to heat through.

Easy-on-the-Cook Lamb Curry Stew

SERVES 6

3 carrots, peeled and cut into bite-size chunks

3 cups chopped cauliflower

1 large boiling potato, diced

1 large onion, chopped

4 cloves garlic, chopped

2½ pounds lamb stew meat cut from the shoulder, neck or shanks (see Cubed Meat Sidebar, Chapter 4)

2 teaspoons fine salt

1 teaspoon ground black pepper

1 tablespoon grated fresh ginger

2 teaspoons ground cumin

1 teaspoon ground cardamom

2 cinnamon sticks

4 whole cloves

¼ teaspoon ground cayenne pepper

1 teaspoon ground turmeric

1 cup tomato sauce, preferably homemade

2 cups meat stock

6 tablespoons plain whole-milk yogurt, for garnish

My favorite slow-cooker recipes are those where all the ingredients can be tossed into the pot with little other prep work required. I can turn it on, walk away, and come back to a full-flavored dinner. This recipe does just that, and thus has become like an old friend over the years.

Add the vegetables to the bottom of the slow cooker. Put the raw meat on top. Add all the remaining ingredients except for the yogurt. Cover and cook on low for 6 hours or until the lamb is fork-tender. Ladle the stew into bowls and serve with a tablespoon of yogurt.

Leftovers: This dish is generally made with the leftovers being the anticipated side-benefit. When you are ready to eat, just plug it in and set it to high to re-warm for 45 minutes to 1 hour.

ESTIMATED CARBOHYDRATES:	
Carrots: 17.53 g	Cardamom: 1.37 g
Cauliflower: 15.95 g	Cayenne pepper: 0.25 g
Onion: 14.01 g	Turmeric: 1.43 g
Garlic: 3.96 g	Tomato sauce: 21.93 g
Black pepper: 1.47 g	Yogurt: 4.28 g
Ginger: 1.07 g	Total number of carbohydrates per recipe: 85.11 g
Cumin: 1.86 g	Total number of carbohydrates per ⅙ recipe: 14.19 g

Ginger and citrus zest: Freeze your tropical ingredients

Ginger and citrus are great for brightening flavor. Since they aren't local to the Northeast, I generally used powdered and cooked with citrus only on occasions when I happened to have some on hand. If I absolutely needed fresh ginger, I'd have to remember to purchase it ahead, and I'd wince as I used one or two tablespoons then watch as the rest of the root withered away. The same was true for citrus. And then my friend Jane from Hawaii told me to freeze it: simply wash the ginger whole, dry it then keep it in a sealed freezer bag. When I need fresh grated ginger, I don't need to thaw it or even peel it; I just grab the frozen root, grate off what I need then put it back in the freezer. One good-sized root will get me through about one year of cooking with virtually no waste. After heeding her advice with ginger, I began experimenting with citrus. I froze the peels from Christmas oranges or if I purchased fresh lemon for a recipe (or a martini!), I saved those peels, too. These brightly colored peels keep beautifully in my freezer and add flavorful zest whenever I need it.

Lamb Meatballs and Crudités with Sun-dried Tomato Aioli

**SERVES 2–4 AS A MEAL,
8 AS AN APPETIZER**

MEATBALLS:

1 pound ground lamb

½ cup onion, finely chopped

3 tablespoons chopped fresh oregano, or 1 tablespoon dried

3 tablespoons chopped fresh parsley, or 1 tablespoon dried

2 ounces soft goat cheese

1 tablespoon chopped fresh mint, or 1 teaspoon dried

1 teaspoon ground cumin

1 teaspoon fine salt

1 tablespoon lard, tallow or butter

An assortment of Crudités, such as 4 carrots, peeled and cut into sticks, 4 celery ribs, strung and cut into sticks, ½ head cauliflower, cut into bite-size florets, ½ head broccoli, cut into bite-size florets, 8 ounces radishes, scrubbed and left whole, 8 ounces fresh cherry tomatoes, left whole, or a selection of seasonal, fresh, local vegetables that are available to you

Sun-dried Tomato Aioli (Recipe follows)

SUN-DRIED TOMATO AIOLI

½ cup sun-dried tomatoes packed in oil, drained

1 tablespoon lemon juice

1 tablespoon fresh parsley or 1 teaspoon dried

2 cloves garlic

1 recipe Mayonnaise, Chapter 7

This is a great dish for a tapas party. The aioli accents the lamb without overpowering it, and it tastes fantastic with the raw veggies, too. Kids like it because they get to eat with their fingers.

Place all the above ingredients in a bowl, except the fat, crudités, and aioli. Using your hands, mix until just blended, then form into 1 ½-inch-diameter balls.

Position a rack 4–6 inches below the heat source and preheat the broiler for 15 minutes. Rub a large cast-iron skillet or baking sheet with the fat. Arrange the meatballs on the pan, allowing at least 1-inch space around each ball. Broil 5 minutes, use tongs to turn them, and broil 3 minutes longer.

To serve, arrange the Crudités and meatballs on a platter. Serve with the aioli on the side for dipping.

Leftovers: The meatballs can be reheated in a covered baking dish in a 200-degree oven until they are warmed through, but they will be slightly drier (the aioli makes up for it, however). The meatballs can also be diced and added to Refrigerator Soup (Chapter 8). The flavor is especially tasty if a cup of tomato sauce is added to the meat broth. They will also work well in Minestra Maritata (Chapter 8).

SUN-DRIED TOMATO AIOLI

Put the tomatoes, lemon juice, parsley and garlic in a food processor fitted with the steel blade and puree until smooth. Gently stir the mixture into the mayonnaise. Refrigerate until ready to serve.

ESTIMATED CARBOHYDRATES:	
Onion: 3.42 g	Garlic: 1.98 g
Oregano: 2.07 g	Carrots: 23.38 g
Parsley: 0.81 g	Celery: 4.75 g
Goat cheese: 2.88 g	Cauliflower: 14.61 g
Mint: 0.24 g	Broccoli: 20.19 g
Cumin: 0.93 g	Tomatoes: 5.80 g
Mayonnaise (homemade): 1.28 g	Estimated number of carbohydrates for entire recipe: 96.41 g
Sundried tomatoes: 12.83 g	Estimated number of carbohydrates per ¼ recipe: 24.10
Lemon juice: 0.97 g	
Parsley: 0.27 g	

Merguez-Style Lamb Burgers

SERVES 6

2 pounds ground lamb, or 1 pound each ground lamb and ground beef

2 teaspoons fine salt

¼ teaspoon cayenne pepper

2 cloves garlic, minced

⅔ cup diced jarred roasted red peppers

1 teaspoon ground black pepper

3 teaspoons sweet paprika

3 teaspoons dried oregano

2 tablespoons red wine vinegar

Olive oil, for the grill

Sun-dried Tomato Aioli (Recipe above, optional)

ESTIMATED CARBOHYDRATES:

Cayenne pepper: 0.25 g

Garlic: 1.98 g

Roasted red peppers: 3.60 g

Black pepper: 1.47 g

Paprika: 3.67 g

Oregano: 2.07 g

Red wine vinegar: 0.08 g

Total number of carbohydrates per recipe: 13.12 g

Total number of carbohydrates per ⅙ recipe: 2.19 g

These lightly spicy burgers are a twist on the popular North African sausage. They have a distinctive bright red color and juiciness from the roasted red peppers, and would pair well with a sprinkling of goat cheese or Sun-dried Tomato Aioli (recipe above).

Put the lamb in a mixing bowl and add all the ingredients except the oil and Aioli; mix well. Loosely shape the meat into 6 balls. Gently flatten them until they are about 1 inch thick. With your fingertips, make a small well in the top of each patty to prevent the meat from getting puffy over the flames. Set the patties aside while you light one side of your grill and clean off the cooking grate with a wire brush.

When one side of the grill is medium-hot and you can hold your hand 5 inches above it for no more than four seconds, brush the rack lightly with oil, then set the patties over direct heat. Cover and cook 4 minutes per side. Move the burgers to indirect heat, cover, and cook 10 minutes longer. Try them with Sun-dried Tomato Aioli.

Leftovers: If my kids leave any leftover burger on their plates, I don't let it go to waste. I toss it into the Minestra Maritata Soup, or Refrigerator Soup. It could also be used with the Meat Canapés with Goat Cheese and Roasted Red Pepper (all three recipes appear in Chapter 8).

Spiced Raw Lamb with Walnuts

SERVES 6–8

2 cups walnuts

1 teaspoon allspice

1 teaspoon cinnamon

⅛ teaspoon nutmeg

¼ teaspoon cayenne pepper

2 small yellow onions, peeled and quartered

1 pound ground lamb, frozen for a minimum of 2 weeks and thawed

Salt and black pepper, to taste

1 tablespoon olive oil

1 small red onion, thinly sliced

1 lemon, cut into 8 wedges

ESTIMATED CARBOHYDRATES:

Walnuts: 27.42 g

Allspice: 1.37 g

Cinnamon: 2.10 g

Nutmeg: 0.14 g

Cayenne: 0.25 g

Onions: 19.62 g

Lemon: 5.41 g

Total number of carbohydrates per recipe: 56.31 g

Total number of carbohydrates per ⅙ recipe: 9.39 g

I first learned about eating raw meat from Sally Fallon's book Nourishing Traditions. *This twist on her recipe for kibbeh, a traditional Arab dish made with bulgur and ground meat, is made with walnuts instead of bulgur. We like the fresh, clean taste, especially as a cool summer evening meal. The importance of using meat that has been frozen for two weeks is to ensure that all possible parasites have been killed. If raw onions trouble your stomach, sauté them in a little butter before adding them to the dish.*

Combine the walnuts, spices and onion in the large bowl of a food processor fitted with the steel blade. Process until the onions are finely diced and the walnuts are ground. Put the lamb in a mixing bowl and add the spiced walnut and onion mixture and mix well. Season to taste with salt and pepper, and mix well. Arrange the lamb on a plate in a mound, drizzle with olive oil, and garnish with the thinly sliced red onion and lemon wedges. Serve spooned on top of lettuce leaves or Parmesan–Parsley Almond Crackers (Chapter 8).

Leftovers: The lamb will be seasoned perfectly for making Moussaka or Stuffed Peppers (both appear in Chapter 8).

Lamb necks—forgotten but delicious

I'm delighted that the vigorous interest in local cuisine has sparked epicureans to spend time with the less glamorous cuts of meat. Restaurant menus and magazines now feature lamb shanks and shoulders, and that in turn sparks my customers' interest in them at the farmers' market. However, one cut that I continually see ignored is the neck.

Neck slices are every bit as flavorful and meaty as the shanks, and they are typically available at an even lower price. Lamb necks can be used interchangeably with shanks and stew meat. Indeed, it can be hard to tell them apart from cross-cut shanks. Those of us farmers who are frequently left with an abundance of necks in our freezer inventory are aware of this, but it is better for us (and for our customers) if everyone knows about this little culinary secret.

Slow-Cooked Spiced Lamb with Root Vegetables

SERVES 4–6

4 teaspoons whole coriander

4 teaspoons whole fennel seeds

¼ teaspoon ground cayenne

2 teaspoons ground black pepper

1 tablespoon fine salt

3 pounds lamb shanks (whole or cross-cut), lamb neck, or lamb stew meat (or as much as your slow cooker will hold)

2 medium onions, sliced into wedges

2 ribs celery, diced

1 cup parsnips, peeled and diced

2 medium apples, skin-on, cored, and cut into wedges

4 carrots, diced

About 2 tablespoons lard, tallow or butter

1 cup meat broth, such as Shannon's Meat Broth, Chapter 3

2 tablespoons port

6 whole cloves

2 whole star anise

2 bay leaves

ESTIMATED CARBOHYDRATES:

Coriander: 3.96 g	Fennel: 4.18 g
Cayenne: 0.25 g	Black pepper: 2.94 g
Onions: 20.54 g	Celery: 2.38 g
Parsnips: 23.93 g	Apples: 50.27 g
Carrots: 23.36 g	Meat broth: 1.40 g*
Port: 3.45 g	Cloves: 1.29 g
Anise: 2.10 g	Bay leaves: 0.34 g

Total carbohydrates per recipe: 140.39 g

Total carbohydrates per ¼ recipe: 35.10 g

* Number of carbohydrates in homemade broth will vary. This figure is calculated using the recipe for Shannon's Meat Broth (Chapter 3).

As the household cook, I am forever partial to one-dish meals that work in my slow cooker. This one, mildly sweetened with the addition of some apple, appeals to my daughters while satisfying my husband's desire for somewhat spicier dishes.

Combine the coriander and fennel in a spice grinder and grind until fine. Combine them in a small bowl with the cayenne, black pepper and salt. Rub the spices into the meat and set aside for 2 hours or overnight, covered and refrigerated (allow the meat to come to room temperature before continuing).

Lay the onions, celery, parsnips, apples and carrots in the bottom of a slow cooker.

Heat a large skillet over a medium-high flame and add half the fat. Add some of the lamb to the pan, taking care to make sure there is ample space surrounding the meat. (If the meat is crowded, it will not brown.) Cook until the meat is browned on all sides, then add it to the slow cooker. Add more fat to the skillet if needed, then brown the remaining meat. (It will take about 10 minutes to sear each batch if you are working with whole shanks, 5–7 minutes for bone-in neck pieces, 3–5 minutes for boneless stew meat). Once all the meat has been added to the slow cooker, add the broth, port, cloves, star anise and bay leaves. Cover and cook on low about 6–8 hours or until the meat is fork-tender. Serve the lamb in shallow bowls, surrounded by the vegetables, with the sauce spooned on top.

Leftovers: This is a braised dish, so the flavors will build if you re-warm it for a second meal. If you don't have enough to serve everyone who will join your table, consider dicing up any remaining meat, then prepare the Onion Soup (Chapter 8). When the soup is nearly ready, add the diced meat, along with the other leftovers from this dish to the soup pot. Bring everything to a simmer and serve immediately. You will have yourself a steaming pot of onion soup with an exotic, fragrant twist. These leftovers would also work well in Mulligatawny (Chapter 8).

Persian-Spiced Lamb Riblets

SERVES 4

2–3 pounds lamb riblets (also known as lamb breast or spareribs)

1 batch Persian Spice Paste, Appendix 1

ESTIMATED CARBOHYDRATES:
Persian Spice Paste: 61.2 g
Total carbohydrates per recipe: 61.2 g
Total carbohydrates per ¼ recipe: 15.3 g

Lamb riblets seem to be the most overlooked cut on the animal . . . which is great for me, because they are my favorite cut of lamb. Roasting these ribs will fill your kitchen with an exotic spice combination of cardamom, cinnamon, cloves, cumin and ginger. The dates in the spice paste lend a mild sweetness that pairs well with the intense flavor in the lamb riblets.

Rub the riblets all over with the spice paste and place bone-side down in a large roasting pan. Allow them to rest 2 hours at room temperature (or overnight, covered, in the refrigerator). Preheat oven to 325°F. Roast for about 1½ to 2 hours, or until the meat is tender and starting to pull away from the bone. The fat in the riblets will eventually break down the connective tissue in the meat.

Leftovers: Riblets can be reheated in a covered dish in a 250-degree oven. The bits of meat can also be pulled off to be stirred into Onion Soup (Chapter 8).

Overlooked bones

As you've probably guessed by now, one of my main intents in writing this book is encouraging you to make use of the bones of all the different grassfed and pastured critters available. Using the whole animal honors their sacrifice, and using the bones maximizes the nutrients available to your family, minimizes waste, and stretches your meat dollars farther. Hence, the chapter I've included that features bones, and the numerous recipes that call for meat broth.

Did you notice those words, "meat broth?" I didn't say "chicken broth," and I didn't say "beef broth." Don't get me wrong, they're both delicious. But somewhere, folks got the idea that there are only two different kinds of bone broth—beef and chicken. Contrary to popular knowledge, pigs and lambs and goats have bones, too, and they all make excellent stock.

In Italy, traditional home cooks make meat broth, not an animal-specific broth. On rare occasion, the delicate flavor of a dish requires only chicken broth. However, in most home-cooking, any kind of bone broth, from any species of animal, will work beautifully. In fact, I often combine bones from different animals to make the broth. There will be subtle differences in the flavor, but it will still taste great. So save that bone from your leg of lamb roast, and keep all those little bones from your chops. They have much to offer you in your stockpot.

Classic Roasted Leg of Lamb

SERVES 6–8

1 (5–6-pound) bone-in leg of lamb

2 recipes Garlic-Parsley Herb Paste, Appendix 1, or other herb paste of your choice

Shallot-Dijon Reduction Sauce (see recipe in Fresh Ham with a Shallot Dijon Reduction, Chapter 6), optional, OR

¼ cup all-purpose flour (if making gravy, optional)

1–2 cups meat broth, such as Shannon's Meat Broth (Chapter 3), or water (if making gravy, optional)

ESTIMATED CARBOHYDRATES:

Garlic-Parsley Herb Paste: (double recipe): 11.02 g

Flour: 43.22 g

Total carbohydrates per recipe (with gravy): 54.24 g

Total carbohydrates per recipe (au jus): 11.02

Total carbohydrates per ⅙ recipe (with gravy): 9.04 g

Total carbohydrates per ⅙ recipe (au jus): 1.82 g

Roast leg of lamb is our quintessential Easter feast. This recipe keeps things simple so that you can taste the delicate flavors of the meat.

Rub the leg of lamb all over with the Garlic-Parsley paste and set it aside for at least 30 minutes so that it can come to room temperature before roasting.

Preheat oven to 300°F. Put the lamb in a roasting pan and roast about 17–20 minutes per pound, until the internal temperature of the meat is between 120 and 145 degrees.

Serve simply au jus (with just the pan juices), with a reduction sauce (see Shallot-Dijon Reduction Sauce), or make gravy as follows: Remove the lamb to a cutting board or platter. Pour off all but ½ cup of the drippings then set the roasting pan over direct heat. Turn on the heat to medium and heat the pan drippings until they are bubbling. Whisk in the flour to form a paste. When smooth, whisk 1–2 minutes longer until slightly browned. Slowly whisk in the remaining pan drippings and 1 cup meat broth or water. Allow the mixture to bubble and thicken. Add additional water or broth until the gravy is at your preferred consistency and simmer 2–3 minutes.

Leftovers: Try using leftover lamb in the following recipes from Chapter 8: Croquettes with Black Pepper and Onion Sauce, Stuffed Peppers, Meat Canapés with Goat Cheese and Roasted Red Peppers, Onion Soup, or Refrigerator Soup.

Roast Leg of Lamb with Fall Harvest Vegetables

SERVES 5–8

1 whole leg of lamb, bone-in, 4–6 pounds

1 batch Oregano-Mustard Paste, Appendix 1

2 pounds butternut squash, peeled and cut into 1-inch chunks

2 pounds beets, scrubbed and diced into 1-inch chunks (skin may be left on)

1 pound yellow onions, cut into wedges

½ cup olive oil

1 tablespoon dried oregano

1 tablespoon coarse salt

1 teaspoon ground black pepper

ESTIMATED CARBOHYDRATES:
Oregano-Mustard Paste: 6.32 g
Butternut squash: 106.03 g
Beets: 86.71 g
Onions: 84.71 g
Oregano: 2.07 g
Black pepper: 1.47 g
Total carbohydrates per recipe: 287.31 g
Total carbohydrates per ⅙ recipe: 47.89 g

This tasty feast comes across as an upscale crowd-pleaser, with a glorious leg perched on a bed of brightly colored fall vegetables. In truth, it's actually an easy-on-the-cook one-dish dinner that is a breeze to clean up.

Preheat oven to 300°F. Rub the lamb all over with the Oregano-Mustard paste and set aside. Place the squash, beets, and onions in a large bowl. Whisk together the olive oil, oregano, salt and pepper. Pour over the vegetables and toss to coat.

Lay the roast, fat-side up, in the center of a very large roasting pan (such as what you might use for a big Thanksgiving turkey). Scatter the vegetables around the outside of the meat. Roast about 17–20 minutes per pound, until the vegetables can be pierced easily with a fork and the internal temperature of the lamb is between 120 and 145 degrees. If the leg is cooked through before the vegetables are finished, remove the meat from the oven and allow it to rest. Turn the heat on the oven up to 400 degrees so that the vegetables can finish cooking while you carve the meat.

Leftovers: To re-warm the lamb with the vegetables, put them all in a baking dish, drizzle with olive oil and bake, covered, in a 250-degree oven until heated through. The lamb can also be used in place of the sausage in the recipe for Creamy Roasted Garlic Soup with Spicy Sausage, in Croquettes with Black Pepper and Onion Sauce, or in Meat Canapés with Goat Cheese and Roasted Red Peppers (all recipes appear in Chapter 8).

Grilled Butterflied Leg of Lamb with Coriander and Herbs

SERVING SIZE VARIES. Allow ½ pound boneless meat per person. If your roast still has the bone in it, calculate slightly less than 1 pound of bone-in meat per person.

1 butterflied leg of lamb

1 recipe Coriander-Herb Paste, Appendix 1

ESTIMATED CARBOHYDRATES:
Coriander Herb Paste: 7.86 g
Total carbohydrates per recipe: 7.86 g

Butterflied leg of lamb on the grill can be a fantastic way to entertain a small crowd on a summer evening without steaming up your kitchen or running yourself ragged with lots of extra work. It is simple to prepare, and it is consistently delicious.

Open boned lamb so that it lies flat. Rub the herb paste on all sides. Set it aside and allow it to come to room temperature while you heat your grill.

Light one side of the grill and allow it to warm up until it is medium-hot. You should be able to hold your hand 5 inches above the grate for no more than 4 seconds. Scrape the grate clean with a wire brush, then lay the meat, splayed open like a book, over direct heat and close the grill. Sear it well on both sides, about 2 minutes per side.

Move it to indirect heat, insert an ovenproof internal meat thermometer into the thickest part of the meat, and close the grill. Cook until the internal temperature is 120 to 145 degrees, about 3–5 minutes per pound.

Allow the meat to rest on a cutting board for about 5–10 minutes before carving it. To guarantee tender slices, cut it diagonally across the grain.

Leftovers. Try slicing the lamb cold and tossing it with cherry tomatoes, raw zucchini squash, some diced fresh basil and Buttermilk Mustard Salad Dressing (Chapter 7).

Lamb Kebabs

SERVES 4

1 recipe Lemon-Garlic Marinade, Dad's Tamari Balsamic Marinade, or Bell Pepper and Garlic Marinade (recipes located in Appendix 1)

2 pounds lamb for kebabs, taken from the leg, cut into 1-½-inch cubes (see Cubed Meat Sidebar, Chapter 4)

ESTIMATED CARBOHYDRATES:

Lemon-Garlic Marinade: 26.81 g

Dad's Tamari-Balsamic Marinade: 66.32 g

Bell Pepper and Garlic Marinade: 22.55 g

Total amount of carbohydrates per serving will depend on which marinade you select and how much of the marinade is absorbed by the meat. To gauge an estimate, weigh the amount of marinade before you begin cooking, and divide the carbohydrates by the number of ounces (which will tell you roughly how many carbohydrates per ounce). Weigh the leftover marinade once you've finished. Subtract it from the original. The difference will be the number of ounces used on your meat. Multiply that by the number of carbohydrates per ounce, and you'll have an estimate for the total number of carbohydrates for the recipe.

Tender, easy and delectable, lamb kebabs require a little advance prep work for the marinade, then leave you a free and easy evening when it comes to putting supper on the table.

Pour the marinade into a large, stainless-steel, porcelain, glass or other nonreactive bowl. Add the lamb and mix well to coat. Cover and refrigerate for a minimum of 2 hours, preferably overnight. Toss periodically to ensure all parts of the meat have an opportunity to absorb the marinade.

When you are ready to grill, remove the meat from the marinade, blot dry with a paper towel, place it on skewers, and allow it to come to room temperature while you prepare the grill.

Heat one side of the grill until the flame is medium-hot. You should be able to hold your hand five inches beyond the flame for no more than 4 seconds. Scrape the grate clean with a wire brush, then brush lightly with oil.

Grill the meat directly over the flame, covered, for 2 minutes. Turn them and grill 2 minutes longer. Move the kebabs off the direct heat, cover, and let them cook over indirect heat for 5 minutes longer for medium-rare. If the lamb kebabs are smaller than 1½ inches, shorten the cooking time. Serve immediately.

Leftovers: Kebabs can be sliced thin and served in Vegetable, Meat and Potato Salad with Warm Bacon Dressing, or Asian-Style Cold Meat Salad (see Chapter 8).

CHAPTER 6

 Pork

As the American food system recovers from factory farms and fossil fuel reliance, one of the great changes in the cultural landscape I look forward to is the noble pig's restoration to its place of honor among human communities. From the time of the first agrarian settlements, pigs have been amiable neighbors, cleaning up after human society, turning food that we wouldn't or couldn't eat into meat. The notion that the pigs' rightful place is in an isolated factory setting, packed cheek to jowl and feeding exclusively off a dull diet of grains grown for their consumption is an indignity they needn't suffer as Americans rediscover that they are truly delightful neighbors.

I could lose myself for hours enjoying the company of pigs. I've been known to gather unsold treats from our farmers' market at the end of the day—Napoleon pastries, brownies, bits of fudge, overripe fruit, muffins and baguettes, and carry them home to them, just for the delight of sitting among them and watching and listening as they sniff the victuals, turn them over with their noses, taste them, and smack their lips to savor the flavor. In my own mouth, those goodies are wasted calories, unnecessary for my nutrition and sustenance. In the pigs' mouths, they will bring untold pleasure, then turn into delicious pork.

A pig may not be as compatible with close-quartered human residences as the chicken. He certainly wouldn't fare as well as a chicken or a honey bee colony on the roof of a Brooklyn apartment building. But he has a place somewhere near a school yard, where he and his siblings can glean the discards of the daily lunches, or on a university campus where he can feast upon food scraps and model far more interesting and honorable behavior than most campus administrations. The pig has a place among neighbors and friends who find a suitable backyard, collect their household food scraps, and turn them into swill, first for the pig's delight and ultimately for their own winter sausage.

As for the grass-based farm, the pig will always have a place there. My hope, however, is that the rest of our culture will embrace the pleasure of working with them, reducing the demand that the farmer keep more pigs than the farm's kitchen scraps, meat waste, forage, bone meal, and garden surplus can sustain.

Yes, I just suggested that farmers feed meat to their pigs. Diversified pasture farms are forever producing potential pig feed as they process chickens, beef, lamb, or whatever critters they may be growing on their pastures. Pigs are omnivores, and they require protein in their diets. Feeding them animal by-products was a long-acceptable practice until fears about so-called "mad cow disease" (bovine spongiform encephalopathy) emerged in the 1990s.

Cattle are herbivores. They are designed to eat grass, not meat. Many believe that the emergence of mad cow disease resulted from factory-farming systems that introduced meat and bone meal to dairy cows' feed rations. Politics, and not sound animal science, consequently mandated that *all* livestock should become vegetarian. Pig feed typically contains soy (a highly problematic crop ecologically and nutritionally) or fish to supply the protein needs. However, they could eat beef, poultry or lamb offal (slaughter by-product) for their protein needs although, for food safety concerns, it should ideally be cooked first. Perhaps gathering on-farm offal and rendering it into pig swill for the area hogs could be yet another locally-based business venture that would help restore economic vitality to our rural, and even suburban, communities. While the image of a vegetarian pig may suit the idyllic pastoral vision, the pig has different ideas about what is tasty, and the pastoral vision generates a lot of meat offal, a valuable source of nutrition that could be recycled through omnivorous farm animals.

This is not to say that pasture-based pork is necessarily fed meat. While some farmers may toss their pigs some offal or some meaty table scraps (and if this practice concerns you, then by all means ask your farmer about it), the vast majority of pasture-raised pigs today graze the fields (and they do actually graze) and are supplemented with grain. When a dairy processor is nearby, pigs often enjoy feasting on milk and whey as well. But as we move toward a more sustainable food system, we will have to open our minds to explore how the animal's natural needs can be part of a flourishing farm ecosystem. Reducing our reliance on grain feeding would probably diminish the number of on-farm pigs, but they would play a more direct role in on-farm nutrient cycling by eating wholesome grassfed meat by-products.

In my vision, the rest of our nation's pork demands will be met as the pigs leave the farm and rejoin neighborhoods, backyards, and school yards, where they can help Americans turn their food waste into something more valuable.

All of this suggests that I expect delicious pork will continue to be a part of the American diet. I can only assume that the factory pigs, overbred in an era of fat phobia to be unnaturally lean, will become a thing of the past. Today, many pasture farms use (and thereby preserve) a variety of the old-style pig breeds, resulting in pork with more fat cover and juicier marbling. Since the pastured pig is more active, the pork will have deeper, more pronounced flavor, and will typically be darker in color than grocery store meat.

Sows play a critical role on the farm raising young piglets out on pasture, and offering themselves as the farmers' confidant. But beware! Don't make them angry. Those Mama omnivores have powerful jaws, strong teeth and plenty of heft!

I love preparing a pasture-raised pork roast for someone who is accustomed to grocery store meat. Upon tasting the meat, they get an entirely overly-inflated view of my culinary abilities, as they have never tasted meat that delicious. Since I write meat cookbooks, they assume it is owing to the skill of the cook. Ha. The secret is in the pig. It just tastes that much better.

When cooking pork, the most important thing is to carefully monitor its internal temperature. Regarding food-borne illnesses, it need only be cooked to a minimum internal temperature of 137 degrees F., the temperature at which *Trichinella spiralis* bacteria are killed. Salmonella bacteria are even easier to thwart. According to the Texas A & M Extension service, exposing meat to cooking temperatures above 150 degrees F. is enough to kill Salmonella bacteria. To clarify, that doesn't mean that the internal temperature of the meat must *reach* 150 degrees, only that the roasting, frying or grilling temperature be set at a minimum of 150 degrees. Most conventional ovens do not go below 170 degrees. Typical frying and roasting temperatures are around 300 degrees.

Like the other four-legged critters, the parts of the pig that do the most work are the shoulders and legs. They contain the most collagen and will benefit most from moist-heat cooking. These cuts include the **hocks**, **shoulder roasts** (also called **picnic roast** and **pork butt**), and **shoulder chops** or **country ribs**. The **spare ribs** also benefit from moist-heat cooking, particularly smoking. The loin and rib primal of the pig generates the **loin, rib and sirloin chops and roasts**, and the **tenderloin**. All of these cuts can be prepared using dry-heat methods. The hind leg of the pork is typically referred to as the **ham**, and it is often cut into smaller roasts that can be cured, smoked on the grill, or roasted in the oven. On occasion, butchers will slice the leg into **ham steaks**. I do not recommend this cut. There are too many different muscle groups that come together in a thin slice of meat, rendering it quite tough unless is it cooked using the super-slow method outlined in Chapter 4. Hams are marbled and delicious and perfectly tender, as long as they are kept as roasts or cut into **kebabs**. The belly of the pig yields the spareribs and the **bacon**, if cured. If left uncured, the **pork belly** can be prepared as Rillons (recipe follows). All parts of the pig can also be used for sausage, one of my favorite products from a pig.

Pork Shoulder Roast with Caramelized Onions and Apples

SERVES 4–6

3 tablespoons unsalted butter or lard

2 pounds onions, peeled and sliced thin

1 3-pound boneless, or 5-pound bone-in pork shoulder roast

1 tablespoon coarse salt

2 teaspoons freshly ground black pepper

5 baking apples, quartered and cored but not peeled

ESTIMATED CARBOHYDRATES:
Butter: 0.03 g
Onions: 84.71 g
Black pepper: 0.94 g
Apples: 125.67 g
Total carbohydrates per recipe: 125.67 g
Total carbohydrates per ¼ recipe: 31.42 g

This recipe is so elegantly simple, it's pure wizardry. The juices and natural sugars in the onions slowly braise the pork shoulder to create a rich, sweet roast with hardly any ingredients. If you've got a food processor, use it to slice the onions. It'll make quick work of your prep time.

Preheat the oven to 250°F.

Melt the butter in a large skillet over medium heat. Add the onions and sauté slowly, about 30 minutes, until they are rich brown and well caramelized (*not burned*). Turn off the heat and allow them to cool until you can handle them easily.

Rub the meat with salt and pepper, and place in a roasting pan. Using your hands, slather the onions onto the surface of the roast, completely coating it. Scatter the apples skin-side up on the bottom of the pan all around the pork shoulder. Roast, uncovered, about 3 to 4 hours, until the internal temperature of the meat reaches 145 to 160 degrees, depending on how done you like it.

Let rest 15 minutes before carving and serve each pork slice with a wedge of baked apple and a spoonful of caramelized onions.

Slow-Cooked Pork Shoulder with Vegetables and a Creamy Red Wine Reduction

ADVANCE PREPARATION REQUIRED.

SERVES 6

3 tablespoons coarse salt

2 tablespoons ground black pepper

1 5-pound pork (bone-in) shoulder roast

2 onions, coarsely chopped

5 cloves garlic, coarsely chopped

2 small carrots, coarsely chopped

4 sprigs fresh thyme (or 1 teaspoon dried)

3 bay leaves

4 cups red wine

4 cups chopped cabbage

1 pound butternut squash, peeled and diced

2 tablespoons lard, tallow or butter

2 cups meat broth, such as Shannon's Meat Broth, Chapter 3

1 tablespoon Dijon mustard

½ cup heavy cream

ESTIMATED CARBOHYDRATES:

Black pepper: 8.82 g

Marinade actually used for cooking and reduction sauce: 25.93 g*

Cabbage: 20.65 g

Butternut squash: 53.03 g

Meat broth: 4.20 g**

Butter: 0.02 g

Total carbohydrates per recipe: 104.71 g

Total carbohydrates per ⅙ recipe: 17.45 g

* This figure was calculated assuming that half of the marinade would be incorporated into the final dish.

** Number of carbohydrates in home-made broth will vary. This figure is calculated using the recipe for Shannon's Meat Broth (Chapter 3).

The roots of this recipe come from an old traditional French preparation for sanglier, *wild boar, where the pork shoulder is marinated in red wine and aromatic vegetables. Here, it is slow-cooked with broth and some of the marinade on a bed of cabbage and winter squash. The juices are then reduced and blended with cream to make a delectable sauce that creates a deeply satisfying one-dish meal. It is a delicious way to feed a hungry crowd, and showcases the terrific flavor and versatility of pastured pork shoulder.*

Rub the pork all over with salt and pepper and put it into a nonreactive (stainless-steel or glass) bowl, along with half the onions and all the garlic and carrots. Add the herbs and wine and turn the meat several times to coat it evenly. Cover and marinate at least 2 hours, or overnight, turning the meat occasionally to be sure it is well coated.

Layer the remaining onions, cabbage and squash on the bottom of a large slow cooker. Remove the meat from the marinade and blot dry. Heat the fat in a large skillet over medium-high heat. Add the pork roast and brown it well, about 3–5 minutes per side (see sidebar, *Searing*, in Chapter 5 for more information). Transfer the pork to the slow cooker. Strain the marinade, discarding the solids, and add 2 cups of the liquid, along with the broth, to the slow cooker. Add the meat and cook on low 6–8 hours, until the meat is fork-tender.

20 minutes before you are ready to eat, remove the liquid from the slow cooker and put it in a shallow saucepan. Bring it to a simmer, and cook it down until it is reduced by half. Whisk in the Dijon mustard, simmer one minute longer, then slowly whisk in the heavy cream. Carve the pork and serve it over a bed of the vegetables, topped with the pan sauce.

Leftovers: This is another one of those dishes that will taste better the second day, once the flavors have had time to ripen. The vegetables, pork and sauce can be re-warmed together in the slow cooker. They will taste delicious without any further effort on your part. To expand the dish to accommodate more diners, dice up any remaining pork into small bits and add more meat broth (figure on 1 cup broth per person), turning it into a stew when you reheat it. Add some extra cooked squash, dice some hearty greens, such as kale or Swiss chard, and sauté them in butter or olive oil and garlic, and stir them into the stew just before you are ready to eat.

How to cook a real, farm-made sausage

One of our hallmark products on Sap Bush Hollow Farm is our line of sausages. At last count, I believe we were making about 16 different varieties of pork, beef and lamb sausages in our on-farm cutting room. Our sausage days are long, as we prepare each individual spice blend, mix great batches of meat, and hand stuff and link all these different varieties. I'm like an over-protective mother when a customer buys their first pack of links from me. We put a lot of time and effort into these products, and I want to make sure my customers know exactly how to treat these babies right. I know that a great sausage isn't great until it's been perfectly prepared, and the fate of the sausage is ultimately in the hands of the cook. So I lecture the customers about how to properly handle them until they can repeat all my instructions back at me. The result, happily, is that they usually return to buy more, claiming ours were the best sausages they ever tasted. If you know a little bit about how sausage is made, you'll understand better how to prepare them.

Don't pierce your sausages. Factory-made sausages are often a mechanism for disposing of lower-quality meat and large volumes of fat, but the opposite is true on the farm. Pork fat is prized for the lard value, and thus most of the sausage is meat. A typical grocery-store sausage can be 35–50 percent fat; but quality farm-produced sausages are often only 20 percent fat (80 percent lean, the same meat-to-fat ratio as a high-quality hamburger). Get to know your farmer, and find out the fat content of their sausages. If they are 80 percent lean, and you pierce your sausages or parboil them, you are going to drain out the fat and juices that are packed in the casing to help braise the meat. When the fat and juices leave, they'll take the seasonings with them, leaving you with a mealy, tasteless link.

Slow down the cook time. The idea of a sausage is that meat and seasonings are stuffed into a little casing where they can braise in their juices, fat and any other liquids (such as beer, wine or vinegar) that may have been included in the blend. As anyone knows with good braising, the longer and slower the cook, the more flavor. The same is true with sausage. If you are grilling them, cook them indirectly, as far from the flames as possible. If you are frying them, keep the heat low and allow them ample time to build flavor. You will know they are done when the skin of the casing is tight around the meat. If the skin shrinks into the meat, you've gone a little too far. However, if you didn't prick your links and you kept the heat under control, the sausage should still be pretty decent.

Sausages, slow-cooked on the grill with indirect heat, are a favorite meal in our home.

Stuffed Acorn Squash

SERVES 4

1 large acorn squash

2 tablespoons lard, butter or olive oil

1 medium onion, chopped

1 pound loose sweet Italian, hot
   Italian or breakfast sausage (or
   1 pound plain ground pork, or
   use the recipe for Fresh Garlic
   Sausage [recipe follows])

½ cup dried cranberries

½ cup raisins

2 tablespoons dried rubbed sage

Fine salt and pepper to taste

1 cup slivered almonds

ESTIMATED CARBOHYDRATES:

Acorn squash: 44.91 g

Onion: 10.27 g

Cranberries: 49.42 g

Raisins: 57.41 g

Sage: 1.22 g

Almonds: 11.70 g

Total carbohydrates per recipe: 174.93 g

Total carbohydrates per ¼ recipe:
   43.73 g

This is a classic autumn meal in our household. It is easy to prepare and makes a dramatic presentation. We especially love serving it at our Halloween parties, where we tell guests it is free-range farmers' brains (I suppose one might consider that a unique brand of grass-farmer humor).

Preheat the oven to 350°F. Rinse the squash and pat dry. Place the whole squash on a baking sheet and roast just until the skin can be broken by the pressure of your fingernail, about 25 minutes. Let it cool enough to handle, cut it in half, then scoop out the seeds and membrane and discard them. Put the squash back on the baking sheet (cut-side up) and return them to the oven. Bake 20–25 minutes longer, or until the flesh is soft enough to be scooped out of the skin.

With a sharp-edged spoon, remove most of the flesh from the skin, leaving a ½-inch shell. Set both aside. Heat a large skillet over a medium flame. Add the fat and swirl to coat. Add the onion and sauté until clear. Add the sausage and cook, breaking up any large chunks of meat with a wooden spoon, until it is no longer pink. Stir in the cranberries, raisins and sage, and cook 2 minutes longer.

Add the meat mixture to a large bowl. Add the reserved squash flesh and mix well. Scoop the mixture into the squash shells, mounding it slightly. Sprinkle the almonds over the top and bake 30 minutes or until heated through and lightly browned on top.

Leftovers: Leftover stuffed squash can be re-warmed in a covered baking dish for 30 minutes in a 350-degree oven. The entire contents of the squash can also be stirred into some simmering broth to make a fragrant fall harvest soup. Stir in some cream just prior to serving to make the dish a little more rich and filling.

Fresh Garlic Sausage

ADVANCE PREPARATION REQUIRED.

MAKES 5 POUNDS

5 pounds fresh (unseasoned) ground pork

3 tablespoons fine salt

1 tablespoon ground black pepper

¾ teaspoon ground coriander

¾ teaspoon ground nutmeg

4 tablespoons minced fresh garlic

1 cup red wine

16 feet medium hog casings (optional)

ESTIMATED CARBOHYDRATES:
Ground black pepper: 4.41 g
Coriander: 0.74 g
Nutmeg: 0.81 g
Garlic: 11.24 g
Red wine: 6.03 g
Total carbohydrates per recipe: 23.23 g
Total carbohydrates per ⅒ recipe: 2.32 g

While spending a winter in France with my family, we repeatedly enjoyed this delicious sausage in our cassoulets. When I got home, inspired by my culinary adventures, I took over recipe development for Sap Bush Hollow's sausages. I was surprised to learn how simple a fresh garlic sausage was to make. Recipes for sausage often assume that the cook possesses a certain amount of equipment— namely, a sausage grinder and a stuffer. To sidestep that problem, this recipe calls for pork that has already been ground. Instructions for stuffing sausages into casings using a simple pastry bag have also been included. However, you can skip that step, if you prefer, and simply cook the sausage as patties (even if you are using them in a cassoulet).

Place the pork and all of the seasonings in a large bowl. Mix the sausage by hand, kneading and squeezing the meat until the spices, garlic and wine are evenly incorporated throughout the meat. Cover the bowl and refrigerate for a minimum of two hours, and up to 24 hours.

When ready to cook the sausages, shape the mixture into patties and fry or place in a cassoulet. Or, you may stuff the sausage into casings as follows:

Hog casings come preserved in salt, so prior to stuffing they must be soaked in a large bowl of warm water for 30 to 60 minutes. Carefully lift out one of the casings, then rinse under running water and thoroughly flush out the inside. Dip it into a second bowl of fresh water to give it a final rinse.

Pull the entire length of the rinsed casing up over the end of a pastry bag (as if pulling on a stocking), leaving about a 2-inch tip dangling off the bottom. Tie a knot in the dangling tip. Fill the pastry bag with the chilled sausage. Squeeze the bag with one hand to fill the casing, while using the other hand to hold it in place and guide the stuffed sausage off the tip. When it is filled, remove the casing from the tip of the pastry bag and prick any air bubbles that formed in the sausage rope.

To form the links, begin at the knotted end and pinch the sausage rope between your fingers about 6 six inches down. Move your fingers down another 6 inches and pinch again. Holding the two pinched points between your thumb and forefinger, with the flick of your wrist spin the sausage link around 3 or 4 times, twisting the casing. Proceed down the casing, repeating the process.

Refrigerate the sausages for use within 2 or 3 days, or package them in freezer bags or butcher paper to be frozen for later use.

Roasted Sausage with Apples

SERVES 6

1 tablespoon tallow, lard or butter

3 pounds linked sweet Italian, hot Italian or breakfast sausage

6 apples, quartered and cored, skins left on

ESTIMATED CARBOHYDRATES:
Apples: 150.81 g
Total carbohydrates per recipe: 150.81 g
Total carbohydrates per ⅙ recipe: 25.14 g

Here is the easiest recipe in the whole book, with only three ingredients. It is dazzling in spite of its simplicity, and a kid-pleaser to boot. I like to serve it in the fall and winter with roasted squash.

Preheat oven to 350°F. Heat a Dutch oven over a medium flame, add the fat and swirl to coat the bottom. Add the sausages and brown on all sides, about 2–3 minutes per side. Lay the apples over the meat, cover, and bake 45 minutes, or until the apples are tender.

Leftovers: Re-warm leftovers in a covered pan in a 250-degree oven for 30 minutes. If you need to stretch the leftovers a little farther, dice them up and toss them with sautéed red cabbage and apples. Season with a little balsamic vinegar and, if you wish, a touch of maple syrup or honey. Round out the repast with a wedge of aged raw cheddar.

A life in touch with the land leads to delicious (and free) discoveries…such as the giant patch of ramps that grows in the woods behind our house.

Fresh Pork Hocks with Sauerkraut
(aka, Great Pop Pop's mashed potatoes)

SERVES 4

1 tablespoon coarse salt

2 teaspoons ground black pepper

1 tablespoon dried parsley

2 cloves garlic, minced

2 fresh (uncured) pork hocks, about 2 pounds each

4 cups sauerkraut, drained

4 cups mashed potatoes

ESTIMATED CARBOHYDRATES:

Black pepper: 2.94 g

Parsley: 0.81 g

Garlic: 1.98 g

Sauerkraut: 24.31 g

Mashed potatoes: 141.2 g

Total carbohydrates per recipe: 171.24 g

Total carbohydrates per ¼ recipe: 42.81 g

My grandfather was Irish, my grandmother was German, and they grew up during the Great Depression. Knowing that, I think it is easy to see how this dish became standard family fare. My grandfather made sure that we continued to serve it at the family table long after my grandmother passed. For years I wouldn't venture near it, assuming it was a wretched combination that served as a perpetual reminder of leaner times. Then, one afternoon, I gave it a try. I loved it! Nope, this dish is definitely not glamorous. But it is inexpensive to prepare and makes for a tasty and filling meal without a lot of prep work.

Combine the salt, pepper, parsley and garlic in a small bowl.

If the hocks have the skin on, use a sharp knife to make a series of gashes (about 10 per hock) through the skin, down to the meat. Insert a pinch of the seasoning mix into each gash, and rub any that remains into the exposed meat on the ends. If the hocks are skinless, simply rub the garlic-salt mix lightly over the entire surface.

Put the sauerkraut in the bottom of a slow cooker. Rest the hocks on top and cook on low 6 hours, or until the meat easily pulls from the bone. Remove the hocks, let cool enough to handle, and pull off the meat, discarding the skin and bones (dogs love the skin). Dice the meat and mix it into the sauerkraut and juices. Serve over mashed potatoes.

Leftovers: Leftovers re-warm beautifully in a covered casserole in a 300-degree oven for 30 minutes, or in the slow cooker, set to low, for an hour. Leftovers can also be incorporated into Meat Pie (Chapter 8).

Pork Hock Rillettes

2 fresh (uncured) pork hocks, about 3 pounds

1 *bouquet garni* made with 4–5 sprigs fresh thyme, 1 small bundle fresh parsley, 2 sprigs fresh rosemary, and 2 bay leaves

1 carrot, cut in half

1 stalk celery, cut in half

1 shallot, peeled but left whole

1 medium onion, peeled but left whole and studded with 6 whole cloves

¼ teaspoon ground black pepper

2 teaspoons coarse salt

4 cups meat broth, such as Shannon's Meat Broth, Chapter 3

Fine salt and pepper, to taste

½ cup lard

ESTIMATED CARBOHYDRATES:

Thyme: 0.59 g
Parsley: 1.90 g
Rosemary: 0.70 g
Bay leaves: 0.45 g
Carrot: 5.84 g
Celery: 1.19 g
Shallot: 5.04 g
Onion studded with cloves: 11.56 g
Black pepper: 0.37 g
Meat broth: 5.6 g
Total carbohydrates per recipe: 33.24 g

The total number of carbohydrates per serving will be quite negligible, as only a small amount of the broth is actually incorporated into the paste that forms the rillettes.

Rillettes are beautiful potted delights that travel well for picnics, provide "fast food" needs for the slow-food gourmet, and dazzle dinner party hosts with something far more extraordinary than a mundane bottle of wine. Rillettes are bits of meat that were braised in a fragrant liquid until they are super-tender, then pounded and mixed until they become a spreadable paste. They are preserved with a layer of lard or duck fat that is poured on top. The entire mixture, fat and paste together, tastes great on a wedge of crisp apple or pear, the tip of a carrot stick, Parmesan Parsley Almond Crackers (Chapter 8), or a slice of baguette. They are a wonderful food to make when the pig harvest comes in, then store in little glass pots until you need them.

Place the pork hocks on the bottom of a slow cooker. Set the *bouquet garni* on top and add the carrot, celery, shallot, and onion, and sprinkle with the pepper and salt. Pour in the broth, cover, and cook on low for 6–8 hours, or until the meat is falling off the bone.

Remove the pork to a cutting board and let it cool enough to handle. Strain the broth and set aside.

Remove the skin and all the meat and soft fat from the bones. Discard the skin (or use it to make Mexican Cracklings) and bones, and put the meat and fat in the bowl of a standing mixer with the paddle attachment. Mix at low speed, then increase to high. Add in just enough of the reserved stock to enable the meat to shred and eventually become a paste. (Cool and refrigerate any remaining stock for another use.) Season to taste with salt and pepper, keeping in mind that the rillettes will be chilled, then eaten at room temperature; the seasonings will not be as pronounced as when the meat is hot.

Loosely pack the pork into glass ramekins, small crocks or wide-mouthed jars, leaving ½ inch of headroom. Cover and refrigerate 1–2 hours, until chilled through. Melt the lard over medium heat and pour over the meat until it is entirely submerged. Cover and refrigerate. They will keep for about 2 weeks (longer if the fat seal remains unbroken). Allow them to come to room temperature before serving (they will spread easier).

Lentils with Bacon, Ham Hocks, and Duck Confit

SERVES 6–8

2 tablespoons duck fat from Duck Confit (Chapter 7), or 2 tablespoons lard

6 slices thick-cut bacon, coarsely chopped

1 small yellow onion, chopped

2 cloves garlic, chopped

1 pound French green lentils, rinsed, drained

6 cups meat broth, such as Shannon's Meat Broth, Chapter 3

2 small to medium smoked ham hocks, or one large one

½ cup chopped fresh parsley, or 4 teaspoons dried

2 tablespoons chopped fresh thyme, or 2 teaspoons dried

1 small red onion, chopped

½ cup chopped celery

1½ cups coarsely chopped Duck Confit (Chapter 7), optional

½ cup olive oil

¼ cup lemon juice

2 tablespoons Dijon mustard

ESTIMATED CARBOHYDRATES:	
Onion: 6.54 g	Garlic: 1.98 g
Lentils: 272.52 g	Meat broth: 8.4 g*
Parsley: 1.90 g	Thyme: 1.17 g
Red onion: 6.54 g	Celery: 1.50 g
Duck confit: 3.35 g	Lemon juice: 3.95 g
Total carbohydrates per recipe: 307.85 g	
Total carbohydrates per ⅙ recipe: 51.30 g	

* Number of carbohydrates in home-made broth will vary. This figure is calculated using the recipe for Shannon's Meat Broth (Chapter 3).

This hearty dish is terrific when served with a robust helping of sauerkraut or red cabbage braised with apples. Toss in a fresh baguette, and the meal will feed a few more folks. If you don't happen to have the duck confit, the dish will still taste excellent without it.

Melt the fat in a large Dutch oven over a medium flame. Add the bacon and fry until crisp. Remove it with a slotted spoon and set it aside. Add the onion and garlic and sauté one minute. Add the lentils and sauté 2 minutes longer.

Pour in the meat broth and add the ham hocks and herbs. Cover and simmer 45 minutes, or until the lentils are tender. Remove the ham hocks with tongs and set them aside on a cutting board to cool. Continue simmering the lentils, uncovered, until all the liquid is evaporated, being careful not to let them scorch. Turn off the heat.

Skin the hocks, pull off the meat, dice it coarsely, and stir it into the lentils. Stir in the red onion, celery and cooked bacon.

If you are using the optional duck confit, heat it briefly in a dry skillet until it is warmed through and the skin is crisp. Add it to the lentils.

In a separate bowl, whisk together the olive oil, lemon juice and mustard until it is emulsified. Pour it over the lentils and toss well to coat. Serve the salad warm or cold on top of salad greens.

Leftovers: Once you've had this as a main dish, serve the leftovers as a side dish to accompany lamb, chicken or pork. It can also be added to some simmering meat broth, along with some tomatoes, for a tasty, smoky soup.

Why can't I buy fresh meat from the farm?

One of our long-time customers often regaled me with stories about her favorite nephew, who had recently graduated from culinary school and was working in a chic urban restaurant. She was eager to introduce him to our farm, and couldn't wait for him to try our meats.

I remember the time she brought the lad up for a weekend so he could come to our farmers' market stall and personally select his dinner. He looked over our offerings, curled his lip, poked at the frozen cuts of beef, pork and lamb and said, "What's fresh?"

"You." Well, that's what I wanted to say. But I didn't. I proudly told him that nothing was "fresh" that day. I explained that we were a small farm, and we didn't process animals every week. At that point, he informed me that the meat used in the restaurant where he worked was *always fresh*, and that our local offerings were unacceptable if they could only be available frozen.

"Fresh" is a great criteria for selecting lettuce. It's not always the best guideline for choosing meat. Conventional meat looks "fresh" because it is wet-aged, vacuum-packed, then shipped all over the country with little regard for the expended fossil fuels. The vacuum bags hold the meat "fresh" for a very long time. Technically the meat has never actually been frozen by the time the consumer gets it, but it has been sitting in a bag of blood for just as long, or longer, than a piece of locally-raised frozen grassfed meat. It has also often been shipped half-frozen (28 degrees F.), even though the vendors may tout "fresh, never frozen" in their labeling or advertising.

With the possible exception of chicken, locally-based grass farmers, if they are working within the confines of their community and their ecosystem, are not likely to have a completely fresh meat inventory every week. A beef harvest in the summer might allow for fresh beef as a special Fourth of July treat, but until the next beef is harvested, that meat will be kept frozen. The same is true for lamb. Pork is a different story altogether. In order to prevent food-borne pathogens in pork, farmers freeze the meat before selling it. That's because *Toxoplasma* oocysts and most *Trichinella* are killed when frozen. Any chef buying "fresh" pork is either buying meat that isn't entirely safe, or he is purchasing a bill of goods and getting thawed meat marketed as fresh.

With an on-farm cutting room at Sap Bush Hollow, my family has probably had more fresh meat than most chefs. Whatever we are cutting in the morning is what we will be eating that day for lunch. It is always delicious, but I honestly cannot discern the difference between a fresh piece of meat and one that has been properly packaged and frozen.

When it comes to chicken, we are in a position to offer fresh birds almost every week at our farmers' market, and our customers are eager to have them. However, in our house, we actually prefer to thaw out a properly stored frozen bird to roast for dinner, as we find the flavor and texture preferable.

In general, frozen pork, if kept in air-tight packages, will hold for six months. Frozen beef, lamb and poultry will maintain their quality for up to a year or longer. If it happens that the day you visit your local farmer coincides with the presence of fresh meat, by all means give it a try. It is nice to pick something up for dinner that you won't need to thaw. Just buy what you are going to eat, however. We inwardly grin at the contradiction when we see our market customers grab as much fresh meat as they can at our market to "stock up the freezer." In fact, your home freezer will take a longer time to bring the unfrozen meat down to the appropriate temperatures, resulting in larger ice crystals. Allow the farmer, who has invested in good-quality super-cold freezer units (or whose butcher has these units) to do that for you. And if you miss the day fresh meat is available, don't fret. Your properly frozen meat will be just as delicious.

Thai-Style Country Ribs with a Dipping Sauce

SERVES 4–6

Thai Marinade, Appendix 1

4 pounds country ribs or spareribs

Thai Dipping Sauce (recipe follows)

THAI DIPPING SAUCE

MAKES ABOUT ¾ TO 1 CUP

2 tablespoons lime juice

2 tablespoons rice wine vinegar

1 tablespoon Tamari or soy sauce

1 teaspoon crushed red pepper

1 tablespoon honey

1 clove garlic, finely minced

1 teaspoon sesame oil

2 tablespoons fresh cilantro, finely chopped

2 tablespoons fresh mint, finely chopped

ESTIMATED CARBOHYDRATES:

Thai Marinade: 32.77 g

Thai Dipping Sauce: 22.65 g

Total number of carbohydrates per recipe: 55.42 g*

Total number of carbohydrates per ¼ recipe: 13.86 g*

* Actual number of carbohydrates will vary based on how much of the marinade is absorbed by the meat.

Use this recipe on spare ribs as well as country ribs. I usually try to grab as many of both cuts as possible whenever I prepare it, because leftovers re-warm so beautifully in a 200-degree oven. When pouring the marinade over the pork, be as parsimonious as possible (while taking care to make sure the meat is thoroughly coated). Any extra marinade that did not have contact with the uncooked meat can be bottled up, stored in the refrigerator and used another time. For another recipe using this marinade, see Thai Shaved Steaks in Chapter 4.

Make a thin paste of the marinade by pureeing it in a food processor fitted with a steel blade. Place pork in a large nonreactive (glass or stainless-steel) bowl, deep stainless-steel or enameled pan or resealable plastic bag. Pour the marinade on top, turn the meat several times to coat it well, and marinate at room temperature for 2–4 hours, turning occasionally to be sure the meat is thoroughly exposed to the marinade.

Fill a porcelain or glass bread loaf pan halfway with water, and set this pan on the bottom rack of the oven. Preheat the oven to 200°F. Remove the ribs from the marinade and lay them in a roasting pan. Set the roasting pan on the middle or top rack and bake 4–6 hours, or until the meat is tender and pulls easily from the bones. Serve with the Thai Dipping Sauce.

Leftovers: This recipe re-warms beautifully. Dice up the leftover pork and put it in a covered, nonreactive pan, pour the dipping sauce on top, cover, and bake in a 200-degree oven until they're warmed to your liking. They can also be reheated in the same way in a slow cooker.

THAI DIPPING SAUCE

Whisk all the ingredients together in a small bowl.

Slow-Cooked Pork Shoulder Chops in a North African Spice Sauce

SERVES 4

3 pounds pork shoulder chops (aka country ribs) or 1 3–4-pound pork shoulder roast

1 recipe Moroccan Spice Rub, Appendix 1

2 tablespoons lard, butter or tallow

1 cup meat broth, such as Shannon's Meat Broth, Chapter 3

1 medium onion, coarsely chopped

2 teaspoons grated fresh ginger

1 tablespoon lemon zest

2 cloves garlic

1 large whole tomato, chopped, or 1 cup canned diced tomatoes

2 tablespoons lemon juice

½ teaspoon ground cinnamon

1 teaspoon ground turmeric

¼ teaspoon ground cayenne

8 ounces pitted green olives, coarsely diced

ESTIMATED CARBOHYDRATES:
Moroccan Spice Rub: 12.68 g
Meat Broth: 1.4 g
Onion: 10.27 g
Ginger: 0.71 g
Lemon Zest: 0.96 g
Garlic: 1.98 g
Tomato: 7.08 g
Lemon juice: 1.94 g
Cinnamon: 1.05 g
Turmeric: 1.43 g
Cayenne: 0.25 g
Olives: 10.44 g
Total number of carbohydrates per recipe: 50.19 g
Total number of carbohydrates per ¼ recipe: 12.55 g

I first read about cooking pork with Moroccan-inspired seasonings in Bruce Aidell's Complete Book of Pork. *Here, I've taken the idea and reworked it for the slow cooker, creating an exotic-tasting dish that is easy on the cook.*

Season the meat on all sides with the spice rub. Allow it to sit for 2 hours at room temperature, or overnight, covered and refrigerated. Bring it to room temperature prior to cooking.

Heat a large skillet over a medium-high flame. Add the fat and swirl to coat. Lay the chops in the pan, taking care to allow one inch of space around each. Working in batches if necessary, sear the chops until well browned on both sides, about 2–3 minutes per side (see the sidebar in Chapter 5, *Searing*, for more details). Transfer them to a slow cooker.

Puree the broth, onion, ginger, lemon zest, garlic, tomato, lemon juice, cinnamon, turmeric and cayenne in a blender. Pour it over the meat, cover, and cook on low 4–6 hours until the meat is tender. Remove the chops to a platter and keep warm. Pour the cooking liquid into a skillet and simmer over medium heat until reduced by half. Add the olives and cook until they are heated through. Serve the chops with the sauce spooned on top.

Leftovers: Braised pork such as this is easily re-warmed for another meal in the slow cooker, or in a covered casserole in the oven. To make a different meal out of it, chill the sauce and remove any fat that solidifies on the top. Dice the remaining meat, stir it into the sauce, then make a soup by adding a few cups more meat broth and some shredded cabbage and carrots. Bring it to a simmer and cook 10 minutes. Leftovers could also be stirred into the Butternut Pork Stew with Bacon and Fennel (Chapter 8).

Pan-Seared Pork Chops

SERVES 2–4

2 bone-in pork rib or sirloin chops, at least 1 ¼ inches thick

3 large cloves fresh garlic, 1 minced and 2 peeled but left whole

2 teaspoons dried thyme

2 teaspoons ground black pepper

1 tablespoon coarse salt

4 tablespoons butter, 2 melted, or 2 tablespoons melted butter and 2 tablespoons lard

1 cup meat broth, such as Shannon's Meat Broth, Chapter 3

2 tablespoons bourbon

1 teaspoon Dijon mustard

2 tablespoons heavy cream

ESTIMATED CARBOHYDRATES:

Garlic: 2.97 g

Thyme: 1.28 g

Black pepper: 2.94 g

Meat broth: 1.40 g

Heavy cream: 0.04 g

Total carbohydrates per recipe: 9.43 g

Total carbohydrates per ½ recipe: 4.71 g

* Carbohydrates in homemade broth will vary. This figure is calculated based on my homemade broth, which uses 1 large onion, 1 large carrot, 4 cups mixed greens and ½ cup cider vinegar in addition to the bones to generate 20 cups of broth.

I never had very good luck turning out a consistently juicy and tender pan-cooked pork chop until I came across this technique, adapted from Bruce Aidell's Complete Book of Pork. *Now I have success every time.*

Blot the chops dry. Stir the garlic, thyme, black pepper and salt into the melted butter. Brush this on the chops and allow them to come to room temperature. Put the whole garlic cloves and broth in a small saucepan. Bring it to a simmer until the garlic is soft and the broth is reduced by half, about 15 minutes. Turn off the heat.

Meanwhile, heat a skillet that is large enough to hold two pork chops without crowding them over a medium-high flame. Add the remaining butter or lard and swirl to coat the pan. Add the chops and sear 2–3 minutes, or until browned on the bottom. Turn and cook 2 minutes longer, then reduce the heat to medium-low. The chops should still be sputtering. If you don't hear this sound, the heat is too low and your chops run the risk of sweating, which causes them to dry out. Once you hear a gentle sizzle, cover and cook until the chops reach an internal temperature between 145–160 degrees—depending on how done you like them—about 10 minutes. Transfer the chops to a platter and allow the meat to rest while you prepare the pan sauce.

Using a fork, thoroughly mash the softened garlic into the reduced broth. Return the skillet to a medium flame. Pour in the garlic reduction and bring it to a simmer, gently scraping up the browned bits from the pan. Simmer until the liquid is reduced by one-third. Stir in the bourbon, simmer a minute more, then whisk in the mustard and cream. Pour over the chops and serve.

Leftovers: Since one typically doesn't prepare more pork chops than there are diners, there are rarely leftovers of this recipe. I've been known, however, to pull the uneaten slices off my daughters' plates and to salvage any tidbits from the bones in order to make a batch of Pork and Greens in a Ginger Tamari Broth (Chapter 8), or whatever version of Refrigerator Soup that I may be able to pull together, often combining these tidbits with whatever bits of extra lamb, beef or pork I have on hand.

Brined Pork Chops in Rosemary Cream Sauce with Caramelized Pears

SERVES 2

1¾ cup water

2 tablespoons coarse salt

3 tablespoons granulated maple sugar, turbinado, sucanat or brown sugar

2 center-cut/loin/t-bone pork chops, 1¼–1½ inches thick

3 pears (any variety that is in season and ripe will do), peeled, cored and thinly sliced

2 tablespoons butter

1 tablespoon lard (or butter)

1 cup dry white wine or meat broth, such as Shannon's Meat Broth, Chapter 3

½ teaspoon dried rosemary

3 tablespoons sour cream

Fine salt and pepper, to taste

ESTIMATED CARBOHYDRATES:

Maple sugar 49.09 g*

Pears: 82.56 g

Meat broth: 1.40 g**

Rosemary: 0.38 g

Sour cream: 1.04 g

Total number of estimated carbohydrates per recipe: 85.38

Total number of estimated carbohydrates per ½ recipe: 42.69 g

* Since the sugar is used in the brine only, very little of it will actually penetrate the meat, thus the amount of carbohydrate it adds to the dish is negligible. Sugar in brines only adheres to the meat surface, where it aids in browning.

** Number of carbohydrates in home-made broth will vary. This figure is calculated using the recipe for Shannon's Meat Broth (Chapter 3).

This autumnal dish beckons when the pears and our pork harvest are ready. While brining balances the lean meat of the center cut (loin) chops, the recipe works well with rib or sirloin chops as well.

In a medium bowl, whisk together the water, salt and maple sugar. Add the pork chops, cover, and refrigerate 4–6 hours. Remove the chops from the brine, rinse well, and pat dry. Discard the brine. If you are not cooking the chops right away, wrap them in plastic or put them in an airtight glass container and store them in the refrigerator for up to two days.

When you are ready to cook the pork, bring it to room temperature for at least 30 minutes. Melt the butter in a medium nonreactive(stainless-steel or enameled) skillet over a medium–high flame. Add the pears and sauté 2 minutes, stirring often. Turn the flame down and cook slowly, stirring occasionally until the pears are caramelized, about 15 minutes.

Meanwhile, prepare the pork chops. Melt the lard or remaining butter over a high flame in a skillet large enough to hold the chops without crowding. Thoroughly pat the chops dry and add them to the skillet. Cook 2–3 minutes or until lightly browned on the bottom. Turn and cook 2 minutes longer, then reduce the heat to medium-low. There should still be a gentle sizzling sound; if not, the heat is too low and your chops run the risk of sweating, and thus drying out. Adjust the heat, cover, and cook until the chops reach an internal temperature between 145–160 degrees—to preferred doneness—about 10 minutes. Transfer to a platter resting the meat while you prepare the pan sauce.

Pour excess fat from the pan and return it to a medium–high flame. Add the wine or broth and rosemary. Bring to a boil, using a whisk or wooden spoon to scrape up any browned bits that are stuck to the bottom of the pan. Simmer until the liquid is reduced by half and is syrupy, about 5 minutes. Turn off the heat. Whisk in the sour cream, season to taste with salt and pepper, and pour the pan sauce over the chops. Serve with the caramelized pears spooned onto the side.

Leftovers: The meat from leftover chops can be sliced and stored in the cream sauce and reused in Croquettes with Black Pepper and Onion Sauce (Chapter 8). If you don't have enough meat to make a full recipe,combine it with some ground meat or any bits of other leftovers you have on hand.

Breaded Pork Chops

MAKES 2 OR 3 LARGE PORK CHOPS

½ cup all-purpose flour

2 teaspoons sweet paprika

1½ teaspoons coarse salt

1 teaspoon ground black pepper

½ teaspoon granulated garlic

1 egg

1 teaspoon Worcestershire sauce

¾ cup dry bread crumbs

1 tablespoon dried parsley

¼ cup freshly grated Parmesan cheese

2 or 3 pork chops, 1½-inch thick

> **ESTIMATED CARBOHYDRATES:**
> Flour: 46.13 g
> Paprika: 2.48 g
> Black pepper: 1.47 g
> Granulated garlic: 1.13 g
> Egg: 0.36 g
> Worcestershire sauce: 1.09 g
> Bread crumbs: 58.30 g
> Parsley: 0.81 g
> Parmesan cheese: 1.01 g
> Total carbohydrates per recipe: 112.78
> Total carbohydrates per ¼ recipe: 28.20 g

When down-home-style cooking is what you crave, this recipe is what you need.

Preheat the oven to 350°F. In a shallow bowl, combine the flour, paprika, salt, pepper, and garlic. In a second shallow bowl, whisk together the egg and Worcestershire sauce. In a third shallow bowl, combine the bread crumbs, parsley, and Parmesan.

Dip the pork chops in the flour, turning to coat both sides thoroughly. Shake off the excess. Repeat with the egg mixture, allowing the excess to flow back into the bowl, and then roll in the bread crumb mixture. Gently shake off the excess, place in an ungreased shallow roasting pan, and bake to an internal temperature of 145–160 degrees—depending on how done you like them—about 45 minutes to 1 hour.

Leftovers: Leftovers can be re-warmed in an uncovered dish in a 250-degree oven, or used in Croquettes with Black Pepper and Onion Sauce, Parmesan-Cheddar One Crust Meat Pie, Meat Canapés with Goat Cheese and Roasted Red Pepper, or Asian-Style Cold Meat Salad (all in Chapter 8).

Choosing pork chops

Pigs offer a variety of chop options, with subtle differences. **Sirloin chops** are closest to the hip and contain a little more bone. If you are diligent about keeping bones for broth, then a little extra bone shouldn't present a problem, especially since the sirloins are very flavorful and are often sold at a lower price. **Loin chops** are located in front of them, and correspond to the porterhouse and t-bone steaks on a beef. The muscle on these chops is leaner, more tender and responds well to brining. If the tenderloin has not been pulled from the pig, these chops will contain a portion of tenderloin muscle where the portion of filet would be on a porterhouse steak. In front of the loin chops are the **rib chops**, which contain more marbling and are slightly less tender. Like the sirloin chops, these are high-flavor cuts, and the marbling keeps the meat juicy. Chops from the shoulder go under different names. Here in Schoharie County they are called "**country ribs**," but they also go by "**blade chops**," "**shoulder chops**," "**country spareribs**" or "**blade steaks**." These cuts contain connective tissue, making them excellent candidates for smoking on the barbecue or slow-cooking with wine or broth.

Simple and Perfect Pork Roast

SERVES 5–6

4 pounds bone-in pork loin or rib roast (preferably with the chine bone removed)

1 recipe Rosemary and Thyme Herb Rub, Appendix 1, *or your choice of herb or spice rub*

Shallot Dijon Reduction Sauce (see Fresh Ham with a Shallot Dijon Reduction), optional

Or, if making pan gravy (optional):

¼ cup all-purpose flour

2 cups meat broth, such as Shannon's Meat Broth, Chapter 3

Fine salt and black pepper, to taste

It amazes me, when reading cookbooks, the number of elaborate treatments prescribed for the bone-in pork loin or rib roast—flavor brines that require you sacrifice precious refrigerator space for a minimum of two days, sticky fruit glazes, directions to bore out the center of the meat, grind it, blend it with odd ingredients then re-stuff it. Embarrassingly, as a cookbook writer, I've been guilty of all these transgressions. But that's not how I actually cook a pork roast. It's not how my dad cooks it. It wasn't how my grandmother cooked it, either. A good old-fashioned pork roast, courtesy of a good old-fashioned pig, has great fat cover insulating the outside of the tender meat, with a tiny bit of fat up next to the bone. Assuming the meat isn't overcooked, it will be juicy and flavorful without all the cookbook magic tricks. Treat a pork roast with some herbs, salt, pepper and garlic, roast it in a moderate oven and serve it up with some gravy, potatoes and sauerkraut, and you will never go wrong. Here's how it's done.

Wipe the meat dry and rub the herb rub into it on all sides, on top of the fat★ and even along the bones on the bottom of the roast. Allow the meat to rest two hours at room temperature, or overnight, covered and refrigerated. Be sure to allow it to come to room temperature prior to roasting.

Preheat oven to 325°F. Place the roast, bone-side down, in a shallow roasting pan or cast-iron skillet. Insert an ovenproof meat thermometer in the eye of the meat and allow it to roast to an internal temperature of 145–160 degrees (depending on how done you like it, but remember that the lower the temperature, the juicier the meat will be), about 30 minutes per pound. Transfer the roast to a platter or cutting board and allow it to rest a few minutes before carving so that the juices, which will have been drawn to the outer surface of the meat, can redistribute throughout the roast. It can be served simply with its roasting juices (au jus), with Shallot Dijon Reduction, or with pan gravy, made as follows:

While the roast is resting, place the roasting pan with the pork drippings over a medium flame. Once the drippings are bubbling and

---

★Are you working with a skin-on roast? Lucky you! You'll have delicious cracklings to munch on as the grease dribbles down your chin. It is a heavenly experience. To season a skin-on roast, simply cut a series of 1-inch gashes throughout the skin, down to the fat layer. Then push the herb rub into the gashes. Season the rest of the roast as described above.

ESTIMATED CARBOHYDRATES:
Rosemary Thyme Herb Rub: 10.23 g
Total carbohydrates per recipe: 10.23 g
Total carbohydrates per ⅙ recipe: 1.71 g
Flour: 23.07 g
Meat broth: 2.8 g*
Total carbohydrates per recipe: 25.87 g

* Number of carbohydrates in homemade broth will vary. This figure is calculated using the recipe for Shannon's
Meat Broth (Chapter 3).

sizzling, whisk in the flour to make a thin paste (if you have a lot of drippings, you may need to use a little extra flour). Cook a minute or two longer, allowing the flour to brown slightly. Stir, scraping any browned bits off the pan to incorporate them into the gravy, then slowly whisk in one cup of broth. Allow the gravy to come to a simmer and thicken. If it is too thick for your liking, or if you need more to serve some gravy-loving diners, add the additional broth or stir in any additional juices from your cutting board after you've carved the meat.

To carve the roast, start with your knife against the bone at the very tip of the ribs on the end of the roast (the thinnest part). Gently work your knife along the bones, underneath the meat, until you reach the curve in the bones under the thickest part of the roast. Curve up and along the bones and work your way back up to the top. You should be able to lift the entire roast right off the ribs, allowing for easy boneless carving. (Don't throw away those bones! The meat is sweetest if you pull them apart and nibble between them! My girls fight over them.) Serve simply with the meat au jus, Shallot Dijon Reduction, or pan gravy.

Leftovers: Leftovers can be re-warmed in a small covered roasting pan or Dutch oven. Add any leftover pan juices, gravy, or reduction sauce, plus 2 teaspoons of butter or olive oil for each serving of meat, cover, and cook at 200 degrees about 30 minutes, or until warmed through. Leftovers also taste great in Parmesan-Cheddar One Crust Meat Pie, Croquettes with Black Pepper and Onion Sauce, or Meat Canapés with Goat Cheese and Roasted Red Pepper (all in Chapter 8).

Five-Spice Pork Roast on a Bed of Mashed Apples and Turnips

SERVES 4–6

1 tablespoon Chinese five-spice powder

1 tablespoon fine salt or more, to taste

2 teaspoons ground black pepper, or more, to taste

3–3 ½ pounds pork roast (fresh ham, loin, rib, or shoulder, bone-in or boneless)

2 apples, peeled, cored and sliced

2 turnips, peeled and diced

1 cup meat broth, such as Shannon's Meat Broth, Chapter 3

1 tablespoon freshly squeezed lemon juice

2 eggs, slightly beaten

ESTIMATED CARBOHYDRATES:

Chinese five-spice powder: 6.g
Black pepper: 2.94 g
Apples: 50.27 g
Turnips: 15.69 g
Meat broth: 1.40 g*
Lemon juice: 0.97 g
Eggs: 0.72 g
Total carbohydrates per recipe: 77.99 g
Total carbohydrates per ⅕ recipe: 15.60 g

* Number of carbohydrates in home-made broth will vary. This figure is calculated using the recipe for Shannon's Meat Broth (Chapter 3).

This is a luscious feast that will work with any type of pork roast you have on hand. Loin and rib roasts, since they are leaner, will cook a little faster. The pork shoulder roast is more marbled and will take a bit more time, which allows the melting fat to break down some of the collagen. Typically, a three-pound bone-in roast will serve three people. I tested this recipe on a bone-in rib roast and discovered that I was able to get five hearty servings, owing to the luscious, naturally sweet bed of mashed apples and turnips, made rich with eggs and meat broth.

Combine the five-spice powder with salt and pepper to taste in a small dish. Rub the mixture all over the pork, then allow the meat to come to room temperature. (Flavor tip: for heightened seasoning, apply the spice rub the night before, cover and refrigerate.) Preheat oven to 350°F. Place meat fat-side-up in a cast-iron skillet or roasting pan, and roast to an internal temperature of 145–160 degrees—depending on how done you like it—about 30 minutes per pound (remember: bone-in meat will cook faster than boneless). Let the meat rest, covered, for 15–30 minutes before carving.

Meanwhile, place the apples, turnips, and broth in a pressure cooker. Seal and cook at 15psi for 3 minutes.★★ Allow the pressure to subside naturally prior to opening the cooker. Move the apples and turnips to a medium bowl, pour in the cooking juices and lemon juice, thoroughly mash with a potato masher, then allow them to cool for 10 minutes before blending in the eggs. Place the mixture in a greased 9-inch-square baking pan and bake alongside the pork for 50 minutes until firm and lightly browned.

To serve, remove the bone from the pork roast, slice thinly, and serve on top of the mashed turnips and apples. Drizzle any pan juices from the meat on top.

Leftovers: Place the sliced pork on top of the mashed apples and turnips, topped with any remaining pan juices, in a covered baking dish. Ideally, you should have about 1 tablespoon of leftover pan juices for each serving. If you don't have enough, top with 1 tablespoon of butter for each serving you are re-warming. Cover and reheat in a 250-degree oven. If you only have pork left over, dice it thinly and use it in Chinese-style stir-fry.

★★ If you don't have a pressure cooker, simmer the apples and turnips in a regular saucepan with enough water to barely cover them, until they are tender. Drain, then mash with the meat broth.

Tenderloin Medallions with Caramelized Onions and Skillet Potatoes

SERVES 2

6 tablespoons butter, lard, or tallow

2 medium potatoes, cut into small chunks

Fine salt and ground black pepper, to taste

1 large onion, cut into wedges

1 teaspoon dried tarragon

1 cup meat broth, such as Shannon's Meat Broth, Chapter 3

1 pound pork tenderloin, cut into 1-inch-thick medallions, or 1 pound pork kebabs

¼ cup sherry

½ cup heavy cream

ESTIMATED CARBOHYDRATES:
Onion: 14.01 g
Meat broth: 1.4 g*
Potatoes (2): 66.92 g
Sherry: 3 g
Heavy cream: 3.32 g
Total number of carbohydrates per recipe: 88.65 g
Total number of carbohydrates per ½ recipe: 44.33 g

* Number of carbohydrates in homemade broth will vary. This figure is calculated using the recipe for Shannon's Meat Broth (Chapter 3).

This is a favorite "date night" meal in our house (it is too good to share with the kids!) If you are on a budget, pork kebabs can be substituted for tenderloin medallions. Their flavor will be more pronounced, but they will be slightly less tender. Also, for those folks who need to avoid potatoes, the recipe is just as delicious without them!

Heat 2 tablespoons of the fat in a cast-iron skillet. Add the potatoes and sauté until browned. Season with salt and pepper, and continue sautéing until they are tender, about 15 minutes.

Meanwhile, heat 2 more tablespoons of the fat in a second skillet. Once it melts, add the onion. The wedges should sizzle as they hit the pan, but if they sputter or splatter, lower the flame. Stir well, coating the onions in the cooking fat and scraping up any browned bits that form in the bottom of the pan. Sauté 2–3 minutes, until the onions collapse and have given up two-thirds of their volume in water. Once they start to brown, lower the flame and cook until they are uniformly caramelized, stirring often, about 10–15 minutes longer. Lower the heat if they start to burn. Add the tarragon and broth, and simmer over a very low flame until it is reduced by half, about 15 minutes.

Pour the sauce and onions into a small bowl. Return the skillet to a medium-high flame, add the remaining 2 tablespoons of fat, and swirl to coat. Sprinkle the pork with salt and pepper then add it to the skillet, making sure there is about 1 inch of space around each medallion, enabling them to brown. Sear 3 minutes per side. Add the potatoes, sauce, and sherry. Bring to a simmer and scrape up any browned bits. Add the heavy cream and mix well over low heat. Serve immediately.

Leftovers: Unless your dinner is interrupted, there won't be any! In such a case, dice the leftover pork, mix it back into the sauce and potatoes, and add them to Creamy Roasted Garlic Soup with Spicy Sausage (Chapter 8).

Rillons

4 tablespoons fine salt

5 teaspoons ground black pepper

1 ¼ teaspoons ground cinnamon

½ teaspoon ground cloves

Pinch ground allspice

3 bay leaves, crumbled

8 sprigs of fresh thyme

Pinch sweet paprika

Pinch ground cayenne

5 pounds skinless pork belly, cut into strips 1 inch wide and 3 inches long

1 bottle dry white wine, preferably Vouvray

4–5 pounds rendered lard or duck fat

ESTIMATED CARBOHYDRATES:
Black pepper: 7.35 g
Cinnamon: 2.62 g
Cloves: 0.64 g
Allspice: 0.34 g
Bay leaves: 0.67 g
Thyme: 0.39 g
Wine: 20.38 g
Total number of carbohydrates in the marinade: 32.39 g

Total number of carbohydrates in the recipe will depend on how much of the marinade is actually absorbed into the meat. To gauge the actual figure, weigh the marinade before the meat has been put in, and after it has been removed. The difference between the two figures will be the amount of marinade absorbed by the meat.

The sleepy French countryside where Bob, Saoirse and I spent the winter of 2005 taught me many wonderful lessons—among them, there is more to a pork belly than sausage or bacon. Rillons, a specialty of the Touraine region where we stayed, have been a local food tradition since at least the 15th century, and with good reason. They're delicious. Every week I would visit my favorite charcutier *at one of the nearby farmers' markets, where I would watch him pull slabs of pork belly that had been cured in white wine and spices out of a giant barrel of bubbling lard. He'd wrap the* rillons *in paper for me, and I would keep them in my refrigerator all week, where I'd carve off slices to eat plain (cold) for breakfast, serve them with mustard on a charcuterie platter with other local sausages and* patés, *or over a salad or sautéed green vegetables tossed with a warm vinaigrette.* Rillons *can be browned in a little fat and served over a warm mountain of sauerkraut, or on a bed of savory white beans cooked in meat broth and herbs.*

Combine the salt, pepper, cinnamon, cloves, allspice, bay leaves, thyme (left whole), paprika and cayenne in a large, nonreactive (stainless-steel or glass) bowl. Mix well. Add the pork and toss to coat. Add the wine, cover, and refrigerate 24 hours, stirring occasionally to ensure all the meat has time to soak in the wine.

Preheat the oven to 200°F. Remove the pork from the wine, blot dry, and place it in an ovenproof pot or Dutch oven. Place the pot over a direct medium-high flame. Add the fat and bring to a simmer. If the meat is not completely submerged, add more fat as needed. Once the fat is gently bubbling, move the pot to the oven and continue to cook until the meat is fork-tender, about 3 hours.

Using tongs or a slotted spoon, remove the pork and place it in an earthenware crock. Pour the fat over the top and refrigerate for about a week, allowing the flavors to ripen before you begin feasting. As long as it remains completely covered with fat, so that no air can get to the meat, Rillons will keep for about 6 months, covered and refrigerated.

Maple Smoked Spare Ribs

ADVANCE PREPARATION
REQUIRED.

½ recipe Maple Mustard Barbecue
Spice Rub, Appendix 1

3–4 pounds pork spare ribs

Several handfuls of hickory, apple or
mesquite chips or chunks (if using
gas, use 2 cups chips, not chunks)

1 cup Apple-Bourbon Barbecue
Sauce, Appendix 1

ESTIMATED CARBOHYDRATES:
Maple Mustard Barbecue Spice Rub
(½ batch): 73.43 g
Apple-Bourbon Barbecue Sauce
(¼ batch): 47.56 g
Total number of carbohydrates per
recipe: 120.99 g
Total number of carbohydrates per
¼ recipe: 30.25 g

The expression that the meat is sweetest when it is closest to the bone has truth behind it. Pork spare rib meat has some of the best flavor on the animal. In honor of that, this recipe calls for a spice rub to get traditional pork spare rib flavor, but then leaves out the cloyingly sweet barbecue sauce at the end, so that the natural pork taste comes through.

The night before you plan to barbecue, trim the ribs and remove the membrane. Sprinkle dry rub evenly over the ribs and massage it into the meat. You may not need all of the rub; store leftovers for another use in an airtight container. Cover the ribs and refrigerate overnight.

On BBQ day, soak the wood chips or chunks for at least 30 minutes in water to cover. Remove the ribs from the refrigerator, unwrap and allow them to come to room temperature.

If using a gas grill, light it, then put the soaked chips in a foil tray set directly over one burner. Close the grill and preheat on high until smoke billows out. Turn off all but the burner beneath the wood, and allow the temperature to come down to about 200–230 degrees. If the chamber won't cool down that low, get it as low as you can and plan for a shorter cook time.

If using charcoal, start the grill and warm it until the temperature inside the cooking chamber is between 200–230 degrees. Make sure there is a cool side directly under the vents. Toss a handful of soaked chips or chunks directly onto the coals.

Lay the ribs bone-side down on the cool side of the grate and cover.

Smoke the ribs without turning for roughly 1 hour and 15 minutes per pound, adding coals and additional wood chips or chunks as necessary for the charcoal grill, or adjusting the flame as needed on the gas grill to maintain a constant temperature between 200 and 230 degrees.

After one hour, if you choose, brush the ribs with sauce. When the meat is tender and the tissue around the ribs has pulled away from the bone, supper is served. Cut the ribs apart and serve.

Leftovers: Spare ribs can be re-warmed in a covered dish in a 250-degree oven.

Pork Kebabs

SERVES 4

2 pounds pork kebabs (1½-inch cubes, cut from the leg)

1 batch of any of the following: Dad's Tamari Balsamic Marinade, Garlic Lime Marinade, Bell Pepper and Garlic Marinade, or Lemon Garlic Marinade (see Appendix 1)

4 metal skewers, or 4 10-inch bamboo skewers soaked 30 minutes in water

---

ESTIMATED CARBOHYDRATES:

Carbohydrates will vary based on which marinade is selected and the amount of marinade that is actually absorbed into the meat. Carbohydrates for each of the following marinades are as follows:

Dad's Tamari Balsamic Marinade: 66.32 g

Garlic Lime Marinade: 11.99 g

Bell Pepper and Garlic Marinade: 22.55 g

Lemon Garlic Marinade: 26.81 g

Easy and inexpensive, pork kebabs can take on any number of flavors, all of which are delicious.

Butterfly the pork cubes by slicing almost through the center of each. This enables the marinade to more fully penetrate the meat.

Place the pork in a nonreactive (stainless-steel or glass) bowl. Pour in the marinade and stir to coat. Cover and refrigerate 4 hours or overnight, stirring occasionally to make sure the meat is thoroughly coated. Do *not* marinate longer than a day, or the meat will become mushy and much of the inherent pork flavor will be overtaken by the seasonings.

Just before grilling, remove the meat from the marinade, pat dry, and thread it onto the skewers. Allow them to come to room temperature while you prepare the grill.

Light the grill, cover it, and allow it to warm until you can hold your hand 5 inches above the grate for no more than 2–3 seconds. If you are cooking with charcoal, you might need to layer the coals a bit higher than usual in order to achieve this temperature.

Scrape the grate clean with a wire brush. Grill the kebabs over direct heat, turning them one-quarter turn every 3 minutes, and covering the grill between turns, until the meat is nicely browned, about 12 minutes altogether.

Leftovers: Depending on the marinade you've selected, the kebabs can be diced and used in Stuffed Peppers, Poultry or Pork Canapés with Peanut Lime Sauce, or Pork and Greens in a Ginger Tamari Broth (Chapter 8).

Fresh Ham with a Shallot Dijon Reduction

SERVES 6–8

1 recipe Rosemary Herb Rub,
   Appendix 1

4 pounds boneless fresh (uncured)
   ham (skin-on or skinless is fine)

2 tablespoons minced shallot
   (optional, for the reduction sauce)

2 tablespoons Dijon mustard
   (optional, for the reduction sauce)

2 cups meat broth, such as Shannon's
   Meat Broth, Chapter 3 (optional,
   for the reduction sauce)

4 tablespoons butter (optional, for
   the reduction sauce)

ESTIMATED CARBOHYDRATES:

Rosemary Herb Rub: 14.68 g

Shallot: 3.36 g

Dijon mustard: 2 g

Meat broth: 2.8 g*

Butter: 0.03 g

Total number of carbohydrates per
   recipe: 22.87 g

Total number of carbohydrates per
   ⅛ recipe: 3.81 g

* Carbohydrates in homemade broth
will vary. This figure is calculated based
on my homemade broth, which uses 1
large onion, 1 large carrot, 4 cups mixed
greens and ½ cup cider vinegar in addition to the bones to generate 20 cups
of broth.

The fresh ham is one of the finest and often least expensive cuts of meat on the pig. While there is not a lot of fat around the outside of the roast, the fat is marbled within the meat, making it juicy and delicious. Fresh hams come in all sizes, from an entire leg, weighing 12–15 pounds, to boneless roasts weighing as little as 3 pounds. The recipe below is for a 4-pound roast. If you need to cook a bigger fresh ham to feed more people, simply double the amount of herb rub, accommodate for the increased size in your cooking time, and be sure to double-check your work with an internal meat thermometer.

Massage the Herb Rub into all surfaces of the meat. If it has not been skinned, use a very sharp knife to cut a series of 1 inch gashes all over the skin, cutting down to the meat without piercing it. Stuff some of the herb rub into each of the cuts. Allow the meat to come to room temperature while you preheat the oven to 325°F.

Place the meat in a roasting pan, insert a meat thermometer, and roast to an internal temperature of 145–160 degrees—depending on how done you like it—about 22 minutes per pound for a boneless roast, 20 minutes per pound for bone-in. Allow the meat to rest for a few minutes before carving so that the juices can settle back down into the meat. Serve *au jus* (with the pan juices), or make a reduction as follows:

Remove the ham to a cutting board, then set the roasting pan over direct medium heat. Heat the pan drippings until they are bubbling. Add the shallots and Dijon mustard. Continue cooking, stirring and scrap-ing, until the shallots are clear and the browned bits from the pan are mixed into the paste with the mustard and pan juices. Add the broth and continue to simmer until the sauce is reduced by half. Add the butter one tablespoon at a time, stirring well after each addition. Drizzle the reduction over the meat and serve.

Leftovers: Slice the ham and put it in a heavy casserole dish. Spoon any pan juices or reduction sauce on top, then top it with a pat of butter or drizzle it with olive oil. Cover, then put it in a 250-degree oven until it is heated through. Diced fresh ham is also delicious in Parmesan-Cheddar One Crust Meat Pie, Pork and Greens in a Tamari-Ginger Broth, or in Meat Canapés with Goat Cheese and Roasted Red Pepper, (Chapter 8).

Pet piggies?

Have you ever taken a tour with your local farmer, gone out to see the pigs, then watched your host lean over the fence and make kissie kissie noises or scratch behind their ears? Perhaps you find this affection between man and his prey disturbing. Wouldn't it be more honest (and easier on the farmer's psyche) to keep an emotional distance between themselves and a critter they plan to slaughter?

Not really. It actually makes the relationship safer for the farmer and for the pigs. Pigs are impressively strong animals, and often they are only contained with a thin roll of portable electric fencing. If a farmer or another stranger comes into their area and the pigs get spooked, they can charge the fence and either break through or get tangled in it. It is better for us and them if they are not easily scared. Keeping relationships friendly also makes it easier to provide care for them whenever needed. One of my farmer friends, Carol Clement of Heather Ridge Farm, used to train her pigs so that, when she touched their backs, they would roll over on their sides. This enabled her to walk into their pasture and safely deliver their grain without getting knocked over. They would lie down until she scratched their bellies, providing her a good opportunity to examine their health. It also made her farm a hot gathering spot for amused farmer neighbors at chore time.

And what about the great betrayal at the end? Remember this: a livestock farmer usually chooses his or her vocation because they *like* animals, not because it is going to make them rich or because they like killing them. The day the pigs are processed is a sad one, but the months leading up to it can be pleasurable for both the farmers and the pigs, especially if both parties take time to exchange a little affection.

It is hard for a farmer not to develop an affectionate bond with pigs. And truthfully, that makes life easier and safer for both.

CHAPTER SEVEN

Poultry and Eggs

Once the last of the icy spring rains have swept across the countryside, farmers can be found outside with an odd assortment of tools: hammers, nails, plastic zip ties, snow fencing, tarps, wire ties, corrugated tin and plastic, chicken wire, and cattle fence panels. Contrary to what it may look like, they're not setting up a gypsy campground. They're getting ready to bring the chicks out of the brooder to introduce them to pasture.

Unlike cattle and sheep, which require only some modest fencing during the summer grazing season, poultry need ready access to shelter for protection from the heat and predatory hawks and owls. While it may be easiest and "safest" to simply keep the chickens permanently in a protective structure, this doesn't guarantee the customer the best meat, the chicken the best life, and it doesn't make full use of the bounty the surrounding ecosystem provides.

By their nature, chickens will not range as far as four-legged farm critters. If confined to one area all their lives, they will be repeatedly foraging through their own feces, the chicken yard will quickly be depleted of insects and grass, and consequently their grain requirements will be quite high. To remedy this, pasture-based farmers (often called graziers) construct lightweight moveable shelters that go out to pasture with the birds. Every few days the farmer comes out and moves the shelter to fresh grass, and the birds travel with it. They soon get accustomed to these short moves and run along eagerly as their pen travels to a fresh patch of grass.

Did I gross you out at the previous mention of birds picking through feces? Try not to let it bother you. Graziers prefer that their chickens don't have to pick through their own feces, which is one of the reasons we keep moving the birds to fresh grass. But chances are the birds are traveling along behind some ruminants who have traversed the pastures ahead of them, and they're finding a goldmine in the form of sheep droppings or cow pies.

Yes, I did use the words *goldmine* and *cow pies* in the same sentence. Ruminant droppings are rich habitats for insects and their eggs, and the chickens are fully aware of this. As they scratch and peck through the manure, they break it up so that it enters into the soil more easily, building its fertility. By eating those bugs, they are also interrupting the cycle of parasites that might otherwise infest ruminants as they move back through the pasture, helping all the different animals on the farm to stay healthy. Better still, those bugs help the birds to grow robust and meaty while reducing the need for grain inputs. Once the flock has been on a patch of grass for a few days, that patch can be quite smelly and trammeled. But, return to that site about a week later, and the ground will be lush and green from the fertilizing droppings they left behind. Within just a short period, the grasses will once again be long enough to bring the ruminants back through for yet another nourishing feast.

Saoirse and Ula have understood from an early age where their food comes from.

That's how poultry rearing happens out on the grass farms, where pasture is plentiful. We typically get laying hen breeds to supply our eggs, and meat bird breeds to supply the meat. When the laying hens are spent, they become soup chickens because there is very little meat on their bones, and the meat birds are the ones we use for roasting and grilling (they don't produce eggs). That's not to say that it can't happen differently.

Urban and suburban farms are springing up across the country, and easy-to-keep poultry are popular urban farm animals. They recycle food waste and turn it into eggs, meat and garden fertilizer, and they are small enough to thrive in limited space. It thrills me to no end to see the ingenuity that is happening on the urban farm front, where more and more citizens are taking responsibility for their food needs. While those of us with enough acreage have ideal set-ups for keeping cattle and sheep, our farms would be far more sustainable if we could share the burden of poultry production and reduce the number of chickens (and pigs) to a size that our own farm ecosystems can support, rather than having to buy fuel-intensive grain.

Naturally, the urban-farmed poultry will not have the same sort of housing conditions that you'll see on the typical pasture-based farm. Their pens are not as likely to be moveable, nor pasture as likely to be available, and their flock size will be smaller. A lot of their food may come from household scraps, supplemented with grain. They should still have access to both shelter and fresh air, with plenty of room to amble about and scratch (this habit can be great for tilling up gardens). Because they don't have much (or any) land, very often urban farmers make use of

Why are pastured birds so darn pricey?

Cheap chicken is one of the great myths of our modern industrialized food system. Chicken is very expensive to produce. In fact, it is the most expensive meat we raise on the farm. Grocery store chicken only looks cheap because you've already paid for it in your tax bill. Through the farm bill, U.S. taxpayers pay approximately $20 billion per year in direct payments to farmers, over one-third of which goes for the production of feed grain. Much of this subsidy is paid out to vertically-integrated industrialized meat production companies who, as a result, are able to feed their livestock grain for less than the price of growing it. Small-scale farmers are generally not in a position to vertically integrate, and therefore cannot gain the same advantage from these grain subsidies.

Furthermore, pasture-raised poultry is extremely labor-intensive compared to raising ruminants like cattle and sheep. On the farm we can visit the cattle once per day to make sure things are going all right, and check the automatic waterers to make sure they are working. Once every few days, we open a gate to allow them to amble into the next pasture. At processing time, one adept butcher in a well-equipped facility can handle the slaughter, and after the dry-aging period, he or she can process

the animal and turn out about 600–800 pounds of saleable meat with one day's work.

By contrast, pasture-raised chickens must be fed and watered three times per day. Depending on the shelter, they must be moved to new pasture once per day or once every three days, and the move requires lifting a heavy portable shelter. At processing time at Sap Bush Hollow, we need a team of 4 people one half day, and two people one whole day, to process 150 birds, generating about the same amount of saleable meat as one beef carcass.

For these reasons, chicken was not historically cheap. In fact, cookbook writers of yesteryear were presented with the culinary challenge of writing recipes for veal, which was the cheap meat at the time, to get it to taste like the costly chicken. Cheap chicken is a relatively new and unrealistic (and unsustainable) phenomenon.

The result, however, is problematic for us farmers. Even though it costs us more to produce, in order to hold onto our customers we must make it the cheapest meat on the farm. We wince every time a customer bristles at paying $20–$25 for a single chicken, knowing the cost to us in terms of time and labor was even greater than that final price. So, the next time your eyes pop at the price of pastured poultry . . . try to remember we're giving you a deal!

dual-purpose birds, breeds of poultry that may not produce as many eggs as laying breeds, nor as much meat as a typical meat bird, but which offer enough eggs to satisfy a family and put on enough meat to make them worthy of the oven. Examples of these dual-purpose breeds include Houdans, Dominiques, and Wyandottes. There are many more than I can name, and every veteran urban farmer will likely have an opinion about which birds make for the best eating and the best eggs. Either way, many breeds that were once falling away owing to industrial farming practices, are now coming back into circulation. They are increasing the diversity of breeds that are available for urban and rural farm settings, helping to increase food security by decentralizing food production, helping us to reuse our food waste, and giving more people access to fresh, healthy nourishment. The turnaround is wonderful and hopeful.

Why won't my farmer sell cut-up chicken parts?

In most states, farmers are permitted to raise and process a limited number of chickens that they can sell directly to consumers without having to build a licensed and inspected processing facility. This "poultry exemption," as it is often called, is actually pretty generous in the eyes of the small farmer without a lot of resources, because he or she can process and sell up to 1,000 birds annually without having to invest in a lot of costly infrastructure. The catch, however, is the limited variety of poultry products the farmer is permitted to sell. They can sell you whole chickens, and that's about it. If a farmer wants to package the breasts separately, or sell just the legs, or a bag containing just the backs and necks, then he or she generally must build a dedicated processing facility and acquire a different license. Since many farmers have little interest in raising more than 1,000 birds, the increase in product diversity simply cannot justify investing thousands of dollars in infrastructure and then working through all the red tape that is required to keep the license up-to-date. It is for this reason that I always write chicken recipes for whole birds, and then for using chicken leftovers. My aim is to help you get out of that grocery store chicken-by-the-piece habit, and help you get comfortable working with the whole bird from beginning to end, making use of it as a main course, as leftovers, and as soup.

BUT, if you want to cut up your own bird, see *How to cut up a whole bird* on page 145.

Indian-Style Chicken

SERVES 6

2 pinches of whole saffron threads

4 tablespoons butter, lard, or olive oil

20 medium cloves of garlic, 12 finely chopped, 8 left whole

2 medium onions, finely sliced

2 cinnamon sticks

20 whole cloves

8 cardamom pods

3 tablespoons fresh ginger, coarsely chopped

1 tablespoon coarse sea salt

1 teaspoon chili powder

1 whole chicken, 4–5 pounds, cut into 8 pieces

4 cups chicken broth, preferably homemade, see Meat Broth, Chapter 3

ESTIMATED CARBOHYDRATES:
Saffron: 0.11 g
Butter: 0.03 g
Garlic: 19.8 g
Onions: 20.54 g
Cinnamon: 3.4 g
Cloves: 2 g
Cardamom: 0.4 g
Ginger: 3.21 g
Chili powder: 1.34 g
Chicken broth: 5.6 g*
Total carbohydrates per recipe: 56.43 g
Total carbohydrates per ⅙ recipe: 9.41 g

This recipe is adapted and simplified for the American kitchen from a traditional Indian recipe called Chicken Handi Lazeez. Ordinarily, one would use only boneless chicken thighs, but since they are not a conventional offering from a local pastured chicken farm, this recipe calls for a whole chicken that is cut into eight pieces. See the sidebar How to cut up a whole bird *for directions on cutting up a chicken.*

Add the saffron to a small glass. Cover with a small amount of water and allow it to soak 10 minutes. Drain off the water, crush, then set aside.

Heat the fat in a large, nonreactive (stainless-steel or enameled) deep-sided pot over a medium flame. Add the chopped garlic and sauté until brown, about 5 minutes. Add the onions and sauté until they begin to brown and caramelize, about 15 minutes. Add the cinnamon, cloves, and cardamom pods and sauté 10 minutes longer, or until the onions are deep gold.

Using the small bowl of a food processor, puree the whole garlic cloves and the fresh ginger to a paste. Add this to the skillet along with the salt and chili powder. Stir well, then add the chicken. Cook about 5 minutes, stirring all the while to make sure the chicken is thoroughly exposed to the onion-garlic mixture. Add the chicken broth, mix thoroughly, then cover and simmer over medium-low heat for about 30 minutes, or until the chicken is cooked through.

Turn off the heat. Remove the chicken and set aside. Strain the sauce, discarding the solids, then return it to the pot and boil 5–10 minutes or until the liquid has reduced by half and thickened. Return the chicken to the pot and let it heat through. Stir in the saffron and serve.

Leftovers: Leftover chicken from this recipe would work well with both Apple Walnut Chicken Salad and Curried Cashew Chicken (or turkey) Salad with Raisins and Cranberries. If you are looking for a way to make use of the leftover sauce and chicken together, follow the basic instructions for Refrigerator Soup, and use cubed butternut squash and diced spinach for the vegetables (all recipes appear in Chapter 8).

Poulet en Cocotte Bonne Femme, Made Simple

SERVES 6

1 4–5-pound chicken

Coarse salt and ground black pepper, to taste

1½ heads of garlic, all cloves peeled but left whole, divided use

6 tablespoons butter or lard, divided use

¼ pound coarsely diced bacon

8 small to medium-size onions, cut into large wedges

1 pound small potatoes (I like Kennebecs or Fingerlings), cut into bite-size chunks

Many recipes for Poulet Bonne Femme require cut-up chicken parts, but in her 1961 classic, Mastering the Art of French Cooking, *Julia Child teaches us to do it with a whole bird, which is very convenient for those of us who'd rather not take the time or energy to cut apart our farm-fresh pastured chickens. What makes this recipe truly special is a wonderful French technique whereby the onions, bacon, and potatoes are each cooked in a casserole that will eventually host the chicken. Although these ingredients are removed before the chicken is added, then reintroduced later, their respective essences actually season the casserole that, in turn, imparts a delicate, yet complex, flavor to the meat. This is a deeply pleasurable dish to prepare—bear with me as I rhapsodize about it—each layer that you cook, starting with the bacon and the onions, creates an entirely new bouquet of scents dramatically different from the isolated ingredients. It is the sort of dish that holds my rapt attention as I tend to it, causing me to engage in dramatic kitchen-time stall tactics (like wiping down my appliances, cleaning my stove burners and oiling my wooden spoons and bowls) just so I can be nearby while it cooks.*

Season the chicken inside and out with salt and pepper, and place 3 cloves of garlic inside the cavity. Set aside.

Melt 2 tablespoons of the fat in a large heavy casserole over medium heat. Add the bacon and onions and sauté until the onions are soft and clear (about 15 minutes). Remove both and set aside. Add 2 more tablespoons of the fat, then toss in the potatoes. Sauté, stirring occasionally, until lightly browned, about 20 to 30 minutes. Remove the potatoes and add them to the bacon and onions. Add the remaining fat and the chicken. Cover and allow the bird to brown on all sides, turning every 7 to 10 minutes.

Turn the chicken breast-down, lower the heat to medium-low, toss in the remaining garlic, cover, and cook 20 minutes, basting occasionally. Flip the bird breast-side up, return the onions, potatoes, and bacon to the casserole, cover, and cook another 20 to 25 minutes, basting occasionally, until the juice between the thigh joint and the main body runs clear, or to an internal temperature of 165 degrees.

To serve, remove the bird to a platter, let rest 15 minutes, and carve, serving each piece with a spoonful of the sauce, potatoes, onions, bacon, and garlic.

ESTIMATED CARBOHYDRATES:
Garlic: 9.9 g
Bacon: 0.75 g
Onions: 67.24 g
Potatoes: 71.26 g
Total carbohydrates per recipe: 149.15 g
Total carbohydrates per ⅙ recipe:
   24.86 g

Leftovers: The leftovers of this dish never last very long, as they taste even better on day two. Place the chicken in a glass or ceramic baking dish, cover it with the onions, potatoes, bacon and sauce, and re-warm (uncovered) in a 250-degree oven until it is heated through. The chicken, potatoes, bacon, onion and sauce also bring a really nice dimension to Onion Soup (Chapter 8) if added right at the end, just prior to serving.

How to cut up a whole bird

1. Hold the bird by the neck. With a boning knife, cut a collar around the muscle that is at the base of the neck, as close to the breast as you can get. Once you've cut through to the vertebrae, bend and pinch between the vertebrae to squeeze the neck off.

2. Pick the bird up by one wing. Cut a ring with the boning knife around the muscle that joins the wing and the breast. Use the tip of the knife to probe for the shoulder joint to make the break, taking care not to cut the breast muscle. Work the joint loose, using the tip of the knife to cut the cartilage as you do so. Eventually the wing should become loose enough that you can break it free. Repeat with the other side.

3. Lay the bird on its back. Spread the legs apart. Push one leg away from the center and gently slice where the skin stretches between the leg and the body. The leg should drop away fairly easily. Lay the side of the knife against the body and slice the muscle where it joins the leg and the body, exposing the ball-and-socket joint. Use the tip of the knife to cut the cartilage free, then separate the joint. Finish by cutting through the skin and muscle on the back side. Repeat for the other leg.

4. To separate the thigh and drumstick, lay the complete leg skin-side-down on the cutting board.

You should see a faint white line between the drumstick and the thigh. Place the knife blade along that line, squeeze the thigh and drumstick together, applying pressure to the knife as you do so. By squeezing those ends, the knife should find its way between the two joints and pass through easily with downward pressure. Repeat for the other side.

5. To remove the back, use shears to cut across the rib bones, as close to the breast as possible on both sides. (Again, there is a slight whitish line to guide you.) Standing the chicken on its neck end, pry the back away from the breast, using a cleaver or butcher knife to cut through any remaining connective tissue and bone.

6. Lay the breast on the cutting board breast-side up. Carefully make an incision along the peak of the breastbone, just down to the cartilage. At the belly end of the breast, behind the keel bone, you should be able to penetrate the knife all the way through to the cutting board. This allows you to spread the breast flat onto the cutting board. Flip the breast over. Anchor the tip of a butcher knife on the cutting board and use downward pressure to split the breast in half.

For a visual demonstration, check out our video at grassfedcooking.com.

Arroz con Pollo

SERVES 6

1 ½ tablespoons fine salt

1 tablespoon finely ground white
pepper

1 tablespoon dried oregano

2 teaspoons ground cumin

1 4–5-pound chicken, cut into 10
pieces (see sidebar, *How to cut up
a whole bird*)

2 tablespoons lard, tallow or butter

1 large onion, diced

1 medium red bell pepper, diced

4 cloves garlic, minced

2 teaspoons paprika

2 cups long grain rice

3 cups meat broth, such as Shannon's
Meat Broth, Chapter 3

1½ cups diced canned (or fresh)
tomatoes (including juice)

2 pinches saffron threads, crumbled

1 bay leaf

6 ounces pimiento-stuffed green
olives, diced

*Here is a fun, festive dish, packed with authentic Spanish flavor to delight kids
and grown-ups alike.*

Combine the salt, white pepper, oregano and cumin. Rub this over all
surfaces of the chicken. Heat the fat in a nonreactive Dutch oven over
a medium-high flame. Brown the chicken on all sides, about 3 minutes
per side, taking care to only brown a few pieces at a time so that there is
about 1 inch of space surrounding each piece of meat. Transfer browned
chicken to a plate.

Add the onion and bell pepper to the skillet and sauté until the
onions are clear. Add the garlic, paprika, and rice and sauté until the
rice is lightly toasted. Add the broth, tomatoes, saffron and bay leaf. Set
the chicken on top, pour in any juices left on the plate, cover, and simmer until the rice is cooked, nearly all the liquid is evaporated, and the
juices from the chicken run clear, about 45 minutes. Uncover and cook
an additional 10 minutes to allow more of the liquid to cook down.
Remove from the heat, sprinkle with the olives and season to taste
with salt and pepper. Allow the dish to rest, covered, 10 minutes before
serving.

Leftovers: Pull any excess meat off the bones and toss it with the
remaining rice. Reheat in a covered dish at 250 degrees until warmed
through. To stretch dwindling leftovers farther, stir whatever remains into
a few cups of meat broth, along with some diced sautéed vegetables for a
chicken and rice soup.

ESTIMATED CARBOHYDRATES:	
White pepper: 4.87 g	Canned tomatoes: 14.40 g
Oregano: 2.07 g	Saffron: 0.11 g
Cumin: 1.86 g	Bay leaf: 0.11 g
Onion: 14.01 g	Olives: 6 g
Red bell pepper: 7.18 g	Total carbohydrates per recipe: 357.06 g
Garlic: 3.96 g	Total carbohydrates per ⅙ recipe: 59.51 g
Paprika: 2.48 g	* Number of carbohydrates in homemade
Rice: 295.81 g	broth will vary. This figure is calculated
Broth: 4.2 g*	using the recipe for Shannon's Meat Broth (Chapter 3).

Chicken with Lemon Cream

SERVES 6

1 4–5-pound chicken, cut in 8–10 pieces (see sidebar, *How to cut up a whole bird*)

2 tablespoons coarse salt

1 tablespoon ground black pepper

3 tablespoons butter, lard or tallow

1 medium onion, finely chopped

1 teaspoon tarragon

1 teaspoon basil

1½ cups meat broth, such as Shannon's Meat Broth, Chapter 3

¼ cup sherry

2 tablespoons lemon juice

1 cup heavy cream

ESTIMATED CARBOHYDRATES:

Black pepper: 4.41 g
Onion: 10.27 g
Tarragon: 0.30 g
Basil: 0.23 g
Meat broth: 2.1 g*
Sherry: 3 g
Heavy cream: 6.64 g
Lemon juice: 1.94 g
Total number of carbohydrates per recipe: 28.99 g
Total number of carbohydrates per ⅙ recipe: 4.83 g

* Number of carbohydrates in home-made broth will vary. This figure is calculated using the recipe for Shannon's Meat Broth (Chapter 3).

I made this recipe one evening while Bob and I were having a date night. Since the kids would be home in the morning, we were counting on serving everyone the leftovers the next day. But there was hardly enough, because it was so delicious we couldn't stop eating. The secret to the intense flavor is twofold: first, as always, a good rich broth makes all the difference. And second, don't cut any corners when browning the chicken pieces at the outset. Allow yourself the time and luxury to brown the chicken slowly and thoroughly, and you will have no regrets. This recipe is an absolute showstopper.

Sprinkle the chicken with the salt and pepper. Place a large Dutch oven over a medium flame. Add 2 tablespoons of the fat, swirl to coat and, working in small batches (no more than 3 or 4 pieces at a time), brown the chicken in the Dutch oven, about 3–4 minutes per side. Make sure there is about 1 inch of space around each piece of chicken as it browns. Remove them to a separate dish. Once all of it is browned, lower the heat slightly and add the final tablespoon of fat to the pot and then the chopped onion. Sauté until clear, sprinkle in the herbs, and mix well. Pour in the broth, bring to a simmer, and simmer 3 minutes, stirring often with a wooden spoon, scraping the browned bits off the bottom of the pan and incorporating them into the sauce. Stir in the sherry, then add all the chicken back to the pot. Cover and simmer for 45 minutes, or until the chicken is cooked through.

Remove the chicken to a serving platter. Simmer the sauce, uncovered, until the volume is reduced by half, about 10 minutes. Stir in the lemon juice.

Meanwhile, in a separate saucepan bring the cream to a simmer over medium heat, then whisk it into the sauce. Pour the sauce over the chicken and serve.

Leftovers: To re-warm, heat the chicken (without the sauce) in a covered pan in a 200-degree oven for 45 minutes. Reheat the sauce separately. Alternatively, pull any remaining meat off the bones and stir it into the sauce to be served over rice or noodles, or add it to Cream of Chicken Soup Florentine. It can also be mixed into the Mulligatawny, adding it right at the end, just before serving, allowing it to just heat through (see Chapter 8 for recipes).

Chicken Roasted with Caramelized Onions, Apples and Cheddar

SERVES 6

1 4–5-pound chicken, cut into 8 or 10 pieces (see sidebar, *How to cut up a whole bird*)

2 tablespoons coarse salt

1 tablespoon ground black pepper

4 tablespoons lard, tallow or butter, divided use

4 large onions, cut into thin wedges

4 medium apples, halved, cored and sliced (skins can be left on)

1 cup grated cheddar (or a locally available Swiss-style cheese)

½ cup coarsely ground walnuts

1 teaspoon dried thyme

4 ounces diced bacon (optional)

¼ cup Calvados, brandy or apple cider

ESTIMATED CARBOHYDRATES:

Black pepper: 4.41 g

Onions: 56.04 g

Apples: 100.54 g

Bacon: 0.75 g

Cheddar: 1.45 g

Walnuts: 8.02 g

Thyme: 0.64 g

Calvados: 4 g

Total carbohydrates per recipe: 175.85

Total carbohydrates per ⅙ recipe: 29.31 g

This is a fun recipe for celebrating a great apple harvest, suited to kids and upscale company alike.

Preheat the oven to 350°F. Sprinkle the chicken with the salt and pepper. Heat 2 tablespoons of the fat in a large skillet over medium heat and, working in batches (no more than 3–4 pieces at a time to make sure there is about 1 inch of space around each piece of meat), brown the chicken well, about 3–4 minutes per side. Remove and set it aside on a platter as it is browned.

Melt the remaining 2 tablespoons fat in the skillet. Add the onions; they should sizzle as they hit the pan, but if they sputter or splatter, lower the flame. Stir well, coating the onions in the fat and scraping up any browned bits from the bottom of the pan. Cook 2–3 minutes longer, or until the onions have given up two-thirds of their volume in water. When they start to brown, lower the flame and cook, stirring often, until they caramelize, about 15–20 minutes longer. Again, lower the heat if they start to burn.

When the onions are deeply caramelized, spread them on the bottom of a greased 9-x-13-inch baking dish. Lay the apples on top. Set the chicken on the bed of apples and onions. Mix the cheese, walnuts and dried thyme in a small bowl. Sprinkle the mixture over the chicken, dot with the optional bacon, drizzle with calvados, and bake for 40 minutes, or until the chicken is cooked through to an internal temperature of 165 degrees.

Leftovers: Leftovers can be reheated in a covered dish for 20–30 minutes at 350 degrees. Leftover chicken can also be used in Chicken and Rice in a Sherry Cream Sauce, or Lemon Chicken Salad (Chapter 8).

Yakitori

SERVES 4

2 pounds boneless, skinless chicken breasts or thighs, diced into 1-inch cubes

Metal skewers, or wooden or bamboo skewers soaked in water for 30 minutes

½ cup green onions, finely diced

½ cup tamari

1 cup sake or dry sherry

1½ tablespoons maple syrup or honey

2 tablespoons grated fresh ginger

3 cloves garlic, crushed

ESTIMATED CARBOHYDRATES:
Green Onions: 2.04 g
Tamari: 8.02 g
Sake: 11.64 g
Maple Syrup: 20.11 g (Honey: 25.96 g)
Ginger: 2.13 g
Garlic: 2.98 g
Number of carbohydrates for entire recipe. 46.92 g (with maple syrup) 52.77 g (with honey)
Number of carbohydrates per ¼ recipe: 11.73 g (with maple syrup) 13.19 g (with honey)

When I was a schoolteacher in Japan, I'd meet my fellow foreign friends in bars, where we'd drink beer, swap stories and jokes, and go through platefuls of this fantastic Japanese invention. I came home at Christmas and made some for my mother, and every time we go near a Japanese restaurant, she asks if we can order it. Trouble is, a lot of yakitori sauce is cloyingly sweet in this country. This recipe isn't quite so sweet, so the chicken and tamari flavor stand out more.

Thread the chicken on skewers and set aside.

Combine the green onions, tamari, sake, maple syrup, ginger and garlic in a saucepan. Bring to a boil and stir until the ingredients are well blended. Reduce the heat and simmer until reduced by half, about 5–10 minutes.

Prepare and light the grill, and allow it to heat, covered, for 5–10 minutes.

When the grill is ready, you should be able to hold your hand 5 inches from the grate for no more than 5 seconds. Scrape the grate clean with a wire brush, then oil it lightly.

Lay the skewers across the grate, directly over the flame. Cover and grill 3 minutes; uncover, brush both sides with sauce, turn, and cook, covered, 3 minutes longer, or until it is done to your liking.

Leftovers: Leftover Yakitori can be added to the Asian-Style Cold Meat Salad, or substituted for the pork in Pork and Greens in a Ginger Tamari Broth (Chapter 8).

Grilled Spiced Lime Chicken with Hot Chilies

ADVANCE PREPARATION
REQUIRED.

SERVES 6

1 4–5-pound chicken, cut into 8 or 10
  pieces (see sidebar, *How to cut up
  a whole bird*)

1 cup lime juice

1 batch Caribbean Chili-Garlic Paste,
  Appendix 1

ESTIMATED CARBOHYDRATES:
Lime juice: 16.46 g
Caribbean Chili-Garlic Paste: 26.64 g
Total carbohydrates per recipe: 43.10
Total carbohydrates per serving will
depend on how much of the marinade is
absorbed by the meat.

This is a fun, spicy recipe that pairs well with a cold beer or kombucha on a hot evening.

Place the chicken pieces in a glass baking dish or a nonreactive (stainless-steel or glass) bowl. Pour in the lime juice, and turn the chicken to coat. Marinate at room temperature for 15–20 minutes, turning occasionally.

Discard the lime juice, pat the chicken dry, and rub it all over with the seasoning paste. Cover and refrigerate for 1–2 hours.

Remove the chicken from the refrigerator and allow it to come to room temperature while you prepare your grill.

Light the grill and, when the coals are ready, dump them out onto one side only and allow the grill to heat, covered, for about 5 minutes. The grill is ready when you can hold your hand 5 inches above the grate for no more than 5 seconds. If using a gas grill, leave one burner on high and turn off the others. Scrape the grate clean with a wire brush, then oil it lightly.

Place the legs and thighs over direct heat. Cover and sear 2 minutes per side, then move them to indirect heat. Now lay the breasts, meat-side down, over the heat, cover, and sear 2 minutes longer. Turn them and move them to indirect heat. Cover and cook over indirect heat for 15 minutes.

During the last 10 minutes, add the chicken wings to the indirect heat side. Cover and continue as before. After 6 minutes, move the wings to the hot side of the grill and sear for 2 minutes per side, until the skin is deep golden brown and crispy.

Remove all the chicken from the grill and serve.

Leftovers: These leftovers would add a spicy twist to the Tomato-Garlic Chicken (or turkey) Salad, Lemon Chicken Salad with Braised Sweet Peppers, or Mexican-Style Chicken and Cheese Casserole (Chapter 8).

Whole Smoked Chicken

SERVES 4–6

1 4–5-pound chicken

½ batch Apple-Bourbon Barbecue Sauce, Appendix 1, or your favorite dry barbecue rub

2–3 handfuls of hickory, maple, mesquite, apple or other hardwood chips or chunks, soaked in water for at least 30 minutes (if you are cooking with gas, use only chips)

ESTIMATED CARBOHYDRATES:
Apple-Bourbon Barbecue Sauce
(½ batch): 95.13 g
Total carbohydrates per recipe: 95.13 g
Total carbohydrates per ¼ recipe:
23.78 g

Chicken has such a light flavor, it easily picks up a great smoky taste when it is cooked out on the grill. The smoke lingers in the leftovers, making them taste great in salads.

Rub the chicken all over, including under the skin, with the spice rub. Allow it to come to room temperature while you prepare your grill.

If using a gas grill, light the grill, turn all burners to high, then put all the soaked wood chips in a foil tray and set it down directly over one burner. Close the grill and preheat (with all burners on high) until smoke billows out. Turn off all but the burner beneath the wood chips, and allow the cooking chamber to come down to 325–350 degrees.

If using charcoal, light your grill, keeping the fire only to one side and, when the coals are ready, cover and allow it to heat until the cooking chamber is about 325–350 degrees. Toss a handful of soaked wood chips or chunks directly on the coals.

Once the grill is ready, put the chicken breast-side up in a cast-iron skillet and set it over indirect heat. Cover and roast 1½–2 hours, adding wood chips or chunks once or twice more during that time until the internal temperature of the meat is 160–165 degrees, measured in the thickest part of the inside of the thigh.

Leftovers: This recipe is delicious in Curried Chicken Salad with Raisins and Cranberries, or Apple Walnut Chicken Salad. For a warmer dish, consider adapting the recipe for Chicken Roasted with Caramelized Onions, Apples and Cheddar, as follows: Remove the meat from the bones. Depending on the amount of leftovers you have, you may want to halve that recipe and switch to a 9-x-9-inch baking dish. Because your meat is already cooked, skip the browning and partial cooking of the chicken. Prepare the rest of the dish as directed, but reduce the final baking time to 30 minutes.

No Frills, Straightforward (and really tasty) Chicken

SERVES 6

3 tablespoons unsalted butter, melted

1 4–5-pound chicken

1 to 2 tablespoons coarse salt

2 teaspoons ground black pepper

1 whole clove garlic, peeled

ESTIMATED CARBOHYDRATES:
Black pepper: 2.94 g
Total carbohydrates per recipe: 2.94 g
Total carbohydrates per ⅙ serving: 0.49 g

Lately, this is the recipe I use to prepare 90 percent of the chickens I roast at home. It is fast, easy, delicious, and the minimal seasonings enable me to take the leftovers in any number of directions. The simplicity of this recipe also lets me use the delay-bake feature on my oven. On farmers' market days, I prepare this chicken before I leave in the morning, then set the oven to begin roasting while we're out of the house. When our family gets home, exhausted at the end of the day, dinner is ready.

Preheat the oven to 350° F.

Thoroughly brush the melted butter over the surface of the bird, sprinkle the outside with salt and pepper, and place the garlic clove in the cavity. Put the chicken, breast-side-up, in a large cast-iron skillet or any roasting pan that can be transferred to the stove top when you are ready to make the gravy.

Roast the bird approximately 1½ hours until the juices between the cavity and the thigh run clear; the internal temperature of the breast should read 160 degrees, and the internal temperature of the thigh, taken on the inside at the meatiest part, 165 degrees. Serve the chicken au jus, or make the gravy recipe that follows.

Leftovers: This chicken recipe sets you up to use any of the chicken recipes from Chapter 8 (Leftovers and Soups). The minimal seasonings make it compatible with everything . . . Don't forget to save the bones for broth!

Pan Gravy for Roasted Poultry and Meat

Fat and pan juices from the roast, separated with a fat separator

2 tablespoons unsalted butter

¼ cup all-purpose flour

2 cups meat broth, such as Shannon's Meat Broth, Chapter 3, or chicken broth, preferably homemade (see Meat Broth, Chapter 3)

Coarse salt and ground black pepper

ESTIMATED CARBOHYDRATES:

Butter: 0.02 g

Flour: 23.07 g

Meat broth: 2.8 g*

Total carbohydrates per recipe: 25.89 g

* Number of carbohydrates in home-made broth will vary. This figure is cal-culated using the recipe for Shannon's Meat Broth (Chapter 3).

This gravy recipe works for any roast meat . . . but it is pretty fun to make it with a roast chicken.

Remove the roast to a warm platter, pouring the fat from the roasting juices back into the roasting pan. Add the butter to the roasting pan and set it on the stove top over medium heat. Once it melts and bubbles, whisk in the flour to make a roux. Continue to whisk 1–2 minutes longer, until the paste has browned. Slowly whisk in the pan juices and broth, and allow the mixture to come to a boil. Reduce the heat and allow the gravy to simmer for 5–10 minutes, until it thickens to your preferred consistency, stirring often to scrape up any browned bits from the bottom of the pan. Season to taste with salt and pepper.

Why can't I get pastured chicken year-round?

Okay, okay. I see your point here. Pasture-based farmers typically have a supply of beef, lamb and pork in the freezers all year. But if you show up at the farm in February and ask for a chicken, a lot of us will tell you that you're out of luck. There are a couple reasons for this.

For starters, broilers are not hearty birds. Those of us in northern climates can only keep them comfortable during the summer months. Laying hens can be moved into the barn for the winter, but the meat birds, which we guarantee are raised on green pastures, need to be processed before the temperatures get too cold and the grass stops growing. If we kept them in the barn all winter, our heating bill would be exorbitant, as would be our grain bill. They can't subsist on hay or rely on thick winter coats like the cattle and sheep can.

For that matter, it isn't easy to winter-over pigs, either. But pork chops store much more efficiently in the freezer than chickens. The awkward shape of the chicken takes up significantly more freezer room than any of the other meats.

There are farms out there that maintain dedicated storage facilities for frozen poultry so that it can be available year-round, but there are just as many who don't. Instead, we encourage you to buy throughout the growing season and store them in your own freezer for the winter months.

Everything you need to know about a pasture-raised Thanksgiving turkey

I launched grassfedcooking.com in 2007, and one of the first stories I posted was a list of tips and explanations about the world of pasture-raised Thanksgiving turkeys. Much to my surprise, farmers across the country began printing them off and distributing them to all their turkey customers. Customers then wrote to me with their further questions and concerns, and once I responded, I added the information to a new edition of the article, which went out in November 2008. Every year since, the list of pastured turkey tips has been revised and updated this way and has become a more salient holiday tradition for many of us than the Thanksgiving Day Parade or football game. Below is my most current list of tips and explanations to date. Check back at grassfedcooking.com each November for updates!

Please be flexible. If you are buying your pasture-raised turkey from a small, local, sustainable farmer, thank you VERY much for supporting us. That said, please remember that pasture-raised turkeys are not like factory-farmed birds. Outside of conscientious animal husbandry, we are unable to control the size of our Thanksgiving turkeys. Please be forgiving if the bird we have for you is a little larger or a little smaller than you anticipated. Cook a sizeable quantity of sausage stuffing if it is too small, or enjoy the leftovers if it is too large. If the bird is so large that it cannot fit in your oven, simply remove the legs before roasting it.

Know what you are buying. If you don't personally know the farmer who is growing your turkey, take the time to know what you are buying! "Pastured" is not necessarily the same as "free-range." Some grass-based farmers use the word "free-range" to describe their pasture-raised birds, but any conventional factory farm can also label their birds "free-range" if they are not in individual cages and if they have "access" to the outdoors—even if the "outdoors"

happens to be feces-laden penned-in concrete pads outside the barn door, with no access to grass. "Pastured" implies that the bird was out on grass for most of its life, where it ate grass and foraged for bugs in addition to receiving some grain.

Brining optional. If tradition dictates that you season your meat by brining your bird, by all means do so. However, many people brine in order to keep the bird from drying out. This is not at all necessary. Pastured birds are significantly juicier and more flavorful than factory-farmed birds. You can spare yourself this extra step as a reward for making the sustainable holiday choice!

Monitor the internal temperature. Somewhere, a lot of folks came to believe that turkeys needed to be roasted until they had an internal temperature of 180 degrees Fahrenheit. Yuck. You don't need to do that. Your turkey need only be cooked to 165 degrees. If the breast is done and the thighs are not, take the bird out of the oven, carve off the legs and thighs, and put them back in to cook while you carve the breast and make your gravy. That entire holiday myth about coming to the table with a perfect whole bird and then engaging in exposition carving is about as realistic as expecting our daughters will grow up to look like Barbie (and who'd want that, anyhow?) Just have fun and enjoy the good food.

Cook the stuffing separately. I recommend doing it this way for a couple reasons . . . First, everyone's stuffing recipe is different. Therefore, the density will not be consistent, which means that cooking times will vary. While I can suggest a cooking time (12–15 min. per pound), you must not take it as an absolute gauge, since I cannot control what stuffing each person uses. Also, because of food safety concerns, I happen to think it is safer to cook the stuffing outside the bird. It is much easier to lift and move both the bird and the stuffing when prepared separately, and it's a lot easier to monitor the doneness of each. And, as an added bonus, the stuffing can be prepared a day or two in advance, then simply re-warmed before the meal, saving a little work on the big day. Rather than putting stuffing in my bird's cavity, I put in aromatics, like an onion, carrot, garlic and some fresh herbs, which are discarded once the bird is cooked. The aromatics perfume the meat beautifully, and the only seasoning I wind up using on the surface is butter, salt and pepper.

No need to flip. I used to ascribe to that crazy method of first roasting the bird upside down, then flipping it over to brown the breast. The idea was that the bird would cook more evenly and the breast wouldn't dry out. When I did this, the turkey came out fine. But I suffered 2nd-degree burns, threw out my back, ruined two sets of potholders and nearly dropped the thing on the floor. Pasture-raised turkeys are naturally juicy. Don't make yourself crazy with this stunt. Just put it in the oven breast-side up like you would a whole chicken, and don't overcook it. Take it out when the breast is 165 degrees (see **Monitor the internal temperature**, above). If, despite the disparaging comments in **Monitor the internal temperature**, you still want to show off the whole bird, then bring it into the dining room, allow everyone to ooh and aah, then scuttle back to the kitchen, and proceed as explained above.

Be ready for faster cook times. Pasture-raised turkeys will cook faster than factory-farmed birds. Figure on 8–10 minutes per pound for an unstuffed bird, uncovered, at 325 degrees, as you plan your dinner. That said, oven temperatures and individual birds will always vary. Use an internal meat thermometer to know for sure when the bird is cooked.

Use a good-quality roasting pan. If this is your first Thanksgiving and you do not yet own a turkey roasting pan and cannot find one to borrow, treat yourself to a really top-quality roaster, especially if you have a sizeable bird. Cheap aluminum pans from the grocery store can easily buckle when you remove the bird from the oven, potentially causing the cook

serious burns or myriad other injuries in efforts to catch the falling fowl. Plus, they often end up in the recycling bin, or worse, landfills. If you buy a good-quality large roasting pan and you own this book of recipes, I guarantee you will have multiple uses for the pan!

Pick the meat off the bird before making stock. If you plan to make soup from your turkey leftovers, be sure to remove all the meat from the bones before you boil the carcass for stock. Add the chunks of turkey back to the broth just before serving the soup. This prevents the meat from getting rubbery and stringy.

Help is available. In recent years, our home seems to have become the unofficial Sustainable Thanksgiving Hotline. Please do not hesitate to write to me with your questions at feedback@ shannonhayes.info. I make a point of checking e-mail often right up through Thanksgiving Day (I stop around noon), so that I can promptly respond to your questions or concerns. Enjoy your holiday!

Turkey and Gravy: Straightforward, Simple and Delicious

1 turkey, any size

1 large onion, cut into quarters

2 carrots, cut into quarters

2 stalks celery, cut into quarters

1 *bouquet garni* (any mix of fresh herbs, including thyme, sage, marjoram, oregano, rosemary and/or parsley, tied together in a bundle with kitchen string will work)

3 cloves garlic, whole, peeled

10 ounces (2½ sticks) butter

Coarse salt and ground black pepper, to taste

Turkey giblets, including the neck, gizzard (make sure it has been cleaned), heart and liver

3 cups meat broth, such as Shannon's Meat Broth, Chapter 3

⅓ cup flour

Cooking a Thanksgiving turkey need not be as intimidating as the mystique surrounding it makes it out to be. If you are working with a good, pasture-raised turkey, your work is significantly easier than the travails one faces with a factory-farmed bird. You've got flavor, juiciness, and texture all working in your favor. To learn more about what to expect from your pasture-raised turkey, refer to the sidebar, Everything you need to know about a pasture-raised Thanksgiving turkey.

When trying to decide what size turkey to order, allow for a minimum of 1 pound for each person around your Thanksgiving table. Lower this figure to ½ pound if you will have a lot of side dishes. If you are hoping for some leftovers, estimate 1½ pounds per person. Thus, for a Thanksgiving dinner for 12, I usually figure on an 18-pound turkey.

Preheat the oven to 325°F. Set the turkey in a large roasting pan, breast-side-up. Insert the onion, carrots, celery, *bouquet garni* and garlic into the cavity. Melt 6 ounces (1½ sticks) of the butter and pour it over the surface of the skin, then sprinkle all over generously with salt and pepper. Put the bird in the oven and roast for 8–10 minutes per pound, until the internal temperature of the breast is 165 degrees.

If the leg meat is not 165 degrees when the breast meat is done, don't panic. Simply carve off the legs and put them back into the oven to cook a little longer while you carve the breast meat.

While the turkey roasts, prepare the giblets for the gravy.

Place a saucepan over a medium-high flame. Add 2 tablespoons of butter and swirl to coat. Blot the neck and giblets dry, then set them in the pan, taking care to leave one inch of space around each piece of meat to enable them to brown well. Sear for 2–3 minutes per side. If the bottom of the saucepan is too small, brown the meat in batches.

Place all the giblets back in the saucepan, pour in the broth, cover, and bring to a boil. Reduce the heat and simmer for 40 minutes. Remove the giblets from the broth and allow them to cool. Reserve the broth.

Once the giblets are cool enough to handle, remove any gristle, then finely dice the gizzard, heart and liver. Pull off the neck meat and dice that as well, if necessary.

When the turkey is fully cooked, remove it to a carving board and pour off any juices. Set the empty pan over the burners on your stove and turn the heat onto medium (if the pan will cover two burners, turn both burners on).

Add the remaining butter to the roasting pan. Once it melts and bubbles, whisk in the flour to make a roux. Continue to whisk 1–2 minutes longer, until the paste has browned. Slowly whisk in the pan juices and allow the mixture to come to a boil. Reduce the heat and allow the gravy to simmer for 5 minutes, until it thickens, stirring often to scrape up any browned bits from the bottom of the pan.

At this point, begin stirring in the reserved meat broth that you used to cook the giblets. Add one cup and simmer until it is reduced by one-third. Stir in the giblets, along with enough of the remaining broth until the gravy is at your preferred consistency. If you accidentally make the gravy too thin, simply let it cook down a little longer until it is thick again. Season to taste with salt and pepper.

Flour-free alternative: If you need to avoid grains, combine the pan juices and giblet broth in the roasting pan and simmer until it is reduce by two-thirds. Whisk in the minced giblets, 1 tablespoon brown mustard and 2 tablespoon butter to create a delicious pan sauce for pouring over your turkey.

Leftovers: First of all, make sure you save those bones and boil them for meat broth! Here are some recipes from Chapter 8 that will all work with your turkey leftovers: Croquettes with Black Pepper and Onion Sauce, Mexican-Style Chicken and Cheese Casserole, Asian-Style Cold Meat Salad, Chicken (or Turkey) with Rice and a Sherry Cream Sauce, Poultry or Pork Canapés with a Peanut Lime Sauce, Chicken (or Turkey) Divan, Tomato Garlic Chicken (or Turkey) Salad, Lemon Chicken (or Turkey) Salad with Braised Sweet Peppers, Curried Cashew Chicken (or Turkey) Salad with Raisins and Cranberries, or Apple Walnut Chicken (or Turkey) Salad.

Duck Confit

SERVES 8

1 ½ pounds coarse salt

2 tablespoons ground black pepper

4 cloves garlic, peeled and cut in half

1 bunch fresh thyme

1 4–5-pound duck, cut into 6–8 pieces (see sidebar, *How to cut up a whole bird*)

About 2½ pounds lard or duck fat*, as needed to completely cover the duck

---

ESTIMATED CARBOHYDRATES:

Black pepper: 8.83 g
Garlic: 3.96 g
Thyme: 0.59 g
Total carbohydrates per recipe: 13.38 g
Total carbohydrates per ⅛ recipe: 1.67 g

Often, modern recipes for duck confit expect the cook to have an abundance of duck legs, and duck legs only, on hand. Maybe that's the way city ducks grow, but farm ducks come with breasts and wings on them, too. Thus, whenever I make duck confit, rather than working with the legs of 3–4 ducks, I work with one whole duck, preserving the breast and wings in the fat along with the legs. Duck confit forms the flavor base for Cassoulet (Chapter 5) and tastes fantastic paddled into Rillettes from Confit (Chapter 8) and spread on Parmesan Parsley Almond Crackers (Chapter 8) or on a crusty slice of baguette. It also has many other uses. I've listed them in the leftovers section, below.

Combine the salt, pepper, garlic and thyme in a large bowl. Mix well, then add the duck and turn well to coat. The goal is to have the meat thoroughly coated with salt. Cover and refrigerate for 24 hours. This curing process draws excess moisture from the meat and builds flavor.

After 24 hours, remove the duck from the salt, rinse well, and blot dry. Preheat the oven to 200°F. Place the duck in a large Dutch oven (layering the pieces is okay). Cover the meat with the fat and bring it to a simmer over a direct medium-high flame. If, when the fat has melted, the meat is not completely submerged in it, add more fat until the duck is completely covered.

Once the fat is gently bubbling and the meat is submerged, transfer the pot to the oven, where the low, steady heat can gently poach the meat for 4 hours, or until it is tender.

Using tongs, remove the duck and place it in an earthenware crock. Pour the fat over the top and refrigerate for about a week, allowing the flavors to meld before you begin feasting. As long as no air can get to the confit, it will keep for about 6 months.

Leftovers: Re-warm duck confit by frying the whole pieces briefly (this also crisps up the skin, making it extra tasty), and serve it as a quick meal. Serve it warm or cold, coarsely chopped, over a field green salad with lemon or red wine vinaigrette. Stir chopped bits of the confit into a risotto, or use it in Lentils with Bacon, Ham Hocks and Duck Confit. Use the fat and any leftover bits of confit in Pommes de Terre Sarladaises (recipes appear in Chapter 8).

* A note to the frugal: The fat that you use for this confit can be reused, either when sautéing or for another confit. Since it will be flavored by the herbs and salt, be mindful that whatever dish you choose to use it in is compatible with the pre-seasoned fat. After a few uses in confit, it will become quite salty and you will want to start with a fresh batch once more.

Behold the fresh egg—it is a thing of beauty.

We rarely keep fresh eggs on display at our farmers' market. A few years ago, when we noticed customers elbowing each other to grab the last dozen and received emails from customers who'd been physically pushed out of the way by an egg grabber, we decided it was safer to keep them behind the counter, available almost exclusively by preorder, unless there was an unusual surplus.

Customers can immediately taste the difference in a fresh, pasture-raised hen's egg. The yolk is firmer and more flavorful, the whites don't run willy-nilly all over the pan when cracked. Grocery store eggs can be several months old by the time they make it home to your kitchen, and so a fresh egg in the heart of farmers' market season is a treat that is not to be missed. But it is also a beautiful item to behold. At first glimpse it may seem like an ordinary brown egg from the grocery store, but there are visual pleasures to take in as well, making them a feast for the eyes as well as the taste buds.

Yolk color: Egg yolks from pasture-raised chickens will be bright yellow or orange from the carotene in the grasses. If they happen to be pale, it is an indicator that the hens have not been moved to fresh pasture recently.

Yolk height: If you crack a factory-farmed egg and a fresh farm egg into a pan, you'll immediately notice a height difference. The yolks of fresh eggs have not collapsed and will stand erect in the pan. Factory yolks are flatter, more fragile, and are harder to keep whole when frying.

Intact Chalazae: No, this isn't some kind of hip new fitness dance. The chalazae are the bands of tissue at either end of the egg that suspend the yolk in the middle of the egg. When the egg is fresh, the chalazae are strong, and when you crack it, the yolk will be in the center. In a stale egg, the chalazae will have deteriorated and the yolk will have fallen to the bottom of the shell.

Two different egg whites: The albumin of a stale egg will be thin and runny. When the egg is fresh, there will be two distinct regions—the thick layer of egg white immediately surrounding the yolk, and the thin layer that is around the perimeter. Thus, when you crack a fresh egg, you should distinctly see a yolk and two layers of white.

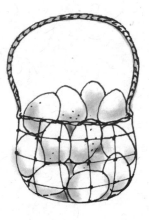

Vegetable Timbales

SERVES 4

4 ounces softened cream cheese

½ cup heavy cream

½ cup meat broth, such as Shannon's Meat Broth, Chapter 3

4 large eggs

½ teaspoon coarse salt

1 pinch of ground cayenne

1 teaspoon dried parsley or 1 tablespoon chopped fresh parsley

2 tablespoons butter

1½ cups finely diced broccoli, (or cauliflower, spinach, beet greens, Swiss chard or a combination thereof), steamed and blotted dry

Grated nutmeg, to taste

1 lemon, cut into 4 wedges (optional)

ESTIMATED CARBOHYDRATES:
Cream cheese: 4.62 g
Heavy cream: 3.32 g
Meat broth: 1.4 g*
Eggs: 1.44 g
Parsley: 0.25 g
Broccoli: 5.58 g
Butter: 0.02 g
Lemon: 5.41 g
Total carbohydrates per recipe: 22.04 g
Total carbohydrates per ¼ recipe: 5.51 g
*Number of carbohydrates in home-made broth will vary. This figure is calculated using the recipe for Shannon's Meat Broth (Chapter 3).

This forgotten, elegant-yet-inexpensive luncheon standby deserves a reprise on the American table. It pairs beautifully with a salad dressed with vinaigrette.

Preheat oven to 350°F. Generously butter 4 8-ounce ramekins. In a large bowl, beat the cream cheese briefly, then gradually beat in the cream, broth, eggs, salt, cayenne and parsley.

Place a medium skillet over a medium flame. Add the butter. Once it is melted, turn off the heat and add the vegetables. Stir until they are well coated. Stir the buttered vegetables into the custard. Spoon the mixture into the ramekins and set them in a shallow roasting pan. Add hot water to the pan until it comes 1 inch up the sides of the ramekins. Cover with foil and bake 35 minutes, or until the custard appears solid to the touch and a knife inserted into the center comes out clean.

Lift the timbales out of the pan and allow them to rest 10 minutes. Run a knife around the perimeter of each ramekin and turn the timbales out onto a serving plate. Garnish with the nutmeg and optional lemon, if using.

Leftovers: Timbales are best eaten fresh, but leftovers can be stored in the refrigerator in a covered container and served cold (although they are not as glamorous).

Potato-Parsnip Blinis

SERVES 10

½ pound boiling white potatoes or sweet potatoes, peeled and cut into ½-inch cubes

½ pound parsnips, peeled and cut into ½-inch cubes

¼ cup heavy cream (or milk)

¼ cup arrowroot (or all-purpose flour)

1 teaspoon fine sea salt

3 large eggs

3 egg whites*

2 tablespoons lard or butter, plus more if needed

ESTIMATED CARBOHYDRATES:

Potatoes: 36.09 g
Parsnips: 40.84 g
Cream: 1.66 g
Arrowroot: 27.5 g
Eggs: 0.72 g
Egg whites: 0.72 g
Total number of carbohydrates per recipe: 107.53 g
Total number of carbohydrates per ⅒ recipe: 10.75 g

These little quick breads are a gift to leftovers. Top them with Slow Cooked Brisket with Sweet Peppers and Caramelized Onions (Chapter 4), a little leftover chicken salad, or use them in place of crackers for the Meat Canapés with Goat Cheese and Roasted Red Pepper (Chapter 8). For Christmas, I top them with gravlox, cream cheese, a caper and a tiny sliver of red onion. My kids devour them.

Place potatoes and parsnips into a pressure cooker and add one cup of water. Cook at 15 psi for 5 minutes, and allow the pressure to subside naturally before opening the cooker.** Strain off the water and puree the two vegetables together, then add them to a large bowl. Whisk together the cream and arrowroot, then stir into the puree. Thoroughly stir in the salt, then each of the eggs, one at a time.

In a separate bowl, use an electric mixer to beat the egg whites until stiff. Fold egg whites into the batter.

Place a griddle over a medium flame and grease using the butter or lard. Drop the batter by tablespoonfuls onto the skillet and cook until lightly browned, about 2 minutes per side. You can hold blinis warm in a 250-degree oven until they are ready to be served. Or, you can make them a day ahead, refrigerate them in an airtight container, then re-warm them on a baking sheet for 5 minutes in a 350-degree oven.

Leftovers: Store blinis in an airtight container, then re-warm them on a baking sheet in a 350-degree oven for 5 minutes.

* Worried about wasting the egg yolks? You can use exactly three egg yolks to whip up a batch of Deep Vanilla Ice Cream. Alternatively, you could make a large batch of Mayonnaise for potato, chicken or egg salads, or Deviled Eggs.

**If you do not own a pressure cooker, simply boil the potatoes and parsnips in water to cover until tender, about 12–14 minutes.

Poached Eggs

SERVES TWO

1 teaspoon vinegar

4 eggs

ESTIMATED CARBOHYDRATES:
Eggs: 0.96 g
Total carbohydrates per recipe: 0.96 g
Total carbohydrates per ½ recipe: 0.48 g

High-end kitchen stores market egg poachers, pricey little gadgets designed to help you poach the perfect egg. What goes unmentioned is that they are only necessary if you are working with factory-farmed eggs from the grocery store, not fresh eggs from the farm. When you have fresh, good-quality eggs, the mystique behind poaching the perfect egg vanishes. They are simple and delicious. Serve over roasted tomatoes and a little ham, or on top of creamed spinach, or topped with Hollandaise. (Or all of the above!)

Fill a wide 3-quart saucepan with an inch and a half of water. Bring the water to a light boil over a medium flame, then reduce to a simmer. Add the vinegar. Break one egg into a small bowl and slowly slide it into the water. Repeat with the remaining eggs, being sure there is plenty of space around each egg. Allow them to cook at a very light simmer until the whites are firm, about 3 minutes. Remove the eggs from the water using a slotted spoon.

Hollandaise Sauce

SERVES 4

8 tablespoons cold butter

4 egg yolks

2 tablespoons lemon juice

1 pinch fine sea salt

1 pinch ground black pepper

I think the single most important sauce to commit to one's memory is the hollandaise. It is the perfect accompaniment for Brussels sprouts, broccoli, cauliflower, poached eggs, hash, steak, chicken and fish. (I'm sure I've left out other possibilities!) It can turn any simple meal into a stellar feast, rich in beneficial nutrients. Don't be discouraged if your sauce gives you trouble at first. Hollandaise can seem fickle. With a little practice, you will develop a sixth sense about persuading egg yolks to thicken and absorb butter, and you will move through the steps easily, drawing effortlessly on the rescue remedies below to coax the sauce along without giving it a second thought. Before starting, I recommend having a glass of cold water on hand in the event you need some of it for the rescue tip mentioned below (when the egg yolk gets too hot).

Melt 6 tablespoons of the butter and set aside (keep warm). Cut the remaining butter into small pieces and set next to your stove. Place the egg yolks in a saucepan and whisk vigorously until they have turned lemon yellow and have thickened slightly. Whisk in the lemon juice, salt and pepper, and set the saucepan over a very, very low flame (or, if you prefer, over a double boiler). Whisk the sauce continuously as the egg yolks heat, watching it very carefully. After a few minutes, you will start to see the bottom of the pan between your strokes. Promptly remove the egg yolks from the heat and whisk in the cold butter, a few pieces at a time. Once the cold butter has melted into the sauce, slowly drizzle in the melted butter, whisking all the while.

Rescue tips:

If the sauce appears too thin, you have probably not given the egg yolks enough time to cook and thicken. Return the pan to low heat and whisk steadily until it starts to thicken. When you are able to see the pan clearly between your strokes, promptly remove from the heat and add some additional cold butter to the sauce.

If the egg yolks get too hot, the egg will start to cook and the butter will be forced out of suspension, causing the sauce to have a curdled appearance. If this starts to happen, quickly whisk in a tablespoon of ice water, adding additional ice water until the sauce recovers.

If the sauce is too thick, slowly whisk in warm water, 1 tablespoon at a time, until it reaches your preferred consistency.

Leftovers: Promptly store unused hollandaise in the refrigerator. Leftovers will keep up to two days. You can use it in place of 1 or 2 of the eggs required for the Hearty Macaroni and Cheese in Chapter 8. It could also be blended into any béchamel sauce to make it richer. If you'd prefer to use the sauce again as a hollandaise, place a saucepan over very low heat. Add 2 tablespoons of the leftover hollandaise and whisk steadily. Once the sauce has softened, gradually whisk in the remaining hollandaise, one tablespoon at a time, until the entire mixture is once more the creamy warm dressing you so fondly remember.

Mayonnaise

MAKES 1 CUP

1 egg yolk

1 teaspoon mustard

1 teaspoon fine salt

½ teaspoon ground black pepper

1 teaspoon apple cider vinegar

1 teaspoon lemon juice

1 cup olive oil or sunflower oil

ESTIMATED CARBOHYDRATES:

Egg yolk: 0.61

Mustard: 0.56

Black Pepper: 0.06

Cider Vinegar: 0.05

Number of carbohydrates for entire recipe: 1.28

Number of carbohydrates per ⅙ recipe: 0.2

For years I never attempted to make my own mayonnaise, as I assumed it required the culinary equivalent of an alchemist master. How wrong I was! Follow these directions exactly, and your mayonnaise will be consistently perfect and unbelievably delicious. You will quickly swear off the jarred alternative from the grocery store, I promise!

Place the egg yolk in a shallow bowl and whisk until it lightens to a lovely lemon yellow. Whisk in the mustard, salt, pepper, vinegar and lemon juice.

And now for the magical part: You must drizzle the oil into the egg mixture *extremely* slowly, whisking it all the while. To be exact on just how slow, set a timer for four minutes. During that 4-minute period, you should whisk in no more than ¼ cup of the oil. After that initial period you can drizzle in the remaining ¾ cup a bit faster (about two or three times that initial rate), whisking steadily the entire time. Use immediately or store covered in the refrigerator for up to two days.

Gathering fresh eggs on the farm feels like receiving a daily gift from the hens.

Buttermilk Mustard Salad Dressing

1 ½ teaspoons grainy mustard

1 batch Mayonnaise, see above

½ cup whole-milk yogurt (or more, see steps)

Heavy cream (optional, see steps)

Coarse salt and ground black pepper

ESTIMATED CARBOHYDRATES:
Mustard: 0.40 g
Mayonnaise: 1.28 g
Yogurt: 11.42 g
Number of carbohydrates for entire recipe: 13.1
Number of carbohydrates per ⅙ recipe: 2.18

Once you've mastered making your own mayonnaise, gourmet homemade salad dressings become a breeze. Making your own will save a lot on your grocery bill, and will also guarantee that you are feeding your family the best ingredients.

Whisk the mustard into the mayonnaise. Add the yogurt and stir until blended. If you prefer a thinner dressing, stir in more yogurt, or add some heavy cream. Season to taste with salt and pepper.

Parmesan Peppercorn Salad Dressing

1 batch Mayonnaise, see above

About ½ cup whole-milk yogurt

2 teaspoons freshly coarse-ground black pepper

½ cup grated Parmesan cheese

ESTIMATED CARBOHYDRATES:
Mayonnaise: 1.28 g
Yogurt: 11.42 g
Peppercorns: 3.71
Parmesan cheese: 2.03
Number of carbohydrates for entire recipe: 18.44
Number of carbohydrates per ⅙ recipe: 3.07

This is a great accompaniment to any leftover bits of steak or rare beef you may have on hand.

Stir together all the ingredients, beginning with ½ cup of yogurt. If you'd like a thinner dressing, add additional yogurt, milk or heavy cream. Serve.

Deviled Eggs

SERVES 6

12 large hard-boiled eggs (see
sidebar, *Hard-Boiling Farm Fresh
Eggs*), peeled and split in half

1 batch Mayonnaise, see above

2 teaspoons Dijon mustard

Smoked paprika, for garnish

ESTIMATED CARBOHYDRATES:

Eggs: 4.32 g
Mayonnaise: 1.28 g
Dijon mustard: 0.67 g
Total number of carbohydrates per
recipe: 6.27 g
Total number of carbohydrates per
⅙ recipe: 1.05 g

Favorite on-the-go fare in our household, I've experimented extensively with finding the perfect deviled egg recipe. I diced up chives, shallots, black olives, bits of roasted red pepper. All of those things were fine, but this pared-down simplified version is hands-down our family favorite.

Remove the yolks from the whites. Set the whites on a platter, cut-side up, and add the yolks to a bowl. Mash the yolks thoroughly with a fork. Add the mayonnaise and mustard and mix well. Spoon this back into the cavities of the egg whites, sprinkle with smoked paprika, and chill for 1–2 hours before serving.

Leftovers: Store deviled eggs in a covered glass container and serve cold. If you have too few left over to make a second meal, repurpose them into an elegant appetizer. Smash them with a fork to make egg salad, then put small spoonfuls on small pieces of the Parmesan-Parsley Almond Crackers (Chapter 8) or sliced cucumbers. If you wish to get fancy, garnish them with a slice of green olive or a small piece of roasted red pepper.

Hard-boiling farm fresh eggs

Every good thing has a down side, as evidenced by the number of invectives uttered by chefs and home cooks across the country as they try to peel hard-boiled eggs fresh from pasture-raised chickens. Much to their despair, the white sticks to the shell, leaving them with little more than a ball of yolk and a few broken stubs of (admittedly delicious) cooked white. If there is one advantage to be found in months-old factory-farmed store-bought eggs, it is that they are stale enough to hard-boil and peel with ease. The game changes when you work with super-fresh eggs, but that doesn't mean hard-boiled eggs are a thing of the past. If you are able to plan three weeks or one month in advance for when you need your hard-boiled eggs, you can set them aside in the refrigerator and allow them to gain a little more age before you cook them. If you are like me, with the exception of Easter, planning that far in advance is impossible. Fortunately, a few adaptations to your traditional methods for hard-boiling eggs should help increase your rate of peeling success.

1. Cover your eggs with one inch of water, put the lid on the pot, and bring to a full boil, then lower the heat and simmer for one minute.

2. Turn off the heat and allow the eggs to rest for 8–10 minutes for gas and induction cooktops, and 4–5 minutes for electric cooktops.

3. Drain, then crack each egg, then cover them with cold water. Let them sit for 5 minutes, then drain the water off and refrigerate them for several hours or overnight before peeling.

My Grandmother's Eggnog—*Improved*

SERVES 16

1 gallon milk

12 egg yolks

½ cup vanilla extract

1 cup maple syrup

1 teaspoon salt

Maple Whipped Cream (recipe follows)

Nutmeg, to taste

MAPLE WHIPPED CREAM

4 cups heavy cream

4 tablespoons maple syrup

4 teaspoons vanilla

ESTIMATED CARBOHYDRATES:
Milk: 187.39 g
Eggs: 2.88 g
Vanilla: 13.16 g
Maple syrup: 211.18 g
Whipped cream: 82.32 g
Total carbohydrates per recipe: 496.93 g
Total carbohydrates per ⅟₁₆ recipe:
31.06 g

My grandmother passed away when I was sixteen, but to this day our entire family considers Christmas incomplete without a few gallons of her eggnog. For years I dutifully adhered to her method of standing over the stove stirring together egg and milk for the better part of an hour until they congealed to make the custard base. Then, last year, while preparing too many different things in the kitchen at once and wearing myself out, I got plain old lazy and decided to experiment by tempering the egg yolks before adding them to the milk. The results were the best 'nog we've ever had (sorry, Grammie!), and in record time.

Pour the milk into a heavy-bottomed large pot, cover, and heat over a medium flame on the stove top. Meanwhile, add the egg yolks, vanilla, maple syrup and salt to a large bowl. Whisk thoroughly and allow them to come to room temperature. Once the milk is steaming hot and just shy of a simmer, turn the heat off and slowly ladle it, ½ cup at a time, into the egg mixture, whisking vigorously all the while. When about 2 cups of the milk has been whisked into the egg, carefully pour the entire solution back into the milk pot. Stir the big batch of yolk and milk together thoroughly, turn the heat back on, and simmer over a medium-low flame, stirring constantly, until the mixture thickens and leaves a silky coating on a wooden spoon.

Remove the eggnog from the heat and whisk until it is cooled, then chill. If the egg has started to cook slightly, quickly whisk in an additional ¼ cup of cold milk, which should reincorporate the egg. If you have taken it so far that you are seeing bits of cooked egg floating around in your eggnog, hold your head high and boldly inform your guests when you serve it later on that you've made it "extra chunky" just for them. Advise them that they might have to chew, and privately note to yourself to not cook it quite so long next time. (You can just strain it through a wire mesh sieve as well.)

Chill the eggnog 2–4 hours, or overnight. Serve in wine goblets or punch glasses, topped with a dollop of Maple Whipped Cream and a dash of nutmeg.

MAPLE WHIPPED CREAM

Pour all the ingredients into the bowl of a stand mixer fitted with a whisk and whip until soft peaks form.

Leftovers: Refrigerate leftover eggnog and serve it whenever guests drop by. It should keep for about a week (but it usually disappears long before then).

Raw Milk Eggnog

SERVES 16 (4-OZ.) GLASSES

6 eggs, separated

3 tablespoons vanilla

¼ cup granulated maple sugar, maple syrup or honey, or to taste (or ⅛ teaspoon Stevia powder)

½ gallon (8 cups) raw milk

2 cups chilled Maple Whipped Cream (optional)

Freshly grated nutmeg, optional

ESTIMATED CARBOHYDRATES:
Eggs 1.44 g
Raw milk: 93.31 g
Vanilla: 4.93 g
Granulated maple sugar: 32.72 g
Sweetened whipped cream: 41.16 g
Total carbohydrates per recipe: 173.56 g
Total carbohydrates per 1/16 recipe: 10.85 g

For those folks who cannot tolerate dairy unless it is unpasteurized, here's a little way to enjoy some holiday cheer while taking good care of your digestive system. Naturally, I am assuming that you have reliably-sourced eggs on hand, since this recipe calls for using them raw, too. Provided you have these two ingredients, this recipe is easy and quick to prepare. Once you've got the proportions in your head, you can whip up eggnog at the drop of a hat . . . or at the wave of a sprig of mistletoe.

Add the egg yolks, 3 tablespoons vanilla, and sweetener to the large bowl of a food processor or blender. Blend well. Pour in as much milk as the container can reasonably hold, and blend again. Whisk the yolk mixture into the remaining milk. Set aside.

Beat the egg whites with the remaining tablespoon of vanilla until stiff. Fold this into the milk mixture.

Serve plain, or topped with whipped cream and a sprinkling of nutmeg.

Leftovers: This is best consumed all in one sitting, as the egg whites do break down over time, and it is best not to leave raw egg products sitting around for very long. If you don't have enough revelers on hand to consume the full shot, cut the recipe in half.

Bittersweet Fudge Pops

YIELDS 6 (4-OUNCE) POPS

1 tablespoon vanilla

4 tablespoons unsweetened cocoa

3 tablespoons maple syrup

4 eggs

1 cup unsweetened kefir or yogurt

6 wooden pop sticks and small paper cups, or a pop mold

ESTIMATED CARBOHYDRATES:
Vanilla: 12 g
Cocoa: 0 g
Maple syrup: 42 g
Kefir or yogurt: 11.42 g
Total number of carbohydrates per recipe: 73.42 g
Total number of carbohydrates per ⅙ recipe: 12.24 g

These rich, creamy fudge pops are packed with protein, making them an excellent treat for little ones and grown-ups alike. If you prefer your chocolate somewhat sweeter, feel free to customize the recipe by adding an extra tablespoon or two of maple syrup to suit your taste.

Combine all the above ingredients in a blender and mix well. Pour into pop molds, insert the sticks or pop holders, and freeze until solid.

Deep Vanilla Ice Cream

MAKES 1 QUART (8 HALF-CUP SERVINGS)

3 egg yolks

¼ cup maple syrup

3 tablespoons vanilla extract

3½ cups heavy cream

ESTIMATED CARBOHYDRATES:
Egg yolks: 1.83 g
Maple syrup: 52.79 g
Vanilla: 4.93 g
Heavy cream: 23.24 g
Total carbohydrates per recipe: 82.79 g
Total carbohydrates per ⅛ recipe: 10.35 g

This recipe takes the vanilla *in vanilla ice cream very seriously. It is a year-round family favorite in our house. In late winter we celebrate sugaring off by topping it with maple syrup. In summer we pair it with fresh fruit. For Bob's birthday I make a Lemon Meringue Ice Cream Pie (recipe follows).*

Beat together the egg yolks, maple syrup and vanilla until smooth. Whisk in the heavy cream, then pour into an electric ice cream maker. Process according to the manufacturer's directions. Pour into a glass container and cover to freeze (for some reason, glass keeps the ice cream from freezing so hard that it can't be scooped). Freeze until firm, about 4 hours. Allow it to soften a few minutes before serving.

Leftovers: Store leftovers in a covered glass container in the refrigerator. Don't count on them lasting for very long. They tend to disappear quickly. I'm pretty certain there are freezer elves that enter most houses at night to eat it.

Lemon Meringue Ice Cream Pie

SERVES 8

FOR THE LEMON CURD FILLING:

2 large eggs

2 large egg yolks

6 tablespoons butter

5 tablespoons honey

½ cup lemon juice

1 tablespoon grated lemon zest

½ teaspoon salt

FOR THE CRUST:

1 cup walnuts

1 cup shredded unsweetened
coconut

1 teaspoon fine ground unrefined
sea salt

6 medjool dates, pitted

1 recipe Deep Vanilla Ice Cream

FOR THE MERINGUE:

4 large egg whites

Pinch cream of tartar

2 tablespoons honey

ESTIMATED CARBOHYDRATES:
Eggs: 2.66 g
Butter: 0.05 g
Honey: 121.13 g
Lemon juice: 7.91 g
Lemon zest: 0.96 g
Walnuts: 13.71 g
Coconut: 11.73 g
Dates: 107.96 g
Deep Vanilla Ice Cream: 82.79 g
Total carbohydrates per recipe: 348.9 g
Total carbohydrates per ⅛ recipe:
43.61 g

Bob's birthday is at the end of April, and this recipe has become a family tradition for celebrating both him and the start of the growing season. This recipe must be started a day before you plan to serve it.

The day before you plan to serve the pie, make the lemon curd: prepare the bottom half of a double boiler with an inch of water and bring it to a simmer. Beat the eggs and egg yolks together in a bowl. Melt the butter in the top half of the double boiler. Whisk in the honey, lemon juice, zest and salt. Pour in the eggs and put the pan over the simmering water bath. Whisk continuously as the egg yolks heat, watching very carefully. After a few minutes, you will start to see the bottom of the pan between your strokes and the curd will have thickened. Remove it from the heat, transfer it to a small bowl and refrigerate for several hours.

While the lemon curd chills, prepare the crust. Place the walnuts, coconut, salt, and dates in the bowl of a food processor. Process until finely ground, then press the mixture into the bottom of a 9-inch glass or ceramic pie dish. Prepare the ice cream and pour half of it over the top of the crust as soon as it comes out of the churn so that it is still soft enough to spread. Freeze for 2 hours (pack the unused ice cream into a separate container and freeze it as well).

Once the first layer of ice cream is firm, remove the remaining ice cream from the freezer and let it soften. Take the pie from the freezer and spread the lemon curd over the top. Spread the remaining ice cream over the lemon curd and freeze 2 more hours, or overnight.

Once the second layer of ice cream is firm, preheat the oven to 475°F. Prepare the meringue. Place the egg whites, cream of tartar and honey in the bowl of a stand mixer fitted with a whisk, and whip until stiff peaks form. Spread the meringue topping over the ice cream pie and bake briefly until the meringue is golden, about 3–5 minutes. Serve immediately, and store leftovers in the freezer.

CHAPTER EIGHT

Leftovers and Soups

While I was writing this book, I would occasionally be asked about my decision to tackle the subject. I habitually explained that I felt compelled to write it because of all the waste I noticed in the meat-cutting room and in our farm inventory. I was frustrated by the accumulation of meaty bones that were destined to go unsold and ultimately to the compost pile, and by my customers' confessions about the amounts of leftover meat they discarded after cooking something that might have easily generated a second delicious meal. In truth (my own confession) there was another reason I wrote recipes that referenced other recipes for leftovers and soups: my own fridge had become a reflection of my own wasteful kitchen habits.

Maintaining the nutrition and well-being of my family is my primary work these days. For quite some time, I've taken that role to mean providing three square meals each day, made largely from foods produced on my family's farm or in my community. Frankly, it was exhausting. While breakfast was homemade yogurt or eggs, lunch and dinner were both full-fledged classic meals: meat, starch, vegetables. My fridge was a mess of leftover bits that I didn't quite know what to do with, we were constantly drawing down the farm's meat inventory, and I felt like I was chained to the kitchen, rarely relieved of the responsibility of preparing a meal. Every few weeks Bob and I confronted the loathsome task of gathering up all the glass dishes of unused leftovers cluttering our refrigerator shelves and spending a morning lugging it to the compost pile and scraping out the unidentifiable moldy contents.

It was on one of these dreary rainy mornings, while simultaneously dumping slimy remains into the compost heap and trying to figure out what I would next cook for lunch, when I had a realization: food was not supporting my life, it was running it. I was working too hard to generate meals, *and* being wasteful with them. Thinking about this forthcoming book, I resolved that by the time I finished the manuscript I would have a clean fridge.

My daughters have joined me in the kitchen and the farm cutting room from the time they were quite young. It's not always easy, but they are becoming confident farm-to-table cooks with lifelong skills.

I started by using the bones to make broth and demi-glace. Once those ingredients had become a regular fixture in my refrigerator, I had a base for making use of the bits of vegetables, the uneaten portions of meat, the occasional cold mashed potatoes. With that innovation at hand, I started changing the way I thought about each piece of meat that I took from the freezer. Like most folks, I had a habit of selecting a piece of meat with only one meal in mind. I realized that this needed to change. While selecting cuts to cook, I began simultaneously planning the primary meal, the meal made from leftovers, and any soups that could be created from the odd scraps.

I don't have any hard figures for changes as a result of this strategy, but I would estimate that we reduced our consumption of meat from the farm by fully two-thirds. Our use of bones, however, increased dramatically. We went from using 30–50 pounds of bones per year, to about 10 pounds *per week*. We didn't reduce the number of calories we consumed, nor did we need to increase the amount of vegetables and starches we ate. We simply made more prudent and thorough use of what we had available.

Furthermore, my kitchen labor reduced significantly. Preparing a dish that incorporates leftovers may require a little more time chopping and dicing or stirring up sauces, but the dishes are usually large enough for us to generate at least two meals for our family of four, reducing several of the meals I prepare each week to merely reheating or recombining. With the ready availability of broth, supper prep work reduced considerably. We prefer to eat lighter in the evening, and with good quality broth already in the fridge, nutrient-rich soups can be prepared in a matter of minutes. The result has been more time for us to sit at the table together, and less time with me standing at the kitchen stove (and fewer dishes for Bob!) By making fuller use of our food stock, we've made our lives a lot easier.

And there is a lot more room these days in the refrigerator. Although, I will admit, the shelves themselves are not exactly *clean* . . .

The recipes on the following pages reflect the core of what this book is really about. But truth be told, I don't exactly expect readers to *follow them*. Once you are in the realm of soups and leftovers, improvisation and serendipity must always play a role. Perhaps, as you learn the concept behind the recipes, you might follow them as written once or twice. Then, by all means, please deviate. Work with what you have available. Make substitutions; broaden your repertoire beyond what's here so that even more food choices are available to you. If the end result is that you, too, have a cleaner fridge, a little more time for yourself and a few extra dollars in your pocket, then I'll have met the resolution I set before myself that dismal morning by the compost pile.

Stuffed Peppers

SERVES 4

2 tablespoons olive oil, butter, lard or tallow

1 medium onion, finely minced

1 clove garlic, minced

2 cups finely shredded cabbage

1–2 cups finely minced leftover meat, or 1 pound ground beef, lamb or pork

1 teaspoon dried thyme (or 1 tablespoon fresh)

1 teaspoon dried oregano (or 1 tablespoon fresh)

1 teaspoon dried basil (or 1 tablespoon fresh)

Coarse salt and ground black pepper, to taste

1 cup tomato sauce or 2 diced fresh tomatoes

4 whole medium sweet peppers, cut in half lengthwise, seeds and membranes removed

8 ounces whole-milk mozzarella cheese, or any other easy-melting cheese, sliced thin

I love simple and satisfying rustic fare like this, which celebrates late summer's bounty. We also cut a few peppers in half each fall to put in the freezer to have them ready for this meal.

Preheat the oven to 350°F. Heat the fat in a large skillet over medium heat. Add the onions and sauté until clear, about 4 minutes. Add the garlic and sauté a minute longer, taking care to control the heat so as not to scorch it. Stir in the cabbage and sauté until crisp-tender. Stir in the meat. If you are working with leftover cooked meat, sauté just until the ingredients are heated through. If you are working with fresh ground meat, sauté about 5–7 minutes until the meat is browned. Stir in the herbs, then season to taste with salt and pepper. Stir in the tomato sauce. Stuff each pepper half with the filling, top with cheese, place in a casserole dish and bake 25 minutes.

Kid alternative: A giant half pepper can be a bit cumbersome for little fingers and mouths. If you need to cook for little ones, I suggest following all the directions as above. Then, instead of filling the bell pepper halves, dice them finely and stir them into the cabbage and meat. Put all the ingredients into a casserole dish, top with cheese, and bake at 350 degrees for 20 minutes. This was extremely popular with my little ones!

ESTIMATED CARBOHYDRATES:
Peppers: 22.09 g
Onion: 10.27 g
Garlic: 0.99 g
Cabbage: 8.12 g
Tomato sauce: 24.35 g
Thyme: 0.64 g
Oregano: 0.69 g
Basil: 0.33 g
Mozzarella cheese: 4.97 g
Total number of carbohydrates per recipe: 72.45 g
Total number of carbohydrates per ¼ recipe (2 stuffed pepper halves): 18.11 g

Meat Canapés with Goat Cheese and Roasted Red Pepper

SERVES 10 AS AN APPETIZER, OR 5 FOR A LIGHT SUPPER WHEN PAIRED WITH A SALAD

1 cup leftover cooked pork, chicken, turkey or lamb, finely diced

½ cup diced roasted red pepper

2 cloves garlic, minced

½ teaspoon coarse salt

½ teaspoon ground black pepper

3 tablespoons olive oil, plus extra for drizzling

4 ounces plain goat cheese

1 teaspoon Dijon mustard

1 recipe Parmesan Parsley Almond Crackers (recipe follows)

This recipe is dazzling for its intense, deeply memorable flavor, its elegance, simplicity . . . and for how very well it pairs with a martini.

Thoroughly combine all the ingredients except the crackers. If time allows, let the mixture sit in the fridge, covered, for 1–2 hours, until the flavors meld.

When ready to serve, preheat the broiler. Spread 1–2 tablespoons of the topping on each cracker. Drizzle with oil, and broil until the mixture browns lightly on top, about 3–5 minutes. Serve immediately.

ESTIMATED CARBOHYDRATES:

Roasted red pepper: 2.73 g
Garlic: 1.98 g
Black pepper: 0.74 g
Goat cheese: 2.88 g
Parmesan Parsley Almond Crackers: 47.66 g

Total number of carbohydrates per recipe: 55.99 g

Total number of carbohydrates per ¹⁄₁₀ recipe: 5.59 g

Total number of carbohydrates per ⅕ recipe: 11.20 g

Can I refreeze my thawed meat?

I am often surprised by the number of times I hear my customers tell me about the uncooked meat that gets discarded, simply because it thaws and they don't get a chance to use it, and they presume it isn't safe to eat.

The primary method to decide whether or not meat is safe to cook is by smelling it. If it doesn't smell bad, it is safe to cook and eat. Be sure, however, to adhere to safe food-handling practices, such as not allowing the raw meat to touch any utensils that might touch foods you will eat raw, and washing your hands after you've handled it.

If you have a thawed piece of meat and your schedule changes, and suddenly you know you won't be eating it, by all means put it back in the freezer. While there may be a few extra ice crystals, it is certainly safe for human consumption, particularly if you are cooking it and using safe handling practices. As sellers of meat, we farmers have to adhere to different criteria. Meat that is completely thawed cannot be refrozen and sold on another day (more often than not, it is refrozen and put into our own freezer for personal use). However, as long as a piece of meat has maintained at least some ice crystals, it is safe to refreeze for retail sale.

Parmesan Parsley Almond Crackers

SERVES 10

2 cups finely ground almonds

1 teaspoon baking soda

3 tablespoons dried parsley

1 cup finely grated Parmesan cheese

1 teaspoon coarse salt

About 2 tablespoons olive oil

About 4 tablespoons water

ESTIMATED CARBOHYDRATES:
Almonds: 41.17 g
Parsley: 2.43 g
Parmesan cheese: 4.06 g
Total carbohydrates per recipe: 47.66 g
Total carbohydrates per 1/10 recipe:
    4.78 g

Okay, okay. There is no meat to be found in this recipe. I'm including it here because so many meaty things taste delicious on these crackers: including the Meat Canapés with Goat Cheese and Roasted Red Pepper, chicken salad, Rillettes from Confit, and any of the pâtés in Chapter 9.

Preheat oven to 350°F. Line a baking sheet with parchment paper. Combine all the above ingredients in a bowl. Use your hands to mix until a sticky dough forms (it may be necessary to add extra water or olive oil). Place the dough on the parchment-lined baking sheet. Flatten the dough out into a uniform thin layer free of cracks. Use a knife to gently score the surface without cutting all the way through (this will enable you to break off uniform pieces later). Bake for 20–25 minutes, or until dough is dry and lightly golden. Cool it in the pan on a wire baking rack, then break into crackers. Store in an air-tight container.

Bob takes advantage of quiet moments during the week to weave baskets that we sell alongside our meats at the farmers' market.

Croquettes with a Black Pepper and Onion Sauce

**SERVES 8 AS AN APPETIZER,
OR 4 AS A MEAL**

1 bunch green onions, minced

8 tablespoons unsalted butter

9 tablespoons all-purpose flour

1½ cups rich meat broth, such as
Shannon's Meat Broth, Chapter 3

1 cup finely diced leftover cooked
pork, chicken, turkey or lamb

Coarse salt and ground black
pepper, to taste

3 eggs, beaten

2 cups dry bread crumbs

Lard or tallow, for frying

Black Pepper and Onion Sauce
(recipe follows)

**BLACK PEPPER AND ONION
SAUCE**

4 tablespoons minced green onions
or shallots

2 tablespoons lard, tallow or butter

1 cup dry red wine

1 cup rich meat stock

2 tablespoons butter

2 teaspoons ground black pepper

1–2 dashes cayenne pepper

Delicate and elegant . . . and oh, so French. A classic example of how lowly leftovers can suddenly turn upscale.

Sauté the green onions in the butter in a large skillet over medium heat until softened and transparent, then blend in the flour until smooth. Cook, stirring constantly, until the flour is browned, about 5–7 minutes. Slowly stir in the stock and simmer, stirring constantly, until thick. Turn off the heat. Fold in the meat, season to taste with salt and pepper, then allow the mixture to rest for 5 minutes. This enables the meat to be well penetrated by the flavors in the sauce. Pour everything into a bowl and chill for 1–2 hours, until firm.

Shape the cold meat mixture into balls about the size of an egg, and partially flatten. Dip each croquette into the beaten egg, then roll in bread crumbs. Do this twice. Fry in one inch of tallow or lard over medium heat until browned, about 3 minutes per side. Serve hot, topped with Black Pepper and Onion Sauce.

BLACK PEPPER AND ONION SAUCE

Sauté the onion in the fat in a nonreactive (stainless-steel or enameled) skillet over a medium flame until clear, about 4 minutes. Pour in the red wine and meat stock and simmer until reduced by half. Stir in the butter and black pepper, and season to taste with cayenne. Serve with croquettes.

ESTIMATED CARBOHYDRATES:

Green onions: 8.27 g

Butter: 0.07 g

Flour: 51.9 g

Meat broth: 3.5 g*

Eggs: 0.48 g

Bread crumbs: 155.48 g

Red wine: 6.03 g

Black pepper: 2.94 g

Total number of carbohydrates per recipe:
228.67 g

Total number of carbohydrates per ¼ recipe:
57.17 g

Total number of carbohydrates per ⅛
recipe: 28.58 g

* Number of carbohydrates in homemade broth will vary. This figure is calculated using the recipe for Shannon's Meat Broth (Chapter 3).

Hearty Macaroni and Cheese

SERVES 6

1 tablespoon olive oil

9 ounces dry pasta (elbow, fusilli, or ziti all work)

2 tablespoons lard, olive oil, butter or tallow

1 medium onion, finely diced

2½ cups broccoli (fresh or frozen), diced

1 pound ground beef or loose Italian sausage, OR 2–3 cups finely diced leftover cooked meat

½ cup sundried tomatoes, diced

1 cup grated cheddar cheese

1 cup grated whole-milk mozzarella cheese

½ cup grated Parmesan cheese

1 cup heavy cream

3 eggs

½ teaspoon cayenne pepper

1 teaspoon salt

1 teaspoon ground black pepper

4 tablespoons butter

1 cup bread crumbs

Okay, one look at this recipe and you'll realize that I am no wimp when it comes to the butterfat. This dish is so rich and creamy that a little goes a long way. If you are not able to tolerate so much butterfat, feel free to substitute milk for the cream. Leftovers are even tastier the next day.

Preheat the oven to 350°F. Lightly grease a 9-by-12 baking pan or casserole dish. Bring 4 quarts water to a rolling boil over high heat. Add the olive oil and stir in the pasta. Cook until just al dente. Drain and arrange it on the bottom of the prepared pan. Melt the remaining fat in a large skillet and put in the onions and broccoli. Sauté until the onions are clear and the broccoli is crisp-tender. Add the meat and continue to sauté until it is cooked through. Sprinkle this on top of the pasta. Scatter the sundried tomatoes on top, then layer the cheddar, mozzarella and Parmesan over everything. In a separate bowl, whisk together the cream, eggs, cayenne, salt and pepper. Pour it over the casserole. Melt the butter in a small saucepan over a medium flame, mix in the crumbs, then scatter them over the top of the casserole. Bake 40 minutes, or until bubbly and lightly browned on top.

ESTIMATED CARBOHYDRATES:	
Pasta: 140.11 g	Eggs: 0.72 g
Onion: 10.27 g	Cayenne: 0.51 g
Broccoli: 15.11 g	Black pepper: 1.47 g
Sundried tomatoes: 12.83 g	Butter: 0.03 g
Cheddar cheese: 1.45 g	Bread crumbs: 77.74 g
Mozzarella cheese: 2.45 g	Total number of carbohydrates per recipe: 271.36 g
Parmesan cheese: 2.03 g	Total number of carbohydrates per ⅙ recipe: 45.23 g
Heavy cream: 6.64 g	

Pressure Cooker Red Beans and Rice

SERVES 6

2 tablespoons lard or butter, plus more, for warming the meat topping

4 ribs celery, diced

1 medium green pepper, diced, or ½ cup diced garlic scapes*

1 medium onion, diced

1 teaspoon ground black pepper

1 teaspoon coarse salt

1 teaspoon crumbled dried thyme, or 1 tablespoon chopped fresh thyme

1 teaspoon granulated garlic (use ½ teaspoon if you are using garlic scapes)

½ teaspoon ground cayenne

3 bay leaves

1 cup dried red beans, rinsed and soaked overnight in 1 quart water and 2 tablespoons yogurt, drained, and rinsed again

1 cup raw long grain rice

2 cups meat broth, such as Shannon's Meat Broth, Chapter 3

1–2 pounds diced cooked Italian, chorizo, andouille, merguez or other mildly spicy sausage, OR 1–2 cups diced leftover chicken or pork

When I was a teenager, one of my favorite musicians was Louis Armstrong. I read everything I could find about his life, including the fact that Red Beans and Rice was his favorite food. I love to prepare this dish, especially with my beloved Satchmo playing in the background. If you remember to soak the beans a day ahead, the pressure cooker makes this dish a quick and easy way to turn leftovers into a soul-satisfying meal.

Melt the fat in a pressure cooker over medium heat. Add the celery, green pepper or garlic scapes, and the diced onion, and sauté until the onions are clear. Stir in the black pepper, salt, thyme, granulated garlic, cayenne, and bay leaves. Add the rice and beans and sauté until the rice grains are lightly browned. Stir in 2 cups broth. Secure the pressure cooker lid in place, and cook for 22 minutes at 15 PSI. Allow the pressure to subside using the natural release method. Warm the sausage or leftover meat in a skillet with a little butter or lard, and serve on top of the rice and beans.

* Garlic scapes are the curling top of the garlic plant, typically harvested in early summer.

ESTIMATED CARBOHYDRATES:		
Celery: 4.76 g		Bay leaves: 1.35 g
Pepper: 5.52 g		Kidney beans: 112.77 g
Onion: 10.27 g		Rice: 147.91 g
Black pepper: 1.47 g		Meat stock: 2.8 g*
Thyme: 0.64 g		Total number of carbohydrates per recipe: 290.25 g
Granulated garlic: 2.25 g		Total number of carbohydrates per ⅙ recipe: 48.38 g
Cayenne: 0.51 g		

Vegetable, Meat and Potato Salad with Warm Bacon Dressing

SERVES 6

FOR THE SALAD:

1 pound potatoes (or sweet potatoes or winter squash), peeled, cut into 1-inch chunks, and boiled in water to cover until tender, drained

½ pound steamed chopped broccoli

½ pound steamed chopped cauliflower

2 medium sweet red peppers, diced

4 hard-boiled eggs, coarsely diced

½ cup Kalamata or other oil-cured black olives, coarsely diced

1 pound room-temperature diced leftover lamb, steak, duck or pork

FOR THE WARM BACON DRESSING:

3 ounces sliced bacon

½ cup extra-virgin olive oil

2 teaspoons Dijon mustard

5 tablespoons cider vinegar

Coarse salt and ground black pepper, to taste

ESTIMATED CARBOHYDRATES:
Potato: 71.17 g (winter squash: 38.96 g)
Broccoli: 15.07 g
Cauliflower: 11.28
Sweet red peppers: 14.35
Eggs: 0.96 g
Olives: 4.21 g
Bacon: 1.27 g
Cider vinegar: 0.28 g
Total carbohydrates per recipe: 118.59 g
Total carbohydrates per ⅙ recipe: 19.77 g

This salad is hearty and a great way to help stretch your leftovers into a feast.

Combine the salad ingredients in a large salad or serving bowl and toss to mix.

To make the dressing, fry the bacon until crisp in a skillet over medium heat. Remove the bacon, reserving the pan drippings, and drain it on absorbent paper. Crumble and set aside. Whisk together the pan drippings, olive oil, mustard and vinegar until emulsified. Season to taste with salt and pepper. Stir in the crumbled bacon and toss with the salad.

Mexican-Style Chicken and Cheese Casserole

SERVES 4

2 cloves garlic, crushed

1 teaspoon fine Celtic sea salt

1 tablespoon lard, butter or olive oil

1 medium onion, diced

2 cups diced canned or fresh tomatoes

1 tablespoon tomato paste

1 green chili pepper, seeded and chopped

1 green bell pepper, diced

1 teaspoon ground cumin

½ cup ripe pitted olives, diced

1–2 cups diced cooked chicken, turkey, pork, or sautéed ground beef

1 egg, beaten

16 ounces whole milk ricotta

1 cup grated cheddar

4 ounces crushed tortilla, sweet potato or vegetable chips (optional)

My kids loved this recipe. They were able to come into the kitchen and help me put it together. Saoirse was able to dice the olives and onion and help stir the sauce, and Ula, with her iron fist and compulsion to break things, was a natural when it came to crushing the chips. Better still, they thought it was delicious.

Preheat oven to 350°F. Mix the garlic and salt together. Melt the fat in a medium saucepan over medium-low heat, add the onion and garlic/salt mixture and sauté until soft, keeping the flame low enough so that they don't brown. Add the tomatoes, tomato paste, both peppers, and cumin. Simmer, uncovered, until sauce thickens, about 15–20 minutes. Remove it from heat and stir in the olives and meat.

Mix the egg and ricotta in a bowl. Pour half the sauce into a 9-inch-square casserole or baking pan. Sprinkle with half the cheddar, then cover with all of the ricotta-egg mixture. Spread the remaining tomato sauce on top, then sprinkle with the remaining cheddar and optional tortilla chips. Bake until bubbly, about 20 minutes. Let it rest 10 to 15 minutes prior to serving so that it can set.

ESTIMATED CARBOHYDRATES:	
Garlic: 1.98 g	Egg: 0.24 g
Onion: 10.27 g	Cheddar: 1.45 g
Tomatoes: 19.20 g	Tortilla chips: 76.06 g
Tomato paste: 3.10 g	Total number of carbohydrates per recipe (with tortilla chips): 142.18 g
Chili: 4.26 g	Total number of carbohydrates per recipe (without tortilla chips): 66.12 g
Bell pepper: 5.52 g	Total number of carbohydrates per ¼ recipe (with tortilla chips): 35.55 g
Cumin: 0.93 g	Total number of carbohydrates per ¼ recipe (without tortilla chips): 16.53 g
Olives: 4.21 g	
Ricotta: 14.96 g	

Asian-Style Cold Meat Salad

SERVES 4

1 pound green and yellow summer squash, diced and lightly steamed

1 large sweet red pepper, seeded and julienned

2 carrots, shredded

3 cups snow peas, lightly steamed and coarsely chopped (or diced large)

2–3 cups leftover cooked chicken, turkey, beef, lamb or pork, sliced into thin strips

½ cup lemon juice, or ¼ cup lemon juice and ¼ cup orange juice, if you prefer a sweeter flavor

¼ cup tamari (available at specialty grocers, Asian food stores, and some supermarkets)

3 tablespoons toasted sesame oil

1 tablespoon honey or maple syrup

3 teaspoons grated fresh ginger

¼ teaspoon crushed red pepper

1 cup salted cashews

ESTIMATED CARBOHYDRATES:
Summer squash 19.55g
Sweet red pepper: 9.89 g
Carrots: 11.68 g
Snow peas: 22.23 g
Lemon juice: 7.91 g
Tamari: 4.01 g
Honey: 17.28 g
Ginger: 3.21 g
Crushed red pepper: 0.25 g
Cashews: 43.05 g
Total number of carbohydrates per recipe: 139.06 g
Total number of carbohydrates per ¼ recipe: 34.765 g

This is a spicy delight for vegetable fans, a cooling meal for a steamy summer afternoon or evening.

Combine the squash, sweet red pepper, carrots, snow peas, and meat in a large bowl. In a separate bowl, whisk together the lemon juice, tamari, sesame oil, honey, ginger, and crushed red pepper. Pour the dressing over the salad and toss well to coat. Serve immediately, garnished with the cashews.

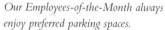

Our Employees-of-the-Month always enjoy preferred parking spaces.

Moussaka

SERVES 8

5 tablespoons lard or butter, or 3 tablespoons lard or butter and 2 tablespoons olive oil

2 medium onions, diced

2 cloves garlic, minced

2 pounds ground beef, lamb, or pork (or a combination thereof), cooked and crumbled, or 2 pounds cooked lamb, beef, pork, chicken, or turkey (or a combination thereof), finely diced

2 cups diced fresh or canned tomatoes

1 cup meat broth, such as Shannon's Meat Broth, Chapter 3

¼ cup chopped fresh parsley or 1 tablespoon dried

1 tablespoon chopped fresh oregano or 1 teaspoon dried

½ teaspoon ground cinnamon

5 tablespoons almond flour (any other conventional flour will also work)

2 cups heavy cream (or milk)

3 eggs, beaten

Coarse salt and ground black pepper

1 cup grated Parmesan cheese

2 eggplants (about 1¼ pounds each), peeled and sliced into thin rounds

This easy-to-prepare one-dish dinner takes advantage of the summer harvest while repurposing your leftover meats into a tasty repast.

Preheat oven to 350°F. Heat 2 tablespoons of the fat or olive oil, if using, in a large skillet over a medium flame. Add the onions and sauté until clear, then stir in the garlic. Sauté 1 minute longer and stir in the meat, tomatoes, broth, herbs and cinnamon. Set aside.

Heat the remaining fat in a saucepan over medium heat. When the foaming subsides, blend in the almond flour until smooth, and stir until lightly browned, about a minute. Slowly whisk in the cream, bring to a simmer, and cook 3–5 minutes, until slightly thickened. Slowly whisk a quarter cup of the hot sauce into the eggs, then stir them into the sauce. Bring to a simmer, whisking constantly, and simmer until thick and creamy. Turn off the heat, season to taste with salt and pepper, and stir in half of the Parmesan.

Lightly grease a 9-by-13-inch glass baking dish and arrange half the eggplant on the bottom. Sprinkle with salt and pepper, then top with all of the meat sauce. Arrange the remaining eggplant over the top, then pour the custard evenly over it and smooth it with a spatula. Sprinkle evenly with the remaining Parmesan. Cover and bake 1 hour, then remove the cover and bake until the top has lightly browned, about 10–15 minutes longer.

ESTIMATED CARBOHYDRATES:	
Onions: 20.54 g	Eggs: 0.72 g
Garlic: 1.98 g	Parmesan: 4.06 g
Tomatoes: 14 g	Eggplant: 31.24 g
Meat broth: 1.4 g*	Total number of carbohydrates per recipe: 97.42 g
Parsley: 0.96 g	
Oregano: 0.69 g	Total number of carbohydrates per ⅛ recipe: 12.18 g
Cinnamon: 1.05 g	
Almond flour: 7.5 g	* Number of carbohydrates in homemade broth will vary. This figure is calculated using the recipe for Shannon's Meat Broth (Chapter 3).
Cream: 13.28 g	

A celebration of the casserole

My graduate school research gave me a wonderful opportunity to interview school food service directors all around New York State. My most memorable conversation was with 70-year-old Rosie, one of my own favorite "Lunch Ladies" from my school years at Cobleskill Central School. Rosie's institutional memory was long. She'd learned to cook in the 1930s and '40s, and recounted the lunches she'd prepared during the 1940s and '50s made from whatever ingredients local farmers had brought to the cafeteria that week. "We cooked from scratch from what we got," she explained, "soups, stews, casseroles." And with that, she stopped abruptly. "Kids, today, they don't even know what a casserole *is*."

A budding home cook at the time, I blushed at my own ignorance. I knew nothing about casseroles, except that they were something thrown together with a can of Cream of Mushroom Soup, as described in countless jokes about Midwestern church ladies. But Rosie was right: the casserole, once a cornerstone in American cookery, was slowly being forgotten.

We take the name "casserole" from the French word used to describe the style of baking dish used, but casseroles can be found in cuisines throughout the world: Moroccan tagines, Greek Osso Bucco, Thai curries, French coq au vin, and Mexican chili con carne. Many casseroles were traditionally poverty food, hence their popularity in the United States during the Great Depression. They were a way, according to *The American Woman's Cookbook*, "to use leftovers in attractive, palatable combinations, to cook tough meats tender, and to prepare vegetables in an almost unlimited variety of ways." The introduction of Campbell's Condensed Soups in 1934 coincided with the casserole's rise in the 1950s. Casserole recipes featuring condensed canned soup (essentially a roux base) became instrumental in a movement to free housewives from the perceived drudgery of the kitchen as the Golden Age of consumerism cleared the runway for our modern industrialized food system. As multinational food corporations devised ever more industrially processed foods, the lowly casserole lost her cultural foothold. But I think she deserves a comeback.

Truly sustainable cuisine requires us to do more than learn how to cook a pork roast, grill a grassfed steak or find a recipe for kohlrabi and rutabagas. We must re-learn to minimize our food waste and maximize our thrift and resourcefulness with every ounce of our locally bountiful nourishment. And here is where the humble casserole shows her truest glory. Casseroles extend servings of our grassfed meats, use whatever vegetables are available from our local farmers and, best of all, they incorporate meat and vegetable into highly nutritious sauce made with mineral-rich, digestible and delicious homemade stock. Adelle Davis elegantly simplifies turning fridge forage into a feast with this most elemental culinary caveat: *"Casserole dishes must depend upon the ingredients you have on hand."* That said, the remaining steps to assembling a casserole are very straightforward:

- Prepare any cream sauce, brown sauce (gravy) or tomato sauce
- Add vegetables and leftover meat and a starch (optional)
- Sprinkle with crumbs (or nuts) and cheese
- Bake

Remember Adelle Davis's principles as you approach the following (or any) casserole recipe, for nearly every ingredient can be substituted with something else. The leftover chicken could be leftover turkey. The stock could be replaced by cream or milk, the vegetables with whatever you have on hand, cheddar can be Parmesan. Perhaps add some bacon or olives if you have them on hand. Work with what you have. What I have written is just a suggestion—a little something to make Rosie proud.

Chicken (or Turkey) Divan

SERVES 6

1 pound lightly steamed broccoli, asparagus or green beans

2–3 cups diced cooked leftover chicken or turkey

1 cup shredded cheddar, Parmesan, or Gruyère, or a combination

6 tablespoons butter

6 tablespoons almond flour (or another flour of your choosing)

2 cups meat broth, such as Shannon's Meat Broth, Chapter 3, or chicken broth, preferably homemade (see Meat Broth, Chapter 3)

2 teaspoons lemon juice

½ cup heavy cream

2 tablespoons sherry

Coarse salt and ground black pepper, to taste

2 eggs

1 tablespoon Dijon mustard

½ cup coarsely ground walnuts (or bread crumbs)

1 tablespoon dried parsley

This dish is one of my personal "comfort foods." I remember my mom preparing it for us when we were kids. It was a one-dish dinner, so we were able to balance our bowls in our laps and sit beside the woodstove while we ate. Unlike typical Divan recipes, there is not a can of cream of mushroom soup anywhere to be found!

Preheat oven to 350°F. Lightly grease a 9-by-13-inch baking dish and arrange the vegetables on the bottom. Top with the chicken and then the cheese.

Melt 4 tablespoons butter in a medium saucepan. Whisk in the flour, and cook, whisking constantly, until it browns, about 1 minute. Slowly whisk in the broth, followed by the lemon juice. Simmer 10 minutes and stir in the cream and sherry. Season to taste with salt and pepper.

Break the eggs into a bowl, add the mustard, and beat until smooth. Whisking constantly, slowly drizzle 1 cup of the hot sauce into the eggs to temper them. Add them to the remaining sauce, mix well, and pour it over the chicken and vegetables.

Heat the remaining butter in a small saucepan. Stir in the ground walnuts and parsley, then sprinkle over the top of the casserole. Bake until heated through and the nuts are lightly browned, about 30 minutes.

ESTIMATED CARBOHYDRATES:	
Broccoli: 30.12 g	Mustard: 1 g
Cheddar: 1.45 g	Walnuts: 16.04 g
Butter: 0.05 g	Parsley: 0.17 g
Almond flour: 9.0 g	Total number of carbohydrates per recipe: 71.55 g
Meat broth: 2.8 g*	
Lemon juice: 0.32 g	Total number of carbohydrates per ⅙ recipe: 11.93 g
Heavy cream: 6.64 g	
Sherry: 3.0 g	* Number of carbohydrates in homemade broth will vary. This figure is calculated using the recipe for Shannon's Meat Broth (Chapter 3).
Eggs: 0.96 g	

Chicken (or Turkey) and Wild Rice with a Sherry Cream Sauce

SERVES 4

4 tablespoons butter or lard

2 medium carrots, diced

2 medium yellow onions, diced

2 ribs celery, diced

3 tablespoons almond flour (or another flour of your choosing)

1 tablespoon Dijon mustard

2 cups meat broth, such as Shannon's Meat Broth, Chapter 3

2 cups diced cooked chicken or turkey

1 cup heavy cream (or milk)

2 tablespoons sherry

Coarse salt and ground black pepper to taste

4 cups cooked wild rice or wild rice blend

This recipe is an easy-to-make treat in our household, giving us something to look forward to the day after we've enjoyed a roasted chicken.

Heat 2 tablespoons of the fat in a large skillet over a medium flame. Add the carrots and sauté 5 minutes, then add the onions and celery. Sauté until the carrots are crisp-tender and the onions are clear. Remove the vegetables to a bowl and return the skillet to the heat. Add the remaining fat and let it melt. When the bubbling subsides, whisk in the almond flour. Cook, whisking constantly, for 1 minute, then slowly whisk in the mustard and 1 cup of the broth, stirring constantly. Simmer until the broth has reduced by half, then slowly whisk in the remaining broth. Simmer 10 minutes, allowing the sauce to thicken further. Stir in the meat and vegetables, cook 1 minute, then stir in the cream. Cook until it is just heated through, about 2 minutes longer. Stir in the sherry, and season to taste with salt and pepper. Remove from the heat and serve over rice in shallow bowls.

ESTIMATED CARBOHYDRATES:

Carrots: 11.68 g

Onions: 20.54 g

Celery: 2.38 g

Flour: 17.3 g

Meat broth: 2.8 g*

Heavy cream: 6.64 g

Sherry: 1.5 g

Wild rice: 139.99 g

Total number of carbohydrates per recipe: 202.83 g

Total number of carbohydrates per ¼ recipe: 50.58 g

* Number of carbohydrates in home-made broth will vary. This figure is calculated using the recipe for Shannon's Meat Broth (Chapter 3).

Black Bean Chili with Dark Roast Coffee

SERVES 8

2 cups black beans, rinsed, soaked overnight in 1 quart of water and 2 tablespoons plain yogurt, drained, and rinsed once more

2 tablespoons butter, olive oil or lard

2 large onions, diced

2 tablespoons chili powder

2 teaspoons ground cumin

2 tablespoons crumbled dried oregano, or 6 tablespoons chopped fresh oregano

¼ teaspoon cinnamon

1 tablespoon unsweetened cocoa powder

4 cups diced canned tomatoes

6 cloves garlic, minced

2 cups strong brewed dark-roast coffee

1 dried chipotle chili

2 teaspoons coarse salt (or to taste)

1–2 cups diced cooked pork, beef, chicken or lamb

Optional garnish toppings: sour cream, chopped fresh cilantro, chopped green onions, shredded cheese, and/or diced hot peppers

Every now and then, there is no food more satisfying than a simmering hot bowl of chili. This recipe, with its exotic twists of cocoa and coffee, creates a center-stage dish, made complete by a previous day's leftovers.

Place beans in a pressure cooker. Cover with the meat stock and water. Cook at 15 psi for 12 minutes, and allow the pressure to subside naturally. (If you don't own a pressure cooker, cover the meat stock and water with 2½–3 cups water and simmer 1½–2 hours, until tender.)

Heat the fat in a large pot over a medium flame. Add the onions and sauté until clear. Stir in the chili powder, cumin, oregano, cinnamon, and cocoa. Cook 1 minute, stirring, then stir in the tomatoes and garlic. Sauté 3 minutes longer, then stir in the cooked beans, coffee and chipotle pepper. Cover and simmer 30 minutes, then remove the lid and simmer until thickened, about 15 minutes longer. Add the leftover meat and simmer until it is warmed through. Remove the chipotle pepper. Serve with the toppings of your choice.

ESTIMATED CARBOHYDRATES:	
Black beans: 241.96 g	Canned tomatoes: 38.4 g
Onions: 28.02 g	Garlic: 5.94 g
Chili powder: 3.98 g	Chili pepper: 2.39 g
Cumin: 1.86 g	Total number of carbohydrates per recipe: 330.34 g
Oregano: 4.14 g	
Cinnamon: 0.52 g	Total number of carbohydrates per ⅛ recipe: 41.29 g
Cocoa powder: 3.13 g	

Summer Harvest Casserole

SERVES 8

3 medium eggplants, peeled and sliced into ¼-inch-thick rounds

Olive oil

3 tablespoons butter, lard, or tallow (or use all olive oil)

1 medium onion, coarsely chopped

2 medium carrots, diced

1 clove garlic, minced

1–2 pounds ground beef, lamb, or loose Italian sausage, or finely diced cooked beef, pork or lamb

6 medium fresh tomatoes, diced

1 tablespoon chopped fresh basil, or 1 teaspoon dried basil

1 tablespoon chopped fresh oregano, or 1 teaspoon dried oregano

1 teaspoon coarse salt

Ground black pepper, to taste

1 pound whole-milk ricotta cheese

2 tablespoons diced fresh chives

1 egg, beaten

8 ounces goat cheese

1 cup freshly grated Parmesan

This one-dish dinner is perfectly suited for a late-summer repast, as it makes use of many of the vegetables spilling out of the garden.

Preheat broiler. Brush both sides of the eggplant rounds with olive oil, then place on a baking sheet. Broil, turning once, until lightly browned on both sides (about 2 minutes per side) and set aside to cool.

Heat the fat in a large nonreactive (stainless-steel or enameled) skillet over medium heat. Add the onion, carrots and garlic, and sauté until the onions are clear. Add the meat and cook until it is lightly browned, stirring often to break up any clumps (note: if you are working with precooked leftover meat, just sauté the meat until it is warmed through, about a minute). Add the tomatoes, basil, oregano, salt, and pepper to taste. Lower the heat, cover, and simmer 10 minutes. Remove the lid and simmer until the sauce has thickened, about 30 minutes longer.

Preheat oven to 350°F. Lightly grease a 9-by-13-inch baking dish. Spoon in enough meat sauce to coat the bottom, and spread it evenly. Cover with half the eggplant rounds. In a separate bowl, mix together the ricotta, egg, and chives, and spread it evenly over the eggplant. Lay the remaining eggplant over the ricotta, sprinkle with the goat cheese, and top with the remaining meat sauce. Sprinkle the Parmesan evenly over the top, cover, and bake 30 minutes. Uncover and bake until the sauce is bubbling and the cheese is lightly browned, about 10–15 minutes longer.

ESTIMATED CARBOHYDRATES:	
Eggplant: 78.32 g	Chives: 0.26 g
Onion: 10.27 g	Egg: 0.24 g
Carrots: 11.68 g	Goat cheese: 5.76 g
Garlic: 0.99 g	Parmesan: 4.06 g
Tomatoes: 28.71 g	Total number of carbohydrates per recipe: 154.84 g
Basil: 0.07 g	Total number of carbohydrates per ⅛ recipe: 19.36 g
Oregano: 0.69 g	
Ricotta: 13.79 g	

Parmesan-Cheddar One-Crust Meat Pie

SERVES 6

6 tablespoons lard or butter

2 cups diced fresh or leftover
vegetables (onions, green
peppers, carrots, peas, corn, or
green beans . . . even lima beans,
will all work)

2 tablespoons all-purpose flour or
arrowroot

2 cups meat broth, such as Shannon's
Meat Broth, Chapter 3

¼ teaspoon mace

¼ teaspoon crumbled dried
rosemary, or ¾ teaspoon chopped
fresh rosemary

Coarse salt and ground black
pepper, to taste

2 cups diced leftover beef, pork or
lamb

Parmesan-Cheddar Pie Crust (see
recipe on next page)

1 egg yolk beaten with 1 tablespoon
water

ESTIMATED CARBOHYDRATES:
Diced onion (1 cup): 14.94 g*
Diced green beans (1 cup): 13.94 g*
Flour: 11.92 g
Broth: 2.8g**
Mace: 0.86 g
Rosemary: 0.19 g
Parmesan-Cheddar Pie Crust: 134.55 g
Egg yolk: 0.61g
Total carbohydrates per recipe: 179.81 g
Total carbohydrates per ⅙ recipe:
    29.97 g
* Number of carbohydrates will vary
based on which vegetables are used.
** Number of carbohydrates in home-
made broth will vary. This figure is cal-
culated using the recipe for Shannon's
Meat Broth (chapter 3).

This is a hearty meal, and is even better when reheated on a second day and served with a wedge of extra-sharp cheddar.

Preheat the oven to 450°F. Heat 2 tablespoons of the fat in a skillet over a medium flame. Add the fresh vegetables and sauté until crisp-tender. Add in any leftover vegetables, if using, and continue sautéing until they are just warmed through. Remove them from the pan and set aside. Add the remaining fat. Heat, stirring constantly, until the butter has melted and is no longer foaming. Sprinkle the flour or arrowroot on top and whisk thoroughly until a paste forms. Slowly stir in the meat stock and bring to a boil, stirring constantly. Reduce the flame intensity and simmer until the sauce is thick, about 7 minutes. Mix in the mace, rosemary, salt and pepper. Stir in the diced cooked meat and the vegetables, then pour into a 10-inch, deep-pie dish or 9-inch-square baking pan. Roll out the pie crust on a floured surface ¼-inch thick, then carefully lay it over the top of the filling. Don't fret if the crust crumbles. Just work it back together and slide it on top. Crimp the edges, then poke a few holes on the surface. Brush the crust with the yolk and water mixture, and bake until the crust is lightly browned, about 20–25 minutes.

Note: For those of you averse to using wheat flour, you can top the pie with potatoes mashed with liberal amounts of butter, then sprinkle the topping with Parmesan or cheddar cheese. The flour in the meat sauce can be replaced with arrowroot powder.

Parmesan Cheddar Pie Crust

1 cup all-purpose flour

½ teaspoon coarse salt

½ teaspoon ground black pepper

⅛ teaspoon baking powder

¼ pound (one stick) cold butter, diced

¾ cup grated cheddar

½ cup grated Parmesan cheese

¼ cup ground walnuts

ESTIMATED CARBOHYDRATES:

Flour: 92.27 g

Black pepper: 0.74 g

Baking powder: 0.14 g

Butter: 0.07 g

Cheddar: 1.08 g

Parmesan: 2.03 g

Walnuts: 2.74 g

Total number of carbohydrates per recipe: 134.55 g

Total number of carbohydrates per ⅙ recipe: 22.43 g

I often double this recipe, then store the extra crust in the freezer for another use.

Combine the flour, salt, pepper, and baking powder. Using a pastry cutter or fork, blend in the butter until the mixture resembles coarse meal. Using your hands, thoroughly mix in the cheese and nuts until the dough forms a solid ball. Chill until ready to use, but allow it to soften at room temperature before rolling it out.

Unlike a conventional pie crust, this dough will be more crumbly and will require your forbearance if it breaks when you lift it over the pie. Simply push the broken pieces together and move forward. The extraordinary flavor and texture will make it well worth any cosmetic imperfections.

Poultry or Pork Canapés with a Peanut–Lime Sauce

SERVES 4–6 AS AN APPETIZER,
2–3 AS A MEAL

2 tablespoons olive oil

2 cups finely diced cooked leftover
   chicken, turkey or pork

1 batch Peanut-Lime Paste,
   Appendix 1

Toasted pita wedges, baguette
   slices, Parmesan Parsley Almond
   Crackers, or sliced cucumbers

Whole cilantro leaves, for garnish

This is a fun way to turn some leftovers into a dazzling appetizer, tapas or a light supper.

Heat the olive oil in a skillet over a medium flame. Add the meat and sauté until it is warmed through. Add the peanut–lime paste and stir until the meat is thoroughly coated. Place a spoonful of the meat on top of each piece of bread, cracker, or cucumber, and garnish with a cilantro leaf before serving.

ESTIMATED CARBOHYDRATES:	
Peanut-Lime Paste: 27.18 g	Total number of carbohydrates without bread, pita or crackers: 27.18 g
Pita, Bread or Crackers: variable	Total number of carbohydrates per ¼ recipe (without bread, pita or crackers): 6.8 g

Tomato Garlic Chicken (or Turkey) Salad

SERVES 4

2 large heads garlic

4 medium fresh tomatoes, diced

½ cup diced green olives (with or
   without pimentos)

2–4 cups diced cooked chicken or
   turkey

½ cup olive oil

¼ cup apple cider or red wine
   vinegar

½ teaspoon coarse salt

¼ teaspoon ground black pepper

1 teaspoon Dijon mustard

4 ounces crumbled goat cheese,
   optional

The whole cloves of garlic are a surprising ingredient for this salad with a pronounced Provençal flavor; but blanching them first turns their bite into a nutty and mildly sweet flavor.

Separate the garlic into cloves and peel them. Bring a pot of water to a light boil over medium heat and drop in the garlic. Boil until they are tender when pierced, about 5–8 minutes. Drain and combine them with the tomatoes, olives, and chicken in a salad bowl.

    In a separate, smaller bowl, whisk together the olive oil, vinegar, salt, pepper, and mustard until it has emulsified. Pour this over the salad and toss to coat. Sprinkle with the goat cheese and serve.

ESTIMATED CARBOHYDRATES:	
Garlic: 11.88 g	Dijon mustard: 0.33 g
Tomatoes: 19.14 g	Goat cheese: 2.88 g
Green olives: 0.96 g	Total number of carbohydrates per recipe: 36.13 g
Cider vinegar: 0.56 g	Total number of carbohydrates per ¼ recipe: 9.03 g
Black pepper: 0.38 g	

Lemon Chicken (or Turkey) Salad with Braised Sweet Peppers

SERVES 6

1 clove crushed garlic

1 tablespoon lemon zest

2 tablespoons chopped fresh parsley (or 2 teaspoons dried)

½ cup olive oil

2–3 cups diced cooked chicken or turkey

2 tablespoons lard, butter or olive oil

1 medium red bell pepper, seeded and cut into strips

1 medium yellow bell pepper, seeded and cut into strips

1 medium green bell pepper, seeded and cut into strips

1 medium red onion, cut into narrow wedges

⅔ cup dry white wine

Coarse salt and ground black pepper, to taste

ESTIMATED CARBOHYDRATES:
Garlic: 0.99 g
Lemon zest: 0.96 g
Parsley: 0.48 g
Red pepper: 7.18 g
Yellow pepper: 7.6 g
Green pepper: 5.52 g
Onion: 0.27 g
White wine: 3.20 g
Total number of carbohydrates per recipe: 36.2
Total number of carbohydrates per ⅙ recipe: 6.03 g

This salad turns leftover chicken into a vibrant palette of summer's colors. While the recipe suggests that you serve it warm, it is also terrific picnic fare, especially when paired with potato salad.

Combine the garlic, lemon zest, parsley and olive oil in a small bowl. Whisk until emulsified. Pour the dressing over the chicken and toss to coat.

Heat the fat in a large skillet over a medium flame. Add all the bell peppers and onion and sauté 1 minute. Pour in the wine, reduce the heat to a simmer, cover, and cook until the vegetables are crisp-tender, about 5–7 minutes. Remove the lid, increase the heat and cook until all the liquid has evaporated. Add the chicken, lower the heat once more, and sauté just until it is warmed through. Serve warm or let cool, cover, and refrigerate until needed.

Curried Cashew-Chicken (or Turkey) Salad with Raisins and Cranberries

SERVES 4–6

2 cups diced cooked chicken

½ cup raisins

⅓ cup dried cranberries

1 cup salted roasted cashews

2 ribs celery, diced

2 tablespoons Muchi curry powder (or to taste)

1 tablespoon turmeric

1 cup Mayonnaise, Chapter 7

6 cups salad greens, rinsed and dried

½ cup olive oil

2 tablespoons lemon juice

Salt and pepper to taste

ESTIMATED CARBOHYDRATES:
Raisins: 65.32 g
Cranberries: 32.94 g
Cashews: 38.91 g
Celery: 2.38 g
Curry powder: 7.33 g
Turmeric: 4.42 g
Mayonnaise: 1.28 g
Salad greens: 5.15 g
Lemon juice: 1.94 g
Total number of carbohydrates per recipe: 159.67 g
Total number of carbohydrates per ¼ recipe: 39.92 g

This is one of my daughters' favorite dishes. Admittedly they do, on occasion, have a tendency to just pick out the cranberries and raisins and leave the chicken behind.

Combine the chicken, raisins, dried cranberries, cashews and celery in a large bowl. Add the curry powder and turmeric, and stir well. Blend in the mayonnaise, season with salt and pepper to taste, and gently stir. If you have the time, refrigerate the salad 2 hours or overnight. The flavors will meld and taste better. However, it is fine to serve it immediately if you are pressed for time.

Put the salad greens in a separate bowl. Whisk together the olive oil, lemon juice, and a pinch each of salt and pepper. Pour the dressing over the greens and toss until they are well coated. Arrange the salad greens on four plates or shallow bowls. Top with the chicken salad and serve.

Apple Walnut Chicken (or Turkey) Salad

SERVES 4

3 cups diced cooked chicken

3 celery ribs, diced

1 medium-crisp, tart apple, diced

1 cup coarsely chopped walnuts

1 cup Mayonnaise, Chapter 7

1 tablespoon lemon juice

1 teaspoon ground cinnamon

Coarse salt and ground black pepper
    to taste

Lettuce leaves, washed and dried
    (optional, for serving)

ESTIMATED CARBOHYDRATES:
Celery: 3.56 g
Apples: 25.14 g
Walnuts: 16.04 g
Mayonnaise: 1.28 g
Lemon juice: 0.97 g
Cinnamon: 2.10 g
Total number of carbohydrates per
    recipe: 49.08 g
Total number of carbohydrates per
    ¼ recipe: 12.27 g

Simple and flavorful, this recipe is great with any chicken or turkey, but it is especially good if you make it with leftovers from the Whole Smoked Chicken (Chapter 7).

Combine the chicken, celery, apple and walnuts in a bowl. Blend in the mayonnaise, lemon juice and cinnamon. Season to taste with salt and pepper and gently stir to combine. Serve alone, or on a bed of fresh lettuce.

*The valley floor of our farm echoes
with the call of turkeys in late fall.*

Pommes de Terre Sarladaises

SERVES 4

1 teaspoon finely ground unrefined
    sea salt (sometimes called Celtic
    gray salt)

1 teaspoon ground black pepper

4 cloves garlic, peeled

3–5 tablespoons leftover fat from
    Duck Confit, Chapter 7

4 medium potatoes, sliced into
    ¼-inch-thick rounds

1 cup chopped fresh parsley

½–1 cup diced Duck Confit or
    leftover cooked diced chicken or
    turkey (optional).

ESTIMATED CARBOHYDRATES:

Black pepper: 1.47 g
Garlic: 3.96 g
Potatoes: 135.47 g
Parsley: 3.80 g
Total number of carbohydrates per
    recipe: 144.7 g
Total number of carbohydrates per
    ¼ recipe: 36.18 g

This rich potato dish, paired with a salad, can be a complete light meal. Or, if you'd rather, serve it up alongside a grilled steak.

Puree the salt, pepper and garlic in the small bowl of a food processor. Set aside. Heat a large pot over a medium-high flame, add 3 tablespoons of the fat, and swirl to coat. Lower the flame to medium, add the potatoes, cover, and cook for 30 minutes.

Using a long-handled spatula, carefully turn the potatoes over so the browned side is on top. If necessary, add 2 more tablespoons of fat. Sprinkle the garlic-salt mixture over the top, cover, and cook for another 10 minutes.

Check to see if the potatoes are browning. If they still seem pale, increase the heat. When the bottom is browned, turn them once more. Add the parsley, cover, and cook until they pierce easily with a fork, about 5 minutes longer.

Use the spatula to lift the potatoes out of the pot and onto a serving platter. If using the confit, return the pot to the flame, add the confit, and sauté until heated through, about 1–2 minutes, adding a little extra fat if needed to prevent the meat from sticking. Sprinkle it over the potatoes and serve.

Rillettes from Confit

MAKES ABOUT ¾ POUND RILLETTES

½ pound leftover confit meat, torn or cut into small chunks

½ cup leftover confit fat or lard

¼ cup Demi-Glace, Shannon-Style, Chapter 3*

ESTIMATED CARBOHYDRATES:
Demi-Glace: 1.4 g (total number of carbohydrates in homemade demi-glace will vary)
Total number of carbohydrates per recipe: 1.4 g

I learned this method from Michael Ruhlman and Brian Polcyn's book, Charcuterie, *an extremely helpful reference as I ventured from farmer, to cook, to butcher. Rillettes are typically made from duck, goose, or pork, but I've made them with confit of lamb and beef tongues as well. I'm especially fond of making rillettes from tongue because, while my daughters will willingly eat tongue in a recognizable form, Bob is a bit more squeamish about putting a cow's tongue on his own. Thus, paddling the meat to a soft paste and spreading it across a crisp cracker has been a great way to ease our marriage through my culinary fascinations.*

Place the torn bits of meat, ¼ cup confit fat and demi-glace into the bowl of a standing mixer. Mix at high speed until creamy, adding more confit fat or demi-glace until the rillettes spread easily.

Pack the rillettes into glass ramekins. Chill 3–4 hours or overnight. To preserve them, melt the remaining confit fat and pour it over the top. Cover and keep refrigerated for 1 month, or freeze for up to 3 months.

*If you do not have homemade demi-glace on hand, use the gel that forms on the bottom of the confit, underneath the fat. However, be aware that this gel is going to be quite salty, since the meat was initially cured in a considerable volume of salt. If the rillettes are too salty for your liking, paddle in a little fresh pork lard (or substitute fresh pork lard for the confit fat) to dilute it. Another substitute for demi-glace would be to reduce 1 cup of meat broth down to ¼ cup.

Cuban Black Beans and Rice

SERVES 12

2–4 cups diced cooked chicken, sausage links (such as breakfast, sweet Italian, hot Italian, andouille, or Fresh Garlic Sausages), beef, or pork

1 cup lime juice

5 tablespoons olive oil, or 3 tablespoons lard or butter and 2 tablespoons olive oil

2 onions, diced

4 cloves garlic, peeled and minced

1½ cups long-grain brown rice

4 cups meat broth, such as Shannon's Meat Broth, Chapter 3

1 pound dried black beans, rinsed and soaked overnight in water and 2 tablespoons yogurt, drained, and rinsed again

2 teaspoons ground cumin

½ teaspoon ground cayenne

2 teaspoons coarse salt

½ teaspoon ground black pepper

Black beans and rice are a special treat in our house. We like to make a big pot of them and invite friends to share.

Put the meat or sausage in a stainless-steel or glass bowl. Add the lime juice, toss to coat, and let marinate while you prepare the black beans and rice.

Heat 3 tablespoons of the oil (or other fat, if using) in a pressure cooker over a medium flame. Add the onion and garlic and sauté until the onions are clear. Add the rice, increase the heat, and sauté until the grains are golden. Add the broth, beans, cumin, cayenne, salt and pepper. Stir well. Lock the lid in place and cook at 15 psi for 22 minutes. Allow the pressure to subside using the natural release method. *If you don't own a pressure cooker, cover the rice and beans with water and simmer two hours, until tender.*

Heat the remaining 2 tablespoons olive oil in a skillet over a medium flame. Drain the meat, discarding the lime juice. Add the meat to the skillet and sauté until it is just warmed through. Turn off the heat. Serve the black beans and rice in shallow bowls, topped with the warm meat.

ESTIMATED CARBOHYDRATES:

Lime juice: 16.46 g
Black beans: 241.96 g
Onions: 20.54 g
Garlic: 3.96 g
Rice: 221.86 g
Meat broth: 5.6 g*
Cumin: 1.86 g
Cayenne: 0.51 g

Black pepper: 0.74 g

Total number of carbohydrates per recipe 513.49 g

Total number of carbohydrates per ¹⁄₁₂ recipe: 42.79 g

* Number of carbohydrates in homemade broth will vary. This figure is calculated using the recipe for Shannon's Meat Broth (Chapter 3).

Rustic White Bean Stew with Bacon, Goat Cheese and Black Olives

SERVES 6

2 cups dried white navy beans, rinsed and soaked overnight in 1 quart water and 2 tablespoons yogurt, drained, and rinsed again

2 cups meat broth, such as Shannon's Meat Broth, Chapter 3

2 tablespoons butter, lard or tallow

4 slices thick-cut bacon, diced

2 small onions, diced

1 carrot, diced

2 ribs celery, diced

1 bay leaf

1 teaspoon dried thyme

1–2 cups diced leftover cooked lamb or pork

4 ounces fresh goat cheese

4 ounces pitted black olives, chopped

ESTIMATED CARBOHYDRATES:
Navy beans; 252.72 g
Broth: 2.8 g*
Onions: 20.54 g
Carrot: 5.84 g
Celery: 2.38 g
Bay leaf: 0.45 g
Thyme: 0.64 g
Goat cheese: 2.88 g
Black olives: 7.07 g
Total number of carbohydrates per recipe: 295.32 g
Total number of carbohydrates per ⅙ recipe: 49.22 g

* Number of carbohydrates in home-made broth will vary. This figure is calculated using the recipe for Shannon's Meat Broth (Chapter 3).

Fragrant, rich and deeply comforting, this dish brings to mind the scents and flavors of the Mediterranean. It is a great way to feed a crowd of hungry farm workers a hearty lunch.

Put the beans into a pressure cooker along with 2 cups broth and 2 cups water. Cover and cook at 15 psi for 8 minutes. Allow the pressure to subside using the natural release method. *If you don't own a pressure cooker, cover the beans with the 2 cups broth and 4 cups water and simmer 1½–2 hours, until tender.* Pour the beans and any remaining cooking liquid into the slow cooker.

Heat the fat in a large skillet over a medium flame. Add the bacon and sauté 2 minutes, then add the onions, carrot and celery. Sauté until the onions are clear and the carrot and celery are crisp-tender. Add all the vegetables to the slow cooker, along with the bay leaf, thyme and diced meat. Cook on low 3–4 hours, or 1–2 hours on high.

Refrigerator soup

Time and again I have tried to think about how to write a recipe for the single most important dish I prepare for my family—Refrigerator Soup. I could say, "use two cups leftover diced meat," but I've often made it with one, or with diced up bits of leftover hamburger from my daughters' plates. I could say "use broccoli," but there might not be any broccoli on hand, and the soup would still be good. Maybe there are only lima beans, carrots, or some mashed potatoes. That could work, too.

Refrigerator Soup simply cannot be reduced (no pun intended) to a recipe. It is a concept. The objective is to use up lingering leftovers, keep your refrigerator clean, and nourish your family as sustainably as possible.

I've written several recipes for soups in this chapter, but this is the one I make most often. My family doesn't know it, however, because it never tastes the same. Here are some guidelines for terrific Refrigerator Soup:

Start by sautéing a few aromatic vegetables; a diced onion is always nice. Add a little minced garlic if you are so inclined, and round it out, if you like, with a diced carrot or rib of celery.

Add good broth. When you are working with genuine meat broth, you are guaranteed a delicious and nutrient-rich repast, no matter what odd ingredients might find their way into the pot. Don't overlook any leftover sauces, reductions or gravies from your various meat dishes. They can take your soup in any number of interesting flavor directions. It is okay to add some water to the pot as well, either to dilute concentrated broths and sauces, or to help stretch the liquid a little farther. For a light supper, I allow 1 ½ cups liquid per person.

If you think you need it, add a filler, such as diced potatoes, diced winter squash, pasta, beans or lentils. We've found in our family that a rich broth is often ample for our appetites, but it makes a nice full dish when it's bulked up a bit.

Once your starches are nearly cooked through, **add your leftovers.** This may be diced up leftover cooked meat in any quantity, cooked vegetables, even mashed potatoes or mashed squash. Take a little extra time to dice things into small pieces. The soup becomes more visually pleasing for children, and the flavors meld better.

Add seasonings. When in doubt, tomatoes, tomato sauce or tomato paste can always transform a pot of bubbling leftovers into a pot of soup. A tablespoon or two of tomato paste brightens the broth flavor; a cup or two of tomato sauce imparts the distinctive tomato taste. Add salt, pepper, perhaps some dried or fresh herbs. If you want to dress it up a bit, add some heavy cream or maybe a splash of sherry, if it's a good match. It is all up to you.

Toss in diced-up greens just prior to serving. To maintain their vivid color and texture, greens should be cooked the least amount of time. You can either add them directly to the soup and let it simmer a few minutes longer, or you can sauté them in lard, butter or olive oil first, then put them in the soup pot right before you ladle it into bowls. Or, you can leave them out all together.

No two pots of Refrigerator Soup are going to taste the same, but I guarantee this: If you are working with good ingredients and genuine broth, they will all taste wonderful.

Winter Squash and Apple Soup

SERVES 8

3 tablespoons butter

1 large onion, diced

2 small tart apples, peeled, cored, and diced

½ teaspoon nutmeg

4 cups pureed cooked winter squash

1 teaspoon Muchi curry powder (available in specialty grocers and Asian food markets)

2 quarts meat broth, such as Shannon's Meat Broth, Chapter 3, or chicken broth, preferably homemade (see Meat Broth, Chapter 3)

½ cup apple cider

ESTIMATED CARBOHYDRATES:

Onion: 14.01 g

Apples: 41.15 g

Nutmeg: 0.54 g

Squash: 60.98 g

Curry: 1.16 g

Chicken broth: 11.2 g*

Apple cider: 14.2 g

Total number of carbohydrates per recipe: 143.24 g

Total number of carbohydrates per ⅛ recipe: 17.91 g

* Number of carbohydrates in home-made broth will vary. This figure is calculated using the recipe for Shannon's Meat Broth (Chapter 3).

This soup is served in my family for the holiday season. It is rather light, ideal as a first course or for a light meal. Rather than using canned pumpkin, we use the squashes harvested from our garden in the fall.

Heat butter in a large soup pot. Add the onion and apples and sauté until the onions are clear and the apples are soft. Stir in the nutmeg and curry powder, then the squash, chicken broth and cider. Simmer 10 minutes, taste, and season to taste with salt and pepper as needed.

My mom takes advantage of our bountiful compost to grow us an abundance of squash to store for the winter.

Stove-Top Stew

SERVES 8–10

3 pounds boneless beef, lamb, pork, or goat stew meat

3 tablespoons coarse salt, or to taste

1½ tablespoons ground black pepper, or to taste

About 1 tablespoon lard, tallow or butter, or more as needed

2 cups water

2 quarts meat broth, such as Shannon's Meat Broth, Chapter 3

2 cups chopped fresh (preferred) or canned tomatoes

6 medium carrots, cut into bite-size chunks

6 medium boiling potatoes, cut into bite-size chunks

5 medium turnips or parsnips, peeled and cut into bite-size chunks

3 ribs celery, chopped

3 medium onions, sliced into wedges

½ medium-head cauliflower, cut into bite-size pieces

3 cups chopped green beans (or shredded green cabbage)

ESTIMATED CARBOHYDRATES:

Black pepper: 6.62 g
Meat stock: 11.2 g*
Tomatoes: 19.20 g
Carrots: 35.04 g
Potatoes: 203.22 g
Turnips: 39.22 g
Celery: 3.57 g
Onions: 30.81 g
Cauliflower: 14.61 g
Green beans: 20.91 g
Total carbohydrates per recipe: 384.4 g
Total carbohydrates per ⅛ recipe: 48.05 g

* Number of carbohydrates in homemade broth will vary. This figure is calculated using the recipe for Shannon's Meat Broth (Chapter 3).

Okay, okay. I know that cooking a stew in a slow cooker is the most energy-efficient way to do it. But growing up, my dad always made stew in a big pot on the woodstove (and what could be more efficient than cooking with your house heat?), and I just got used to the idea that a good stew was made in large volumes, allowing for multiple meals. I can't get a slow cooker big enough to hold all the stuff I like to put in it (although a scaled-down slow-cooker version of this recipe follows). This is a rather unusual recipe because it calls for relatively few seasonings. Surprisingly, whenever I serve it to guests, they ask me what assortment of exotic spices went into it. When they press me for the secret ingredient, I can only tell them "time." The meat broth simmers for at least two days before I deem it worthy of this stew, concentrating flavor all the while. The vegetables are added at different stages, allowing them to hold onto their inherent flavors and natural texture without sacrificing them to the liquid.

Dry the meat, arrange it on a large platter, and sprinkle with salt and pepper. Heat a large, 8-quart soup pot over a medium–high flame. Add the fat and swirl to coat. Working in small batches so as not to crowd the meat (crowded meat tends to steam rather than brown), brown it on all sides (about 2 minutes per side). Add more fat if needed.

Once all the meat has browned, return it all to the pot, add the water, and bring it to a simmer, using a wooden spoon to scrape up all the seared-on bits of meat on the bottom of the pan. Once the bottom of the pan is clean and your water is a rich, dark, pan juice, add the broth. Bring to a simmer and lower the heat. Cook on very low heat for 2–3 hours, until the meat is *mostly* (but not *entirely)* tender. Add the tomatoes, carrots, potatoes and turnips, and simmer for 30 minutes longer. By this point the meat should be tender. If not, continue simmering until the meat is fork-tender before proceeding to the final step.

Add the remaining vegetables and cook until the potatoes are easily pierced with a fork and the cauliflower is cooked to your liking, about 20 minutes longer. If you prefer a thicker stew, simmer with the lid off to allow the liquid to cook down.

Serve immediately, or cover and refrigerate and allow the flavors to meld for a day or two before feasting.

Slow-Cooker Stew

Simple. Easy. Tasty. Cooks while you're away. What more is there to say?

SERVES 6

1 medium onion, cut into wedges

3 carrots, cut into bite-sized chunks

2 ribs celery, diced

2 medium boiling potatoes, cut into bite-sized chunks

2 pounds boneless beef, lamb, or pork stew meat

1 ½ tablespoons coarse salt

2 teaspoons ground black pepper

About 1 tablespoon lard, butter or tallow, or more as needed

1 quart meat broth, such as Shannon's Meat Broth, Chapter 3

1 cup diced canned tomatoes

2 bay leaves

2 cups green beans, chopped and lightly steamed

ESTIMATED CARBOHYDRATES:
Black pepper: 2.94 g
Onion: 10.27 g
Carrots: 17.52 g
Celery: 2.37 g
Potatoes: 33.46 g
Meat broth: 5.6 g*
Tomatoes: 15.78 g
Bay leaves: 0.9 g
Green beans: 13.94 g
Total number of carbohydrates per recipe: 102.78 g
Total number of carbohydrates per ⅙ recipe: 17.13 g

* Number of carbohydrates in home-made broth will vary. This figure is calculated using the recipe for Shannon's Meat Broth (Chapter 3).

Place the onion, carrot, celery, and potatoes on the bottom of a slow cooker. Sprinkle the meat with salt and pepper. Place a skillet over a medium-high flame. Once it has heated through, add the fat and swirl to coat the pan. Working in smaller batches so as not to crowd the meat, brown the cubes well on all sides, about 2 minutes per side. Add additional fat to the pan as needed.

Transfer the meat to the slow cooker. Add the broth, tomatoes, and bay leaves, cover, and cook on low until the meat is fork-tender, about 6 hours. Add the green beans and cook 10 minutes longer, or until they are heated through and done to your liking.

Leftovers: Leftovers taste even better on day two, as the flavors have had more time to meld. If you need to generate a meal to feed more mouths on dwindling leftovers, serve the stew over rice (or rice and beans) that is cooked in meat broth, or on top of buttered noodles.

Butternut Pork Stew with Bacon and Fennel

SERVES 8–10

3 cups butternut squash, peeled and diced into bite-sized pieces

2 bulbs fennel, shoots and core removed, diced into bite-sized pieces (reserve some of the fronds for garnish)

1 clove garlic, chopped

1 medium onion, chopped

1 batch Ginger-Cayenne Spice Rub, Appendix 1

2–3 pounds boneless pork stew meat, cut from the shoulder into 1-inch cubes

About 1 tablespoon lard or butter, or more as needed

3 ounces diced bacon

4 cups meat broth, such as Shannon's Meat Broth, Chapter 3

4 cups diced fresh tomatoes (canned will also work)

ESTIMATED CARBOHYDRATES:

Butternut squash: 49.10 g

Fennel: 34.12 g

Garlic: 0.99 g

Onion: 10.27 g

Ginger-Cayenne Spice Rub: 7.18 g

Meat broth: 5.6 g*

Tomatoes: 28.01 g

Total number of carbohydrates per recipe: 135.27 g

Total number of carbohydrates per ⅛ recipe: 16.91 g

* Number of carbohydrates in home-made broth will vary. This figure is calculated using the recipe for Shannon's Meat Broth (Chapter 3).

This is a fantastic stew to warm up a chilly night or to comfort anyone suffering from a cold. It is fragrant, spicy, and full-flavored. If you are serving it to children, I recommend either reducing the cayenne in the spice rub to ⅛ teaspoon or eliminating it altogether. But if you relish a little heat in your chest, leave it in there. It is delicious.

Layer the squash, fennel, garlic and onion on the bottom of a slow cooker. Pat the meat dry, then sprinkle it with the spice rub.

Heat 1 tablespoon of the fat in a skillet over a medium flame. Working in batches, brown the pork and add it to the slow cooker. Add more fat as needed. Add the bacon to the skillet, sauté 2–3 minutes, and add that to the slow cooker as well. Pour half of the meat stock into the skillet and simmer 5 minutes, using a wooden spoon to scrape up any browned bits and incorporate them into the stock. Add it and the remaining broth to the slow cooker. Add the tomatoes, cover, and cook on low until the pork is tender, about 6–8 hours. Serve garnished with the fennel fronds.

Portuguese Kale Soup

SERVES 6

2 medium onions, coarsely chopped

2 medium carrots, coarsely chopped

2 ribs celery, coarsely chopped

2 medium potatoes, coarsely chopped

2 cups diced green cabbage

1 cup dried kidney beans, soaked overnight in 1 quart of water and 2 tablespoons yogurt

2 cloves garlic, crushed

2 quarts meat broth, such as Shannon's Meat Broth, Chapter 3

1 teaspoon dried oregano

1 teaspoon dried basil

2 tablespoons lard or butter

1 pound fresh (uncured) chorizo or other spicy sausage

1 pound kale, stems and center rib removed, coarsely chopped

Coarse salt and ground black pepper, to taste

The slow cooker does the majority of the work all day on this recipe. Shortly before dinner, all you need to do is sauté the sausage and the kale and stir them in. This method helps to ensure that the sausage and kale maintain their characteristic flavors and textures for this classic soup.

Layer the onions, carrots, celery, potatoes and cabbage on the bottom of a slow cooker. Drain and rinse the kidney beans. Add them to the slow cooker, along with the crushed garlic. Pour in the meat broth, then add the oregano and basil. Cover and cook on low until the beans are tender, about 8–10 hours.

Heat a large skillet over a medium-low flame. Add the lard or butter and swirl to coat. Lay the sausage in the pan and cook, turning once, until they are well browned and the skins are taut, about 10–15 minutes per side. Remove them from the pan and set aside to cool.

Add the kale to the pan drippings and sauté until bright green and crisp-tender. Turn off the heat. Cut the sausage into bite-size pieces. Stir it and the kale into the hot soup, season to taste with salt and pepper, and serve.

ESTIMATED CARBOHYDRATES:

Onions: 20.54 g
Carrots: 11.68 g
Celery: 2.38 g
Potatoes: 67.73 g
Cabbage: 10.32 g
Garlic: 1.98 g
Kidney beans: 110.03 g
Meat broth: 11.2 g*
Oregano: 0.69 g

Basil: 0.33 g
Kale: 45.41 g
Total number of carbohydrates per recipe: 282.29 g
Total number of carbohydrates per ⅙ recipe: 47.05 g

* Number of carbohydrates in homemade broth will vary. This figure is calculated using the recipe for Shannon's Meat Broth (Chapter 3).

Creamy Roasted Garlic Soup with Spicy Sausage

SERVES 4

4 large heads garlic

2 tablespoons butter or lard

1 pound link sausage (Cajun andouille, hot Italian, merguez or any savory and mildly spicy links that your local farm has to offer will work)

6 cups meat broth, such as Shannon's Meat Broth, Chapter 3

1 teaspoon coarse salt

½ teaspoon ground black pepper

2 teaspoons dried thyme

½ cup heavy cream

Paprika for garnish

ESTIMATED CARBOHYDRATES:
Garlic: 25.79 g
Broth: 8.4 g*
Black pepper: 0.74 g
Thyme: 1.28 g
Heavy cream: 3.32 g
Total number of carbohydrates per recipe: 39.53 g
Total number of carbohydrates per ¼ recipe: 9.88 g

* Number of carbohydrates in home-made broth will vary. This figure is calculated using the recipe for Shannon's Meat Broth (Chapter 3).

This soup is just perfect for feasting beside a crackling fire as snow flies past your window.

Preheat the oven to 350°F. Remove any soiled parchment-like peeling from the heads of garlic, but leave them whole. Place them in a lightly greased baking dish and roast 1 hour, or until tender when pierced. Set aside to cool.

Melt 2 tablespoons of the fat in a large saucepan. Add the sausages and cook over medium-low heat until they are browned and the skins are taut, about 6–10 minutes per side. Remove the pan from the heat, remove the sausages, and set them aside to cool.

Return your attention to the garlic, which should now be cool enough to handle. Separate the heads and peel the cloves.

Set the saucepan back over a medium flame. Once it is heated and the pan juices are bubbling, slowly whisk in the meat broth. Let it come to a boil, adding the salt, pepper, thyme and roasted garlic as it reduces down. Simmer, uncovered, 10 minutes. Turn off the heat, let cool slightly, then puree in a blender or food processor.

Return it to the saucepan and bring to a simmer over medium heat. Slice the sausages into bite-sized rounds and stir them into the soup. Stir in the heavy cream and cook just until the sausages and soup are heated through. Garnish each serving with a sprinkling of paprika.

Potato Cabbage Soup

SERVES 6

4 cups green cabbage, diced

3 medium potatoes, diced

2 medium red onions, diced

1 teaspoon coarse salt

1 teaspoon ground black pepper

1 teaspoon dried thyme

¼ teaspoon allspice

2 quarts meat broth, such as Shannon's Meat Broth, Chapter 3

1 pound diced cooked sausage or cooked lamb, pork, goat, beef or poultry

---

ESTIMATED CARBOHYDRATES:
Cabbage: 20.65 g
Potatoes: 101.60 g
Onions: 20.54 g
Black pepper: 1.47 g
Thyme: 0.45 g
Allspice: 0.34 g
Meat stock: 11.2 g*
Total number of carbohydrates per recipe: 156.25 g
Total number of carbohydrates per ⅙ recipe: 26.04 g

Inexpensive, filling, colorful and tasty. This is a great soup that is easy to prepare, and a terrific way to use up some leftovers.

Layer the cabbage, potatoes and onions in a slow cooker. Add the salt, pepper, thyme, allspice and meat broth. Cover and cook on low until the potatoes are tender, about 6 hours. Add the cooked meat, cover and cook until the meat is heated through, about 15 minutes longer.

I think the greatest reward my parents enjoy for starting this farm is being able to share it daily with my daughters.

Beef Borscht

SERVES 8

2 tablespoons lard, butter or tallow

1 tablespoon coarse salt

2 teaspoons ground black pepper

2 pounds beef shanks, cross-cut 1-inch thick

1 pound red beets, trimmed, peeled, and diced into bite-size pieces

2 medium onions, coarsely chopped

2 medium turnips, peeled and diced into bite-size pieces

2 medium carrots, cut into bite-size pieces

2 cups chopped cabbage (optional)

⅛ teaspoon ground allspice

2 tablespoons tomato paste

4 cloves garlic, crushed

2 quarts meat broth such as Shannon's Meat Broth, Chapter 3

1 cup sour cream

3 tablespoons dried dill weed

This is a nourishing soup that is inexpensive to make, super-nutritious, and leaves lots of leftovers for subsequent meals. Don't forget to add the sour cream and dill at the end, as they brighten both the flavor and the color.

Heat a large skillet over a medium–high flame. Add the fat and swirl to coat. Dry the beef shanks and rub them with the salt and pepper. Brown them, in batches if necessary, about 4 minutes per side. Set aside. Pour a cup of water into the skillet and bring it to a simmer, stirring and scraping up any browned bits from the pan.

Put the beets, onions, turnips, carrots, and cabbage (if using) into a large slow cooker. Set the browned beef shanks on top. Add the tomato paste, garlic, and broth, cover, and cook on low until the beets are tender and the beef is falling off the bone, about 8 hours. Take out the shanks, let them cool enough to handle, and remove the meat from the bones. Cut it up into bite-sized pieces and return it to the slow cooker. Remove any marrow from the bones and add it back to the slow cooker, discarding the bones. (When no one is looking, I do this by first allowing the bone to cool, then raising one end to my lips like it is a blowgun, and blowing the marrow back into the soup. Anyone with a more hygienic method is welcome to write and tell me about it.) Serve garnished with a generous dollop of sour cream and a sprinkling of dill.

ESTIMATED CARBOHYDRATES:	
Black pepper: 2.94 g	Sour cream: 6.62 g
Beets: 43.36 g	Dill weed: 5.19 g
Onions: 20.54 g	Total number of carbohydrates per recipe: 137.86 g
Turnips: 15.69 g	
Carrots: 11.68 g	Total number of carbohydrates per ⅛ recipe: 17.23 g
Cabbage: 10.32 g	
Allspice: 0.17 g	* Number of carbohydrates in homemade broth will vary. This figure is calculated using the recipe for Shannon's Meat Broth (Chapter 3).
Tomato paste: 6.19 g	
Garlic: 3.96 g	
Meat broth: 11.2 g*	

Cream of Chicken Soup Florentine

SERVES 4–6

2 tablespoons butter or lard

1 medium onion, chopped

2 ribs celery, chopped

2 medium carrots, chopped

1 tablespoon fresh chopped parsley
(1 teaspoon dried)

1 tablespoon fresh chopped thyme
(1 teaspoon dried)

2 quarts chicken broth, preferably
homemade, see Meat Broth
(Chapter 3)

2 bay leaves

2 cups diced cooked chicken

2 cups diced spinach (or other fresh
greens), lightly sautéed in a
tablespoon of butter

1 cup heavy cream

3 tablespoons sherry

Coarse salt and ground black
pepper, to taste

ESTIMATED CARBOHYDRATES:
Onion: 10.27 g
Celery: 2.38 g
Carrots: 11.68 g
Parsley: 0.24 g
Thyme: 0.59 g
Chicken broth: 11.20 g*
Bay leaves: 0.90 g
Spinach: 2.18 g
Heavy cream: 6.64 g
Sherry: 13.5 g
Total number of carbohydrates per
recipe: 59.58 g
Total number of carbohydrates per
¼ recipe: 14.90 g

* Number of carbohydrates in homemade broth will vary. This figure is calculated using the recipe for Shannon's
Meat Broth (Chapter 3).

This is a real kid favorite, a super way to use leftover chicken

Heat the butter or lard in a large saucepan. Add the onion, celery and carrots, and sauté until the onion is clear. Stir in the parsley and thyme. Slowly stir in the broth and add the bay leaves. Simmer until the vegetables are cooked through, about 15–20 minutes. Stir in the chicken, spinach, and cream. Simmer until the meat is heated through, about 5 minutes longer. Stir in the sherry, then season to taste with salt and pepper. Remove and discard the bay leaves before serving.

Mulligatawny

SERVES 6–8

3 tablespoon butter

4 medium onions, thinly sliced

4 cloves garlic, chopped

2 ribs celery, chopped

1 medium carrot, diced

1 medium-tart apple, peeled and diced

2 tablespoons Garam Masala, Appendix 1

1 teaspoon ground coriander

1½ teaspoons turmeric

¼ teaspoon cayenne pepper (or to taste)

1 cup dried red lentils, picked over, rinsed, and drained

2 quarts meat broth, such as Shannon's Meat Broth, Chapter 3

2 bay leaves

1 (13.66 oz) can unsweetened coconut milk, or 1½ cups heavy cream

2 cups cooked rice

2 cups diced cooked chicken, turkey, lamb or beef

3 tablespoons lemon juice

Here's a hearty stew of Anglo-Indian origin. It's a fun way to turn leftovers into something wildly different.

Melt the butter in a large saucepan over medium heat. When it is hot and the foaming subsides, add the onions. They should make a pleasant sizzle as they hit the butter. If they sputter and splatter, lower the heat. Stir well to evenly coat the onions. Cook 2–3 minutes, stirring, until the onions have wilted and started to brown. Lower the flame and cook, stirring often, until they are caramelized, about 10–15 minutes longer. Lower the heat if they start to burn.

Add the garlic, celery, carrot and apple. Sauté until hot and the apple is beginning to color, about 2 minutes, then stir in the garam masala, coriander, turmeric and cayenne, and sauté until fragrant, about half a minute. Add the lentils, sauté 1 minute longer, then stir in the broth and bay leaves. Raise the heat and bring it to a boil, then lower the flame until it is just at a simmer. Simmer 20–30 minutes, until the lentils are tender. Turn off the heat and let cool slightly. Discard bay leaves, then puree the soup in batches in a blender or food processor or with a hand-held blender. Return it to the saucepan. Stir in the coconut milk, meat and cooked rice. Heat, stirring often, until it just starts to simmer, then turn off the heat. Stir in the lemon juice and serve immediately.

ESTIMATED CARBOHYDRATES:

Onions: 41.08 g
Garlic: 3.96 g
Celery: 2.38 g
Carrot: 5.84 g
Apple: 25.13 g
Garam Masala: 6 g
Coriander: 0.99 g
Turmeric: 2.14 g
Cayenne: 0.25 g
Lentils: 115.35 g
Meat broth: 11.2 g*

Bay leaves: 0.45 g
Coconut milk: 3 g
Lemon juice: 2.92 g
Rice: 89.02 g
Total number of carbohydrates per recipe: 309.71 g
Total number of carbohydrates per ⅙ recipe: 51.62 g

* Number of carbohydrates in homemade broth will vary. This figure is calculated using the recipe for Shannon's Meat Broth (Chapter 3).

Mexican-Style Pork Stew

SERVES 8–10

2 tablespoons chili powder

1 tablespoon finely ground sea salt

2 teaspoons ground black pepper

2 fresh (uncured) pork hocks

1 cup dried kidney beans, soaked overnight in 1 quart water and 2 tablespoons yogurt

1 large onion, diced

2 medium carrots, peeled and chopped

6 garlic cloves, chopped

1 dried ancho chili

2 chipotle chilies

1 cup fresh or frozen corn

4 ounces diced thick-cut bacon

1½ cups diced fresh (or canned) tomatoes, with their juice

1 12-ounce bottle of beer

1 cup meat broth, such as Shannon's Meat Broth, Chapter 3

1 teaspoon oregano

About 1 cup sour cream, for serving

Smokey, spicy and deeply warming, this stew simmered in our slow cooker on a wintery day, and the scent that filled the kitchen was as delightful as the repast.

Combine the chili powder, salt and black pepper in a small bowl. If the hocks have the skin on, use a sharp knife to make a series of 1-inch slits through the skin and down to the meat (make about 10 slits per hock). Insert a pinch of the spice mix into each slit. Rub the remaining spices into any exposed meat. If the hocks have no skin, simply rub the spices directly onto the surface of the flesh. Cover and refrigerate overnight.

The morning before you'd like to eat, drain and rinse the kidney beans. Put them in a pressure cooker and cover with water. Cook at 15 PSI for 10 minutes. Allow the pressure to subside using the natural release method. *If you don't own a pressure cooker, cover the drained and rinsed beans with 3 cups water, and simmer 1½ hours, until mostly cooked through.*

Layer the onion, carrot, garlic, chilies and corn on the bottom of a large slow cooker. Add the bacon and kidney beans. Pour in the tomatoes, beer and broth, and sprinkle in the oregano. Lay the pork hocks on top and cook on low 6–8 hours, until the meat pulls easily from the bone.

Remove the hocks. Let them cool enough to handle, pull them apart, and remove all the bits of meat. Add the meat back to the stew and discard the skin, sinew, and bones (by the way, dogs LOVE chewing the skin). You may just let the meat heat through and serve the soup immediately, or allow it to thicken by simmering for 30–60 minutes longer with the lid off. Serve with sour cream.

ESTIMATED CARBOHYDRATES:

Chili powder: 7.95 g

Black pepper: 2.94 g

Kidney beans: 112.78 g

Onion: 14.01 g

Carrots: 11.68 g

Garlic: 5.94 g

Chilies: 16.74 g

Corn: 29.29 g

Tomatoes: 10.5 g

Beer: 12.65 g

Meat broth: 1.4 g*

Oregano: 0.69 g

Total carbohydrates per recipe: 226.57 g

Total carbohydrates per ⅛ recipe: 28.32 g

* Number of carbohydrates in homemade broth will vary. This figure is calculated using the recipe for Shannon's Meat Broth (Chapter 3).

Sausage and Squash Soup

SERVES 4

2 tablespoons lard, tallow or butter

1 pound breakfast sausage links

6 cups meat broth, such as Shannon's Meat Broth, Chapter 3

2 cups canned tomatoes or 3 whole fresh tomatoes, diced

2 cloves garlic, minced

2 cups winter squash, peeled and diced into bite-size pieces

2 cups green cabbage, diced

1 large onion, diced

Coarse salt and ground black pepper, to taste

ESTIMATED CARBOHYDRATES:

Meat broth: 8.4 g*

Tomatoes: 19.20 g

Garlic: 1.98 g

Butternut squash: 32.73 g

Cabbage: 7.52 g

Onion: 14.01 g

Total number of carbohydrates per recipe: 83.84 g

Total number of carbohydrates per ¼ recipe: 20.96 g

* Number of carbohydrates in home-made broth will vary. This figure is cal-culated using the recipe for Shannon's Meat Broth (Chapter 3).

This soup has a lovely balance of mild sweetness from the squash and onion, heartiness from the cabbage, a light tang from the tomatoes, and just a hint of spice from the sausage to keep it interesting. My girls loved it, and I was able to have the meal on the table in under 40 minutes.

Heat a large skillet over a medium flame. Add the fat and swirl to coat. Add the sausages, taking care to make sure there is about 1 inch of space around each link to enable browning. Fry until they are cooked through (see Cooking Sausages, Chapter 6). Turn off the heat.

Combine the broth and tomatoes in a soup pot. Bring them to a simmer over medium heat, then add the garlic and squash. Turn the heat up until the soup comes to a light boil. After 10 minutes, add the cabbage and onion and simmer 10–20 minutes longer, or until the veg-etables are tender.

Meanwhile, cut the sausages into bite-size pieces. Once you are certain the squash and cabbage are sufficiently cooked, add the sausage and simmer just until the sausage is heated through, no more than 5 minutes longer. Season to taste with salt and pepper.

Pork (or Chicken) and Greens in Ginger–Tamari Broth

SERVES 4

6 cups meat broth, such as Shannon's Meat Broth, Chapter 3

¼ cup tamari (available at specialty grocers, Asian markets, and some supermarkets)

⅓ cup rice vinegar

1 cup diced green onion

2 tablespoons grated fresh ginger

2 cups diced cooked pork (or chicken)

4 cups chopped Swiss chard (or any other braising greens you have on hand)

When you have an ongoing supply of meat broth at the ready in the fridge, this recipe is fast food at its best. I like it so much, I often have it for breakfast.

Pour the broth into a saucepan and bring to a simmer over medium heat. Stir in the tamari, rice vinegar, onion and ginger. Simmer 5 minutes, then add meat and greens. Simmer, uncovered, until the greens are barely wilted and bright green, and the meat is heated through.

ESTIMATED CARBOHYDRATES:	
Meat broth: 8.4 g*	Total number of carbohydrates per recipe: 26.18 g
Tamari: 4.01 g	Total number of carbohydrates per ¼ recipe: 6.55 g
Rice vinegar: 0.73 g	* Number of carbohydrates in homemade broth will vary. This figure is calculated using the recipe for Shannon's Meat Broth (Chapter 3).
Green onion: 5.51 g	
Ginger: 2.14 g	
Swiss chard: 5.39 g	

A good hay crop amuses the farm dogs until it is needed in the depths of winter.

Minestra Maritata

SERVES 8

1 pound ground beef

1 pound ground pork

1½ cups freshly grated Parmesan cheese

1 tablespoon dried oregano or 3 tablespoons finely chopped fresh oregano

1 tablespoon dried parsley or 3 tablespoons finely chopped fresh parsley

2 teaspoons coarse salt

1 teaspoon ground black pepper

2 quarts meat broth, such as Shannon's Meat Broth, Chapter 3

4 cups braising greens (any combination of Swiss chard, cabbage, kale, or collard greens), diced and lightly sautéed

Good-quality extra-virgin olive oil, to taste

The bastardized translation for this recipe is Italian Wedding Soup. No, this soup has nothing to do with Italian weddings. Its American title is the result of a poor translation from the Italian, which celebrates the delicious marriage of meat and vegetables. This soup, another recipe from a glorious but impoverished tradition, allows for myriad variations. Here is the version we enjoy in our home. My daughters love to make the meatballs.

Combine the beef, pork, ½ cup of the Parmesan, the herbs, salt, and pepper in a large bowl. Using your hands, mix well and form into small (½-inch-round) meatballs.

Bring the broth to a boil. Carefully drop in the meatballs. Stir gently to keep them intact, but don't worry if a few break. Cover and simmer until the meatballs rise to the surface, then stir in the braising greens. Simmer a minute longer, until the greens are warmed through.

Serve immediately in shallow bowls topped with the remaining Parmesan and drizzled with olive oil.

ESTIMATED CARBOHYDRATES:	
Parmesan cheese: 6.09 g Oregano: 2.07 g Parsley: 0.76 g Black pepper: 1.47 g Broth: 11.2 g* Braising greens: 15.27 g ** Total carbohydrates per recipe: 36.86 g Total carbohydrates per ⅛ recipe: 4.61 g	* Number of carbohydrates in homemade broth will vary. This figure is calculated using the recipe for Shannon's Meat Broth (Chapter 3). ** This figure is an average taken from the braising greens mentioned. 4 cups of the suggested braising greens would contain carbohydrates as follows: Swiss chard 5.39 g, cabbage 20.65 g, kale 26.83 g, collards 8.2 g.

Coconut Soup

SERVES 4

1 quart meat broth, such as Shannon's Meat Broth, Chapter 3, or chicken broth, preferably homemade (see Meat Broth, Chapter 3)

1 14-ounce can organic coconut milk

¼ teaspoon ground cayenne pepper

1 tablespoon grated fresh ginger

2 tablespoons lemon juice

1 cup finely diced cooked chicken, pork, lamb or beef (optional)

Salt, to taste

3 tablespoons thinly-sliced fresh chives (or 1 teaspoon dried)

ESTIMATED CARBOHYDRATES:
Meat broth: 4.2 g*
Coconut milk: 4 g
Crushed red pepper: .25 g
Ginger: 1.07 g
Lemon Juice: 1.94 g
Chives: 0.39 g
Number of carbohydrates for entire recipe: 10.78 g
Number of carbohydrates per ¼ recipe: 2.70 g

* Number of carbohydrates in homemade broth will vary. This figure is calculated using the recipe for Shannon's Meat Broth (Chapter 3).

I stumbled upon this recipe in my Nourishing Traditions *cookbook and was intrigued. Because coconuts weren't available locally, I made it with canned coconut milk from our health food coop. It has become a classic cold and flu remedy in our home.*

Bring the chicken broth to a boil, then stir in the coconut milk, red pepper, ginger, lemon juice and meat, if using. Simmer 10–20 minutes, or until the meat is heated through, then season to taste with salt. Garnish with the diced chives and serve.

Onion Soup

SERVES 4

2 tablespoons butter

4 large onions, sliced thin into rings

1 cup finely diced cooked lamb, pork or beef

1 teaspoon dried thyme

6 cups meat broth, such as Shannon's Meat Broth, Chapter 3

Coarse salt and ground black pepper to taste

1½ cups grated Swiss, Gruyère, or Cheddar cheese (or a locally made equivalent)

ESTIMATED CARBOHYDRATES:

Onions: 56.04 g

Thyme: 0.64 g

Meat broth: 8.4 g*

Cheese: 8.72 g

Total number of carbohydrates for entire recipe: 73.8 g

Total number of carbohydrates per ¼ serving: 18.45 g

* Number of carbohydrates in home-made broth will vary. This figure is calculated using the recipe for Shannon's Meat Broth (Chapter 3).

This recipe is a constant standby in our home. Even when ingredients start to grow slim, there is always enough stuff on hand to make a batch of onion soup, enabling us to create a rich repast from only a few ingredients.

Heat a soup pot over a medium flame. Add the butter, let it melt, and swirl to coat. Add the onions. They should sizzle as they hit the pan; if they sputter or splatter, lower the flame. Stir well, coating the onions in the butter. Continue to cook 2–3 minutes longer, until the onions have given up two-thirds of their volume in water. Once they start to brown, lower the flame and cook, stirring often, until they are caramelized, about 15–20 minutes longer. Lower the heat if they start to burn.

Add the meat, sprinkle in the thyme, and stir well. Pour in the broth and bring to a boil. Lower the flame and simmer until the onions are very tender, about 15–20 minutes longer. Season to taste with salt and pepper. Serve sprinkled with cheese.

Become reacquainted with your broth

Like many people, I appreciated homemade broth as essential for making high-quality soups and stews. I'd make a batch of it now and then, and keep it frozen until I decided to make a dish that required it; then I'd have to wait a full day for it to thaw. But I'd never fully appreciated just how much more a good, rich broth could add to life.

Over the course of writing this book, I changed my relationship with broth. At first, to conserve fridge space, I started making broth once every six weeks. I'd make a large stockpot of it, boiling it down to just a few cups to make a gelatinous demi-glace. Once the fat chilled to seal over the top, I could keep it in the fridge for about six weeks, drawing on it for my soups and sauces. Demi-glace, stored this way, was far more useful to me than chunks of frozen broth, and certainly better than store-bought cans of insipid broth or those foil-wrapped bouillon cubes of MSG.

Then, while battling a series of family illnesses, we added bone broth to our breakfast menu. When we discovered how our vitality was restored and how much more satisfied we were after breakfast, Bob and I made it a daily ritual. Soon I was making broth every week, about 1½ gallons at a time. We now store it in half-gallon jars in our fridge, and it is as much a staple as milk and eggs. We use it as a snack, for quick on-the-fly meals, and as a primary ingredient in much of our cooking.

Because broth is always on hand, I notice that I tend to make more use of the lower-grade cuts of meat. I'm more inclined to make stews and pot roasts than I was before, because I have the essential ingredients readily available at an affordable price. Where I once made soups only occasionally, now I make them at least three or four times per week. With broth ready to use, soups are fast, tasty dishes that are easy for little children to enjoy.

This simple change we made in our kitchen is at the heart of this book. It is written with the presumption that there is always broth on hand to add to a recipe. I've done this because broth increases the nutritional density of the dishes, because it is so very flavorful, and because for those of us who don't have backyard vineyards, it is less expensive than flavoring dishes with wine. It is my hope that, after spending time with these recipes, you too will discover a deep and enduring love for your stockpot of simmering broth.

CHAPTER NINE

HEADS, TAILS, AND OTHER
Under-Appreciated Treasures

'll admit it. I did not look forward to researching and writing this chapter of the book. Organ meats, heads, feet and other such odious (in my opinion) cuts were an over-glorified salvation effort—the affected cuisine of die-hard nutritional fanatics, stoic old-world hausfraus or pretentious epicureans. According to my own eco-sensibilities, if a person chose to forsake the organ meats, but made full use of the bones and fat of the beasts that gave their lives for our well-being, well, that was ample thrift to earn the omnivore's atonement. As far as I was concerned, the kidneys, livers and hearts could go to the dogs, the heads and feet to the compost or the renderer. I have just enough customer demand for oxtails to equal our supply, so I rarely ate those, either (though they never repelled me as hearts and heads did).

I didn't waste *all* of it. When my children were infants, I blended chicken livers with butter, onions, cream (and a splash of cognac), portioned it in small covered dishes, and carried the pâté as their baby food when going to the market or traveling. When my customers at the farmers' market noticed, then tasted it, they demanded I produce it for them as well. Soon I was making pâté for market-goers' consumption, and stopped making it for our own household. Organ meats had no place in our family kitchen for a good four years . . . until my eldest daughter, who rarely eats sweets, mysteriously began developing cavities.

My dentist commented that this was common in country kids whose parents refused fluoride supplements, but I could not reconcile myself to administering the pills to my child, nor could I accept that a human body was so imperfectly constructed that our teeth could not serve us for the full lifetime that we'd require them, let alone to age eight. Faithful to the nutritional principles proposed by the Weston A. Price Foundation, but abashed by my failure to adopt their enthusiasm for organ meats, I revisited their research, as well as the research presented in Ramiel Nagel's recent book *Cure Tooth Decay*. One of the keys to re-mineralizing my daughter's teeth (in addition to removing grains from the family diet and exploring a number of other environmental and health factors) could quite possibly be found in those very meats I'd spurned. Organ meats are rich in a wide array of macro and trace minerals, as well as fat-soluble vitamins A, D, E, and K, all which aid in addressing biochemical disturbances in the calcium-phosphorus ratio, which is critical to dental health.

And so, eager to avoid the dentist's drill and facing a pile of recipes to test for this book, our family embarked on (quite literally) this new chapter in our lives. And, much to our surprise, we discovered that we *like* these cuts. My kids still love pâté and terrines, and they actually hop up and down with enthusiasm when they see me spearing chicken hearts on a skewer. At their encouragement, I dice heart into one-inch chunks and add it to stews, I reserve the cooking stock when simmering livers for pâté and use it for refrigerator soup, and I dice organ meats into fine pieces and incorporate them into the Stuffed Peppers in Chapter 8. They relished all of it, finally emancipated from my anti-organ tyranny.

Then we moved on to the more grotesque forms of cookery, namely the heads and feet. There, too, came an ebullience I never expected. Saoirse and Ula stood on stools at the kitchen counter, fascinated as I worked a knife around the sockets to remove pigs' eyes, peered into the pot as I added lemon and herbs to the head that faced back up at them, studied the muscles and bones of the pigs' feet before joyously splashing them into the stockpot. The next day, after the headcheese had been prepared, chilled and ripened in the refrigerator, they tucked into it with enthusiasm, and they continue to enjoy it for farm picnics and pre-made meals, as do Bob and I. In her book *How to Cook a Wolf*, M.F.K. Fisher writes, "Why is it worse, in the end, to see an animal's head cooked and prepared for our pleasure than a thigh or a tail or a rib? If we are going to live on other inhabitants of this world we must not blind ourselves with illogical prejudices, but savor to the fullest the beasts we have killed."

It may be true that heads, tails and organ meats comprise a smaller percentage of the ordinarily wasted parts of the animal than the bones and fat, but they are proportionally nutrient-rich, and thus, I've learned, their waste is just as tragic, particularly in light of how critical they are to our overall health. And, yes, even I can attest that they are truly tasty.

Apple Pecan Pâté

SERVES 8–10 AS A MEAL,
16–20 AS AN APPETIZER

¾ pound plus 2 tablespoons
    (3¼ sticks) softened butter

1 cup finely chopped pecans

1 cup meat broth, such as Shannon's
    Meat Broth, Chapter 3

1 cup apple cider

1 medium onion, sliced thin

1 medium apple, diced

1 pound chicken livers

1 teaspoon finely ground sea salt

½ teaspoon finely ground white
    pepper

¼ cup bourbon

1 cup heavy cream

ESTIMATED CARBOHYDRATES:
Pecans: 30.73 g
Meat broth: 1.40 g*
Apple cider: 28.4 g
White pepper: 0.82 g
Heavy cream: 6.64 g
Total number of carbohydrates per
    recipe: 103.39 g
Total number of carbohydrates per
    ⅛ recipe: 12.92 g

* Number of carbohydrates in homemade broth will vary. This figure is calculated using the recipe for Shannon's
Meat Broth, Chapter 3.

When the wild apples ripen in the fall, this pâté becomes the perfect way to celebrate the final days of the hectic growing season.

Heat 2 tablespoons butter in a skillet over medium heat and sauté the pecans until golden. Remove the pecans and set aside. Add the broth and cider, and bring to a simmer. Add the onion, apple and chicken livers, cover, and simmer 10 minutes. Strain the mixture, reserving both solids and liquids, and return the liquid to the skillet. Simmer until it is reduced to ½ cup.

Once the liver, apples and onions are cool enough to comfortably handle, puree them in a food processor with the cooking liquid, pecans, remaining butter, salt, pepper and bourbon, working in batches if necessary, adding a small portion of each ingredient to each batch. Place the pureed mixture in a large bowl (mixing to combine batches if necessary) and refrigerate for 20 minutes.

Whip the cream until stiff peaks form and fold it into the pâté. Pour into a lightly oiled bowl and refrigerate several hours. Turn out onto a cutting board before serving with crusty bread, crackers, carrot and celery sticks, cucumber slices, or sliced apples and pears. If you can't eat an entire batch, refrigerate leftovers in covered glass containers for up to a week, or freeze for up to 3 months.

Chicken Liver Pâté

MAKES ABOUT 1 POUND

1 medium onion, thinly sliced

1 cup meat broth, such as Shannon's Meat Broth, Chapter 3

1 pound chicken livers

¾ pound softened butter

½ teaspoon finely ground sea salt

¼ teaspoon ground black pepper

3 tablespoons good brandy

½ cup heavy cream

ESTIMATED CARBOHYDRATES:
Onion: 10.27 g
Meat stock: 1.40 g*
Butter: 0.20 g
Ground black pepper: 0.37 g
Heavy cream: 3.32 g
Total number of carbohydrates per recipe: 15.56 g
Total number of carbohydrates per ⅙ recipe: 2.6 g

* Number of carbohydrates in home-made broth will vary. This figure is calculated using the recipe for Shannon's Meat Broth (Chapter 3).

This pâté, my daughters' first solid baby food and a perennial favorite at our farmers' market, is great served plain with crusty bread or crackers, as a crudités dip garnished with cornichon pickles or capers, or on toasted baguette slices topped with caramelized onions and drizzled with a little balsamic vinegar.

Place the onion, broth, and chicken livers in a medium saucepan. Bring to a boil over medium heat, then lower the flame and simmer until the livers are cooked through, about 10 minutes. Strain the liver and onions through a colander, reserving the broth for another use.

Once the liver and onions are cool enough to comfortably handle, puree them in a food processor with the butter, salt, pepper and brandy, working in batches if necessary, adding a small portion of each ingredient to each batch. Place the pureed mixture in a large bowl (mixing to combine batches if necessary) and refrigerate for 20 minutes.

Whip the cream until stiff peaks form and fold it into the pâté. Allow it to set in the refrigerator before serving. It can also be molded like the previous pâté. If you can't eat an entire batch, refrigerate leftovers in covered glass containers for up to a week, or freeze for up to 3 months.

Rustic Country Terrine

MAKES 2 (10-INCH) LOAF PANS (ABOUT 15 SERVINGS)

1 medium onion, cut in half

3 cloves garlic

1¼ pounds pork, lamb, chicken or beef liver

1½ pounds ground pork (not sausage)

1½ pounds ground veal (if unavailable, double the amount of pork)

1 egg, lightly beaten

½ teaspoon freshly grated nutmeg

1½ tablespoons coarse salt

1 teaspoon ground black pepper

¼ cup good brandy

¼–½ pound thin-sliced uncured pork backfat, or ¼ pound lard

½ pound lard

ESTIMATED CARBOHYDRATES:
Onion: 10.27 g
Garlic: 2.97 g
Nutmeg: 0.54 g
Ground black pepper: 1.47 g
Total number of carbohydrates per recipe: 15.25 g
Total number of carbohydrates per ¹⁄₁₅ recipe: 1.02 g

During our family's time in France, these French country pâtés became a convenient household standby for us, perfect for picnic lunches and quick snacks. They were available at every farmers' market we visited, each recipe tasting slightly different, and every variation every bit as delicious as the last.

Preheat oven to 350° F.

Place the onion and garlic in the large bowl of a food processor and finely chop. Add the liver and purée. Pour into a large bowl, and add the pork, veal, egg, nutmeg, salt, pepper, and brandy.

Line two loaf pans with the strips of backfat, or thickly coat with ¼ pound of lard. Divide the meat mixture between the pans. It you have extra strips of backfat, layer them over the top of the meat. Otherwise, generously coat sheets of waxed paper with butter or lard, and lay them directly over the meat.

Cover the terrines tightly with aluminum foil and set in a large roasting pan. Carefully add boiling water around the terrines to about halfway up the outside of the loaf pans. Bake 1½ hours, adding more boiling water as needed. The terrine is done when it has shrunk slightly and the juices and surrounding fat show no traces of a rosy color.

Remove the terrines from the oven and cool for about 30 minutes. Spread the remaining lard over the top, cover and refrigerate for 24 hours before feasting.

To serve, set the loaf pan in a bowl of hot water for a minute to loosen the terrine. Unmold it onto a platter, garnish with fresh herbs, and serve with crusty bread and/or cornichon pickles. Alternatively, just use a butter knife to scoop it directly out of the pan.

Because of their generous dressing in pork fat, these terrines will keep for a long time (about 10 days) in the refrigerator. If you can't eat an entire batch in that time, unmold the extra pans, wrap tightly and freeze.

Homesteader's Terrine

SERVES 6–8

½ pound pitted prunes

12 ounces (1½ cups) hot tea

2 tablespoons brandy

10 chicken necks, skins removed and reserved

10 chicken hearts

10 chicken gizzards, cleaned and trimmed (not diced)

2 whole chicken legs

Coarse sea salt

1 bunch fresh thyme

2 cups room-temperature lard

12 ounces diced pork belly

¼ pound smoked bacon, finely diced

1 teaspoon ground allspice

½ teaspoon ground mace

½ teaspoon ground black pepper

14 ounces thinly sliced fatback (about ⅛-inch thick)

I came up with this after reading Fergus Henderson's recipe for Duck Neck Terrine, where he lamented how problematic it was for him to locate duck necks. While homesteaders and farmers may or may not keep ducks, many of us have chickens, and we face the opposite problem. We are positively overrun with underappreciated chicken necks, not to mention gizzards and hearts. Since a lot of us keep a few pigs around as well, we have a bounty of pork belly and lard, too. So, thanks to Fergus Henderson's genius, here is a highbrow dish that takes full advantage of the gloriously abundant meats that so many of our customers fail to appreciate.

Two days before you plan to feast, place the prunes in a nonreactive glass or stainless-steel bowl. Pour the tea and brandy on top, and soak 24 hours.

On the same day, set the skinless necks (remember that you are reserving the skins for later), hearts, gizzards, and chicken legs in a separate nonreactive (glass or stainless-steel) container. Sprinkle generously on all sides with salt and thyme sprigs. Toss to coat. Cover and refrigerate 24 hours.

On the day you wish to prepare the terrine, preheat the oven to 350° F. Remove the meat from the salt and brush off most of the crystals. Lay it in a clear glass baking dish, then add the lard. Cover and bake 15 minutes, then check to see that the meat is completely submerged in the fat. If not, remove it from the oven and add more lard. Once you are certain the meat is amply covered, bake until the meat on the necks pulls easily off the bone, at least 2 hours.

Using tongs, remove the meat from the hot lard, reserving the lard. Let the fat cool, then pour into a clean glass storage container, cover, and refrigerate for another use. Allow the meat to cool slightly, and then pull it all off the bones and finely dice it. Combine it in a bowl with the pork belly and bacon, season with the allspice, mace and pepper, and mix well.

Spread a large piece of plastic wrap on your counter. Lay out the thinly sliced backfat so that it is as long as your terrine (if you don't have a terrine, a 10-inch glass loaf pan is ideal), and about as wide. Set a row of prunes down the middle, lengthwise, then use the plastic wrap to help you lift the fat and fold it over the prunes, making a fat and prune roll that is the length of your terrine. Set aside for the time being.

Line the terrine with the reserved skins from your chicken necks, leaving flaps hanging over the sides. Fill the pan one-third of the way up with the meat mixture. Unwrap the prune roll and set on top, then cover with the remaining diced meat. Fold the chicken skin over the top and cover (use foil if not using a lidded terrine). If you have enough extra filling, put together a second terrine.

Fold a kitchen towel in half and set it on the bottom of a 9-by-12-inch baking pan. Set the terrine on the towel and set the pan in the oven. Carefully pour water ⅔ up the side of the terrine and bake at 350 degrees for 2 hours longer.

Carefully lift the terrine from the baking pan and uncover. Cut a piece of cardboard that will fit perfectly inside the top of the terrine. Wrap the cardboard with foil or waxed paper, then press it down on the terrine. Weight it with a brick or rock to compress the meat, and refrigerate 24 hours.

When you are ready to feast, remove the terrine from the loaf pan (it may help to set the pan in a dish of hot water to loosen it). Allow it to sit at room temperature for about 30 minutes prior to digging in.

Gizzards and other goodies in your broth

One of the ways I've been incorporating organ meats into my family's diet is by adding them to my stock pot, capturing their nutrients in my supply of broth, which we then drink for breakfast or use for soups and sauces. On occasion, however, I've been a bit heavy-handed with the liver additions and discovered that it can impart an overwhelming liver flavor into every dish I subsequently cook with the broth. On one of my broth-cooking days, I also had a few cleaned chicken gizzards in the refrigerator. Eager to use them, I added the gizzards to the broth and discovered that they re-balanced the broth flavor. The results were amazing: an even more nutrient-rich stock with a pronounced chicken flavor unlike any I'd ever had, without a trace of liver taste.

Lamb or Veal Kidneys with Brandy and Mustard

**SERVES 2 AS A MEAL,
4 AS AN APPETIZER**

1 pound veal or lamb kidneys

Milk

Coarse salt and ground black pepper

5 tablespoons unsalted butter

2 shallots, sliced

1 teaspoon chopped fresh thyme

½ clove garlic, chopped

1 medium tomato, peeled, seeded
   and chopped

1 cup brandy

½ cup chicken broth, preferably
   homemade (see Meat Broth,
   Chapter 3)

1 cup heavy cream

2 tablespoons Dijon mustard

1 tablespoon grainy mustard

2 cups cooked noodles, mashed
   potatoes, or sautéed greens, for
   serving, optional

ESTIMATED CARBOHYDRATES:
Butter: 0.04 g
Shallots: 7.56 g
Thyme: 0.64 g
Garlic: 0.50 g
Tomato: 4.78 g
Broth: 0.7 g*
Heavy cream: 6.64 g
Mustard: 2.4 g
Total number of carbohydrates per
   recipe: 23.26 g
Total number of carbohydrates per
   ½ recipe: 11.63 g

* Number of carbohydrates in homemade broth will vary. This figure is calculated using the recipe for Shannon's
Meat Broth (Chapter 3).

Gordon Hamersley originally included this recipe in his classic book Bistro
Cooking at Home. *His editors removed it, however, concluding that a recipe
featuring kidneys was "a waste of space in a modern book." Happily, he was
gracious enough to let me share it with you here. Until someone figures out how
to breed healthy livestock without kidneys, no such recipe would be a waste of
space. He writes, "this is an old-fashioned style dish using cream and mustard,
but kidneys can be nicely grilled, too, and served as a salad with mustard
vinaigrette."*

If using veal kidneys, peel off the outer membrane and trim off the fat.
Cut into 2-inch pieces. Trim off the inner fat. If using lamb kidneys, cut
in half to form crescents, and trim off the fat. Put them in a nonreactive stainless-steel or glass bowl, cover with milk, and let them soak for 1
hour to draw out the blood and bitterness. Drain, discarding the milk.

Pat the kidneys dry and season with salt and pepper. Heat 3 tablespoons butter in a large sauté pan over medium-high heat until hot, but
not smoking. Add the kidneys to the pan and brown lightly, about 1
minute per side, in batches if necessary to keep from crowding the pan.
They should be medium-rare to medium-pink. Remove from the heat
and pour the kidneys into a sieve; set into the sink and let them drain.

Wipe out the pan, return it to the heat, and add the remaining
butter. When it stops foaming, add the shallots and cook, stirring, for
5–7 minutes until soft. Add the thyme and garlic and cook for 2 minutes
longer. Add the tomato and stir to combine.

Remove the pan from the heat and add the brandy. Carefully place
it back on the heat, bring it back to a simmer, and simmer 2 minutes.
Add the chicken broth and simmer until it is reduced by half. Add the
cream, bring it to a boil, and stir in the mustards. Reduce the heat; do
not let it boil again, or the sauce will become quite bitter. Season to taste
with salt and pepper.

Return the kidneys to the pan and gently reheat them for about
1 minute. Serve with fresh noodles, mashed potatoes or fresh greens, or
alone in a shallow bowl with the sauce spooned on top.

Yes, my kids eat this stuff

I approached the idea of introducing heads, tongues, feet, tails and organ meats to my daughters with not a little trepidation. They have always been good eaters but, as many of their friends' parents suggested, this culinary foray might be pushing things a bit too far. I saw my daughter Saoirse's suddenly regressing dental health as an alarming indicator, and I felt I needed to adopt these foods as part of our normal family kitchen repertoire.

Rather than hiding the foods from them, disguising them without revealing the ingredients (that has NEVER worked in this house), I decided to introduce the foods honestly. I started with a beef heart. I left it out on the counter to thaw, then allowed them to explore it. Seeing their interest, Bob grabbed their attention by helping them dissect it, and made a full-on homeschool lesson examining the valves, ventricles, and marveling at the glorious functions it performs. They were so intrigued by the subject, they pleaded for the following day's homeschool lesson: now that they had learned about the role of the heart in the body, they wanted to learn how to cook it. And so we did.

It is in this way that we worked through the tongue, the livers, the heads, kidneys, feet and oxtails. My children have been raised on real food (at the time of this writing, their understanding is that McDonald's is a public rest room . . . that serves food), and I believe this has contributed to their development of a more adventurous and sophisticated palate. That helped pave the way through the recipes in this chapter. However, I think

their final decision to embrace these meats came from first allowing them to satisfy their curiosity. By the time the foods appeared on the table, Saoirse and Ula had grown familiar with them in their raw state; the "gross-out" factor had diminished, replaced by a "dare ya'" challenge. They had appreciated the purpose of the organ in the animal's body, and they'd explored how its living function translated into the appropriate culinary methods (hard-working cardiac muscle needs braising, kidney needs a cleansing soak, etc). Thus, by the time we were ready to eat, the feast on the table nourished their minds as well as their stomachs and senses.

Grilled Jerk Chicken Hearts

SERVES 4

1 recipe Jerk Marinade, Appendix 1

2 pounds chicken hearts

Olive oil

ESTIMATED CARBOHYDRATES:

Jerk Chicken Marinade: 48.41 g

Total number of carbohydrates per recipe and per serving will vary based on how much of the marinade is actually absorbed by the meat. To get an estimate, measure the weight of the marinade before adding the chicken hearts, and then the amount that is left afterward. The difference will be the amount that was absorbed by the meat.

Here's a spicy way to enjoy the bounty of a fresh chicken harvest. My kids beg for this dish.

Pour the Jerk Marinade into a nonreactive (glass or stainless-steel) bowl or large zipper-locking plastic bag. Add the chicken hearts, toss to coat, and marinate 2–4 hours at room temperature, or overnight refrigerated. Turn them at least once during that time.

Just before grilling, drain the hearts, thread them onto skewers, and blot dry. Brush with a little olive oil. If you have refrigerated the hearts while they marinated, allow them to come to room temperature while you prepare the grill.

If using a gas grill, light one side and allow it to warm with the lid down until it is medium-hot. If using charcoal, ignite the coals and let them burn until glowing and then spread them on only one side of the grill. The grill is ready when you can hold your hand 4 inches above the grate for no more than 5 seconds.

Scrape the grate clean with a wire brush. Place all the skewers directly over the flame, cover, and grill 2 minutes. Turn and grill 2 minutes longer. Move the skewers to indirect heat, cover, and grill until just cooked through, about 8–10 minutes longer. Serve immediately.

Fresh grilled chicken hearts with sautéed veggies is a favorite feast for Saoirse and Ula.

"Hearty" Stew with Mashed Potato Dumplings

SERVES 6–8

For the stew:

1 beef heart, or 3–4 lamb hearts, or 2 pork hearts

1 pound stew beef (ideally from the chuck), cut into 1-inch cubes

2 tablespoons coarse salt

1 tablespoon ground black pepper

3 tablespoons butter, lard or tallow

1 large onion, thinly sliced

2 cloves garlic, crushed

⅛ teaspoon caraway seeds

1 tablespoon sweet paprika, plus more, for garnish

1 tablespoon hot Hungarian paprika

4 cups meat broth, such as Shannon's Meat Broth, Chapter 3

3 medium tomatoes, diced, or 2 cups diced canned tomatoes

4 medium boiling potatoes, diced

2 carrots, coarsely chopped

1½ cups chopped bell peppers

FOR THE MASHED POTATO DUMPLINGS:

1 cup cold mashed potatoes

½ cup all-purpose flour

1 egg, lightly beaten

1 teaspoon coarse salt

The day I brought a beef heart out of the freezer to write a recipe, Saoirse became completely fascinated, studying the chambers, the ventricles, etc. We wound up changing the homeschool lesson plan for that morning to accommodate her curiosity. We wound up changing it the next day, too, as she was eager to learn how to cook her science experiment! This stew features beef heart, along with the stew beef, as a way to intensify the meaty richness of the dish. The dumplings just make it plain old fun. And my kids loved it. Yours might, too, if you let them explore the heart and then cook it with you.

Trim any sinew and excess fat from the heart, and remove any blood clots from the ventricles. Slice it in half and clean the inside. Cut it into 1-inch cubes. Combine the heart and stew beef, and season with salt and pepper.

Heat a large, nonreactive (stainless-steel or enameled iron) Dutch oven over a medium-high flame. Add 1 tablespoon of the fat and swirl to coat. Working in small batches, brown the meat well, about 2 minutes per side, adding more fat as needed. Add the remaining fat and onions and sauté, stirring often, until they are caramelized, about 15 minutes.

In a small bowl, use a fork to mash together the garlic, caraway seeds, and both paprikas, and stir it into the onions.

Return the meat to the pot and pour in the broth. Bring to a simmer, cover, and reduce the heat. Simmer 1 hour or until the meat is very tender. Add the tomatoes and potatoes, and simmer 30 minutes longer. Add the carrots and peppers and simmer until the carrots are crisp-tender, about 10–15 minutes longer.

In a medium mixing bowl, combine the mashed potatoes, egg, flour and salt, and mix well, then roll it into 1-inch-round balls.

Drop the dumplings into the simmering stew and cook until they float to the surface, about 15 minutes. Sprinkle with paprika and serve.

ESTIMATED CARBOHYDRATES:	
Black pepper: 4.41 g	Bell pepper: 10.37 g
Onion: 14.01 g	Mashed potatoes: 35.30 g
Garlic: 1.98 g	Flour: 46.13 g
Caraway: 0.13 g	Total number of carbohydrates per recipe: 251.34 g
Paprika: 7.34 g	
Meat broth: 5.6 g*	Total number of carbohydrates per serving: 41.89 g
Tomatoes: 14 g	
Potatoes: 100.39 g	* Number of carbohydrates in homemade broth will vary. This figure is calculated using the recipe for Shannon's Meat Broth (Chapter 3).
Carrots: 11.68 g	

Headcheese with Trotters

SERVES 15

1 pig's head, or calf's head, or 2 lamb's heads, quartered (whole is okay if you have a pot big enough)

4 pig trotters (feet) or 2 fresh (uncured) ham hocks (optional)

2 whole onions, peeled

3 whole carrots, halved

3 stalks of celery, halved

1 bouquet garni made with a sprig each of rosemary, oregano and parsley

1 lemon, cut in half

6 cloves of garlic, whole, peeled

2 bay leaves

1 cup red wine or apple cider vinegar

Coarse salt and ground black pepper, to taste

Lard, for frying the pig's ears, optional

Okay, this is a big project. But it isn't that difficult; it simply requires some direct kitchen time with a smiling pig's face. Take a deep breath and go for it. You can do this, and the rewards are worth the effort. And the squeamishness will fade. Cold sandwich meat can include so much more than just bologna and ham! Headcheese is rich in proteinaceous gelatin, easy to digest, and a convenient treat to have in your refrigerator. Serve it on crackers or crusty bread, topped with olive oil and salt (Louisiana folks prefer hot sauce), toss it in with red beans and rice or scrambled eggs, or serve it as part of a cold lunch buffet surrounded by pickles and potato salad, and garnished with a hearty helping of brown mustard and sauerkraut. My favorite way to eat it is diced up and scattered over field greens, then tossed with a lemon vinaigrette and some coarse salt. The trotters or uncured ham hocks are optional, but they do help to add a little extra meat and to put extra gelatin in the stock.

If it hasn't been done already, remove the brains and eyes. If the head is fresh, the brains can be cooked separately (see Sally Fallon's wonderful cookbook, *Nourishing Traditions*). If you are working with a pig head, leave the ears on for the time being.

Place all the ingredients except for the salt and pepper and lard in a large pot. Cover with cold water and let it rest for about 30 minutes.

Put the pot over a medium-high flame. As it approaches a boil, skim off any foam that rises to the surface. Once it has come to a full boil, lower the flame and simmer gently for an hour. If using a pork head, remove the ears. Dice and refrigerate them to be cooked separately.

Continue simmering for another 1–2 hours, until the meat pulls easily off the bone.

Remove the head and trotters to a platter and let them rest until cool enough to handle. Meanwhile, strain the broth, return it to the pot, and boil until it is reduced at least by half (⅔ is better, if you have the patience). Season to taste with salt and pepper.

Once the meat is cool enough to handle, remove it from the bones and coarsely chop it. Peel the skin from the tongue and chop the tongue as well. Don't be afraid of the snout if you are working with a pig head. That can be diced and added to the mix, too.

Toss all the diced meat into a terrine or stainless-steel bowl. Completely cover it with the reduced broth (you may not need all of it), stirring to eliminate any bubbles, then cover and chill overnight. If you have some broth left over, simply pour it into a glass storage container, cover, and refrigerate for another use.

When ready to serve, invert the terrine onto a cutting board. If the headcheese doesn't come out easily, loosen it by briefly setting the terrine in a pan of hot water.

Let it sit at room temperature for about 30 minutes prior to serving.

While the headcheese comes to room temperature, remove the pig ears from the refrigerator. Add enough lard to fill a cast-iron skillet ½ inch deep when melted. Place skillet over medium-high heat. When hot but not smoking, add the pig's ears and fry, stirring often to prevent them from sticking together, until crispy. Remove and drain them on brown paper. Season with salt to taste, and serve as an accompaniment to the headcheese, alone, or over a bed of fresh greens dressed with a vinaigrette. A pig's ear salad is a perfect accompaniment for cold sliced headcheese.

Rethinking cold cuts

As the growing season pulses through Sap Bush Hollow Farm and the ewes are birthing their lambs in the wood hedge, and the hay needs cutting, and the broilers need moving to fresh pasture, and the farmers' market season revs up, and the kids beg constantly for trips up to the farm pond for a swim . . . the temptation is greater than ever to head to the grocery store for some cold cuts to keep in the fridge for fast food. Who has time to cook?

For years, we sought a nutritious alternative to factory-farmed sliced turkey breast and sandwich ham. Eventually we bought a smoker and a meat slicer for the farm to address some of these demands. While that's a relatively rational purchase for a farm with a meat-cutting facility, it may not be realistic for most families. But many of the recipes in this chapter are. Headcheese, drizzled with olive oil and a little unrefined sea salt, with its slippery coolness and soft flavors, is far more satisfying than any ham sandwich I've ever known. The pâté and terrine recipes pair well with crackers, carrot and celery sticks, or crusty baguettes, making them a far more nutritious, flavorful and elegant alternative than factory-farmed turkey breast. For further cold-cut inspiration, try the Duck Confit (Chapter 7), the Rillons (Chapter 6), the Pork Hock Rillettes (Chapter 6), or the Rillettes from Confit (Chapter 8). All of these recipes provide long-lasting convenience, flavor and nutrition in exchange for a little advance kitchen time. A summer morning is dawning just now as I write this chapter, and my fridge is packed with all of these little treasures I made when the early spring weather was still dreary. Now, there they sit, stored in glass jars, sealed and preserved in fat, and ready to satisfy our hunger at a moment's notice.

Tongue Confit

SERVES 4

1 cup coarse sea salt

2 teaspoons crumbled dried thyme

2 teaspoons ground black pepper

4 lamb tongues, or 2 pork tongues, or 1 beef tongue

2–3 cups lard, or duck or goose fat (for lamb or pork tongues), or 4–5 cups for a beef tongue

Grainy or Dijon mustard, for serving

> **ESTIMATED CARBOHYDRATES:**
> Thyme: 1.28 g
> Black pepper: 2.94 g
> Total number of carbohydrates per recipe: 4.22 g
> Total number of carbohydrates per ¼ recipe: 1.06 g

For surviving the chaotic throes of the growing season, I am forever seeking ways to have nutritious, cold meats on hand that make for easy on-the-go lunches and snacks, without having to succumb to plain 'ol cold cuts. Confits have historically been a way to preserve meats for months on end. However, for them to work properly, the stored meats must be cooked and covered in fat. Duck or goose fat is often the traditional choice for such a project, but since most of us find it easier to have lard on hand than goose or duck fat, I've written this recipe for lard. If you have the good fortune of having goose or duck fat, use it!

P.S. My girls really enjoyed watching me prepare this (especially the part where I peeled the tongue). And, after watching, they really enjoyed eating it.

Combine the salt, thyme and black pepper. Pour this out on a cutting board. Lay the tongues on the salt, then roll them around until they are thoroughly coated. Seal in an airtight container and refrigerate overnight.

On the day you are ready to cook them, preheat the oven to 200° F. Remove the tongues from the salt, rinse, and blot dry, then place them in a nonreactive stainless-steel or enameled iron Dutch oven or other heavy-bottomed flameproof pot. It is okay if they are layered. Cover with fat and bring them to a simmer over direct medium-high heat. If, once the fat melts, the tongues are not completely submerged, add more fat until they're completely submerged.

Bring the fat to a gentle simmer, cover, and bake gently until the tongues are tender, about 4–6 hours (lamb and pork tongues will cook faster than beef).

Using tongs, lift the tongues from the fat, let cool enough to handle, and carefully peel the skin. Set the tongues in an earthenware crock (or any container that will keep the light out). Pour the hot cooking fat on top, let cool, and refrigerate. Once it is completely cooled and the fat has congealed, seal the container tightly. It will be ready to eat the next day, but is better if allowed to ripen for a week. Tongue Confit will keep, covered and refrigerated, for up to six months. Serve cold, sliced thin and accompanied by grainy or Dijon mustard. You may also make it into Rillettes from Confit (Chapter 8).

A note to the frugal: The fat that you use for this confit can be reused, either when sautéing or for another confit. Since it will be flavored by the herbs and salt, be mindful that whatever dish you choose to use it in is compatible with the preseasoned fat. After a few uses in confit, it will become quite salty and you will want to start with a fresh batch once more.

Corned Beef Tongue with Horseradish Cream and Grainy Mustard

SERVES 6

2 quarts water

1 12-ounce bottle beer

1½ cups coarse salt

3 tablespoons pickling spices

5 bay leaves

1 cup granulated maple sugar, sucanat, or turbinado sugar

1 large or 2 small beef tongues

1 large onion, coarsely chopped

6 whole allspice berries

½ teaspoon whole black peppercorns

1 whole star anise

1 cup sour cream

4 teaspoons bottled horseradish, or more, to taste

Parmesan Parsley Almond Crackers (Chapter 8), 1 baguette, thinly sliced, or 1–2 sliced cucumbers

Grainy mustard

ESTIMATED CARBOHYDRATES:
Brine: 256.16 g*
Onion: 14.01 g
Bay leaves: 0.9 g
Allspice: 1.37 g
Peppercorns: 0.93 g
Anise: 1.05 g
Sour cream: 6.62 g
Horseradish: 2.26 g

* The total number of carbohydrates for this recipe will vary based on how much of the brine is actually absorbed into the meat. In researching other brined meats, I've learned that most of them wind up containing 1.5 g or less of carbohydrates per serving, in spite of the sugars in the brines. Thus, the sour cream and horseradish are the essential ingredients to consider in carb-counting.

Anyone who has ever expressed disdain over trying tongue must have forgotten that he or she has one in their mouth all the time. Ok. Ok. Maybe that's a bit off-color for this recipe . . . but the joke was as irresistible as this simple recipe, which will make tongue-lovers out of even the greatest skeptics. Since the tongue is brined, begin the initial (and very easy) prep work at least a week before you plan to eat it.

It can be served with crackers, baguette, or sliced cucumber, as given here, but is also delicious served as a traditional corned beef dinner, paired with cabbage and potatoes simmered in the cooking liquid.

Put the water, beer, salt, pickling spices, 3 bay leaves, and sugar into a soup pot. Bring to a boil and simmer until the sugar and salt are dissolved. Pour this into a stainless-steel or other heatproof, nonreactive container and let it cool.

Add the tongue, cover, and refrigerate 7 days, turning every few days.

On the morning of the 7th day, drain the tongue, discarding the brine. Set the tongue on the bottom of a slow cooker. Add the onion, 2 bay leaves, allspice, peppercorns, and star anise. Completely cover with water (at least 1 quart) and turn on the heat to low. Bring slowly to a simmer and cook gently until the skin of the tongue peels easily and the flesh pierces easily with a fork, about 8–10 hours.

Remove it from the cooking liquid and allow it to cool enough to handle. Peel the skin and slice thinly.

Mix together the sour cream and horseradish in a small bowl. Season to taste with additional horseradish, if necessary.

Serve hot or cold with crackers, sliced baguette, on cucumber slices, or alone, garnished with a dollop of your choice of horseradish cream or grainy mustard.

Leftovers: Corned tongue makes great grilled Reuben sandwiches garnished with sauerkraut, Swiss cheese, and a little Russian dressing, or serve it cold on pumpernickel bread with tomato, mustard and capers. I like to make a platter with cold tongue, horseradish cream, mustard, pickled beets, dilly beans and a nice, sharp, raw cheddar.

Salsa Soup with Meatballs and Oxtails

SERVES 6

1 tablespoon coarse salt, plus 1 teaspoon, finely ground

3 teaspoons ground black pepper

2 pounds oxtails

2 tablespoons butter or lard

1 tablespoon olive oil

4 cloves garlic, minced

1 jalapeno chili, seeds and membrane removed, diced

2 medium onions, diced

2 medium carrots, diced

4 cups canned chopped tomatoes, with their juices

4 cups meat broth, such as Shannon's Meat Broth (Chapter 3)

1 teaspoon smoked paprika

1 pound ground beef or pork, or a combination

½ teaspoon ground cumin

½ cup chopped fresh cilantro

½ cup long grain rice

While this mixed-meat dish can be made with ordinary stew beef as a substitute for oxtails, these gelatinous-rich delights lend a lovely unctuous quality that balances the brightness of the salsa soup base.

Combine the coarse salt and 2 teaspoons pepper, and sprinkle it over the surface of the oxtails. Heat a large, nonreactive stainless-steel or enameled iron Dutch oven over a medium-high flame. Add 2 tablespoons of the fat and swirl to coat. Add the oxtails and sear 2–3 minutes per side, taking care to ensure that, as you brown the meat, there is about 1 inch of space around every piece (work in batches if necessary). Remove the oxtails to a separate dish.

Lower the heat. Add the olive oil to the pot and swirl to coat. Add the garlic, jalapeno, onions, and carrots, and sauté until the onions are translucent, stirring often to scrape up any browned bits. Pour in the tomatoes and broth and add the paprika. Return the oxtails to the sauce, cover, and simmer gently 1½ hours.

Meanwhile, combine the ground meat, ground salt, 1 teaspoon pepper, cumin and ¼ cup of cilantro in a bowl. Mix well and form into 1-inch balls.

Once the oxtails have simmered about 1½ hours, add the rice, if using. Simmer 45 minutes, then add the meatballs and simmer until they float in the broth and the rice is tender, about 15–20 minutes longer.

Serve in shallow bowls to unfussy dinner companions who will delight in sucking the bits of meat off the oxtail bones, garnished with the remaining cilantro. Consider offering small side plates as bone repositories.

ESTIMATED CARBOHYDRATES:

Black pepper: 4.41 g
Garlic: 3.96 g
Jalapeno chili pepper: 4.26 g
Carrots: 11.68 g
Onions: 20.54 g
Tomatoes: 38.40 g
Broth: 5.6 g*
Paprika: 1.24 g
Cumin: 0.46 g
Cilantro: 0.29 g
Rice: 73.95 g

Total number of carbohydrates per recipe (with rice): 164.79 g

Total number of carbohydrates per ⅙ recipe (with rice): 27.47 g

Total number of carbohydrates per recipe (without rice): 90.84 g

Total number of carbohydrates per ⅙ recipe (without rice): 15.14 g

* Number of carbohydrates in homemade broth will vary. This figure is calculated using the recipe for Shannon's Meat Broth (Chapter 3).

Where are the pig tails?

I very much wanted to include a recipe for pig tails in this book, and I even wrote one. However, pig tails from the pasture-based farm are quite small, and a large number of them are required in order to create a meal. I estimate that, in order to test a recipe that serves 4, I'd need between 20 and 30 pig tails, which is far more than we ever have on the hoof at any given time. The typical small pasture-based farm simply doesn't have the kind of production that makes a dish exclusively featuring pig tails a realistic (read "sustainable") culinary adventure. Since I couldn't test the recipe on pasture-raised meat, I opted to leave it out. When I do have a single tail here and there, I add it to my headcheese recipe and think of it as a Head-to-Tail-cheese recipe.

There are also a few other organ meats missing from this chapter, owing to the freshness issue. Sweetbreads and brains, for example, are supposed to be prepared and served fresh, something that is very difficult for most folks to access without the coincidence of a skilled butcher, a processing day and a visit to the farm all at once. For those readers who are raising their own livestock and want to learn how to prepare them, I strongly recommend Fergus Henderson's outstanding work, *The Whole Beast* (Ecco), as well as Sally Fallon's *Nourishing Traditions* (New Trends Publishing).

Meat Seasonings

RUBS, PASTES, AND MARINADES

RUBS

Coriander–Cinnamon Spice Rub

Poultry, beef, pork, lamb

MAKES ABOUT ¼ CUP

2 teaspoons granulated garlic

2 teaspoons fine-ground unrefined (Celtic gray) sea salt

1 teaspoon ground black pepper

2 teaspoons paprika

2 teaspoons ground coriander

1 teaspoon ground cumin

1 teaspoon ground cinnamon

⅛ teaspoon ground cloves

Total Carbohydrates: 13.63 g

Cuban White Pepper and Cumin Rub

Poultry

MAKES ABOUT 3 TABLESPOONS

1 tablespoon fine-ground unrefined (Celtic gray) sea salt

2 teaspoons finely ground white pepper

2 teaspoons dried oregano

1½ teaspoons ground cumin

Total Carbohydrates: 7.16 g

Garam Masala

This spice blend works with beef, lamb, pork and poultry. It is also an essential ingredient in a number of Indian dishes. The recipe below is for the spice blend alone. If directly seasoning meat with it, add 1 tablespoon of unrefined salt once you've ground the spices.

MAKES ABOUT ⅓ CUP

1 (5-inch) cinnamon stick, broken into pieces

6 black cardamom pods

8 green cardamom pods

1 teaspoon whole cloves

2 teaspoons whole cumin seeds

3 teaspoons whole black peppercorns

2 teaspoons whole fennel seeds

4 bay leaves, torn into pieces

Heat a skillet over a medium flame, then add all the ingredients. Dry roast the spices, stirring often, until they are lightly browned and fragrant. Store in an airtight container and grind just prior to using (I have a spare coffee grinder that I use just for spices so my coffee doesn't taste funny).

1 carbohydrate per teaspoon of spice blend

Garlic Spice Rub

Beef, pork, poultry, lamb

If using fresh garlic, plan to use all of the rub immediately, or cover and refrigerate untouched portions and plan to use them within a few days. (The garlic will go sour in a few days.)

MAKES ABOUT ¼ CUP

2 tablespoons coarse unrefined (Celtic gray) sea salt

1 tablespoon ground black pepper

1 tablespoon granulated garlic (or 3 cloves chopped fresh garlic)

Total carbohydrates: 11.46 g

Ginger–Cayenne Spice Rub

Chicken, pork

MAKES ABOUT 3 TABLESPOONS

1 tablespoon fine-ground unrefined (Celtic gray) sea salt

1 tablespoon ground black pepper

1 teaspoon rubbed sage

½ teaspoon ground cayenne pepper

½ teaspoon freshly grated nutmeg

1 teaspoon ground ginger

Total carbohydrates: 7.18 g

Maple Mustard BBQ Spice Rub

Pork, poultry

MAKES ABOUT 1¾ CUPS

½ cup granulated maple sugar (if this is not available near you, use Sucanat or another unrefined sugar from a local health food store)

¼ cup dry mustard

2 tablespoons ground cinnamon

1 tablespoon ground ginger

2 teaspoons ground cayenne pepper

½ cup coarse sea salt

¼ cup ground black pepper

Total carbohydrates: 146.86 g

Moroccan Spice Rub

Pork, lamb, beef

MAKES SLIGHTLY MORE THAN ¼ CUP

1 teaspoon ground ginger

1 tablespoon sweet paprika

2 teaspoons ground turmeric

1 teaspoon ground cumin

1 teaspoon ground coriander

1 tablespoon fine-ground unrefined (Celtic gray) sea salt

2 teaspoons ground black pepper

Total Carbohydrates: 12.68 g

Rosemary and Thyme Herb Rub

Pork, poultry, lamb, beef

MAKES ABOUT ⅓ CUP

2 tablespoons coarse sea salt

1 tablespoon ground black pepper

2 cloves garlic, minced

1 tablespoon crumbled dried rosemary

1 tablespoon crumbled dried thyme

Total carbohydrates: 10.23 g

Rosemary Herb Rub

Beef, lamb, pork, poultry

MAKES ABOUT ½ CUP

2 tablespoons crumbled dried rosemary

1 tablespoon crumbled dried oregano

2 tablespoons coarse unrefined (Celtic gray) sea salt

1 tablespoon ground black pepper

4 cloves garlic, minced

Total carbohydrates: 14.68

PASTES

For all the following recipes, combine the listed ingredients in the small bowl of a food processor and blend to a paste.

Caribbean Chili Garlic Paste

Poultry, beef, pork, lamb

MAKES ABOUT 1⅓ CUPS

1 small onion, peeled and cut in half

3 cloves garlic, peeled

2 hot chilies, cut in half with seeds and white membrane removed

2 teaspoons crumbled dried thyme, or 2 tablespoons chopped fresh thyme

2 tablespoons sweet paprika

1 tablespoon coarse unrefined (Celtic gray) sea salt

½ cup olive oil

Total carbohydrates: 26.64 g

Coriander-Herb Paste

Lamb, beef

MAKES A LITTLE MORE THAN ½ CUP

2 tablespoons coarse salt

1 tablespoon ground black pepper

1 tablespoon chopped fresh rosemary, or 1 teaspoon crumbled dried rosemary

1 tablespoon chopped fresh thyme, or 1 teaspoon crumbled dried thyme

1 teaspoon ground coriander

1 teaspoon ground fennel

¼ cup olive oil

Total carbohydrates: 7.86 g

Garlic and Parsley Herb Paste

Lamb, beef, pork, poultry

MAKES ABOUT ⅓ CUP

1 clove crushed, minced garlic

1 tablespoon coarse unrefined (Celtic gray) sea salt

2 teaspoons ground black pepper

4 tablespoons olive oil

1 tablespoon dried parsley

Total Carbohydrates: 5.51 g

Oregano–Mustard Paste

Lamb, beef, pork, poultry

MAKES ABOUT ¾ CUP

¼ cup olive oil

1 tablespoon crumbled dried oregano

2 cloves minced garlic

1 tablespoon Dijon mustard

1 tablespoon coarse salt

2 teaspoons ground black pepper

Total Carbohydrates: 6.32 g

Peanut–Lime Paste

Poultry, beef, pork

MAKES ABOUT 1 CUP

¼ cup natural peanut butter

3 tablespoons unsalted roasted peanuts

¼ cup chopped fresh cilantro

3 tablespoons lime juice

3 tablespoons water

1 tablespoon grated fresh ginger

1 small shallot, peeled

½ teaspoon ground coriander

½ teaspoon Tabasco or other hot sauce

½ teaspoon coarse salt

Total carbohydrates: 27.18 g

Persian Spice Paste

Lamb, pork, poultry

MAKES ABOUT ¾ CUP

⅓ cup olive oil

3 Medjool dates, pitted and diced

1 tablespoon coarse unrefined (Celtic gray) salt

1 teaspoon ground cardamom

1½ teaspoons ground cinnamon

¼ teaspoon ground cloves

½ teaspoon ground cumin

1½ teaspoons ground ginger

Total carbohydrates: 61.2 g

MARINADES

Bell Pepper and Garlic Marinade

Beef, pork, lamb, poultry

MAKES ABOUT 1½ CUPS

½ cup chopped onion

1 medium bell pepper, cored, seeded, and minced

4 cloves garlic, minced

½ teaspoon crushed red pepper

2 tablespoons grated fresh ginger

1 tablespoon coarse unrefined (Celtic gray) sea salt

2 teaspoons ground black pepper

¼ cup peanut or olive oil

Total Carbohydrates: 22.55

Dad's Tamari Balsamic Marinade

Beef, pork, lamb, poultry

MAKES ABOUT 1½ CUPS

½ cup olive oil

¼ cup tamari

½ cup Balsamic vinegar

2 cloves garlic, crushed

2 tablespoons honey

Total carbohydrates: 62.31 g

Garlic-Lime Marinade

Beef, pork

MAKES SLIGHTLY MORE THAN 1 CUP

2 cloves garlic, crushed

2 teaspoons coarse unrefined (Celtic gray) sea salt

¼ teaspoon ground cumin

½ teaspoon ground black pepper

1 tablespoon dried parsley

½ cup lime juice

½ cup olive oil

Total Carbohydrates: 11.99 g

Jerk Marinade

Chicken, pork

MAKES ABOUT 1½ CUPS

3 scallions, chopped

4 garlic cloves, chopped

1 small onion, chopped

3 teaspoons crushed red pepper

¼ cup lime juice

2 tablespoons tamari

3 tablespoons olive oil

1½ tablespoons coarse unrefined (Celtic gray) salt

1 tablespoon honey

1 tablespoon fresh thyme leaves (left whole)

2 teaspoons ground allspice

2 teaspoons ground black pepper

¾ teaspoon freshly grated nutmeg

½ teaspoon ground cinnamon

Total carbohydrates: 48.41 g

Lemon–Garlic Marinade

Lamb, pork, poultry

MAKES ABOUT 1½ CUPS

⅓ cup lemon juice

¼ cup olive oil

1 small onion, finely chopped

4 cloves garlic, crushed

2 tablespoons paprika

3 tablespoons chopped fresh parsley, or 1 tablespoon dried parsley

2 teaspoons coarse unrefined (Celtic gray) sea salt

2 teaspoons ground black pepper

Total carbohydrates: 26.81 g

Paprika–Lime Marinade

Pork, poultry, beef

MAKES ABOUT ¾ CUP

½ cup lime juice

1½ tablespoons honey

½ teaspoon ground cumin

½ teaspoon sweet paprika

¼ teaspoon ground coriander

1 teaspoon coarse unrefined (Celtic gray) sea salt

½ teaspoon ground black pepper

½ teaspoon crumbled dried thyme

Total Carbohydrates: 27.92 g

Tequila–Lime Marinade

Pork, chicken, beef

MAKES ABOUT 1⅓ CUPS

½ cup tequila

½ cup lime juice

3 tablespoons olive oil

Total Carbohydrates: 8.23 g

Thai Marinade

Poultry, Pork, Beef

MAKES ABOUT 1½–2 CUPS

¼ cup Asian fish sauce

2 tablespoons tamari or soy sauce

3 tablespoons lime juice

3 tablespoons peanut oil

3 medium cloves of garlic, minced

1 tablespoon chopped lemon grass (optional)

¼ cup chopped fresh cilantro

1 tablespoon coarsely chopped fresh ginger (or 1 teaspoon ground dried ginger)

1 tablespoon honey

1 tablespoon sesame oil

1 teaspoon crushed red pepper

2 tablespoons coarsely chopped fresh chives

½ cup chopped onion

Total carbohydrates: 32.77 g

BARBECUE SAUCES

Tamarind-Ginger Barbecue Sauce

MAKES SLIGHTLY MORE THAN 2 CUPS

2 cups chicken broth, preferably homemade (see Meat Broth, Chapter 3)

½ cup honey

2 tablespoons grated fresh ginger

1 tablespoon chopped fresh parsley, or 1 teaspoon dried parsley

1 tablespoon chopped fresh chives, or 1 teaspoon dried chives

1 teaspoon spicy brown mustard

1 teaspoon ground cinnamon

¼ teaspoon ground cayenne pepper

1 clove garlic, minced

½ cup strong black coffee

1 tablespoon tamarind paste

Combine all the ingredients in a saucepan. Bring the mixture to a boil, then reduce the heat and allow the sauce to simmer until it is reduced by one-third.

Total carbohydrates: 159.71 g

Apple-Bourbon Barbecue Sauce

MAKES 3½–4 CUPS SAUCE

½ cup butter

1 yellow or white medium onion, finely chopped

½ cup maple syrup

½ cup bourbon

½ cup cider vinegar

½ cup apple butter

¼ cup Dijon mustard

⅓ cup apple cider

Melt the butter in a saucepan over medium heat. Add the onion and sauté until translucent. Whisk in the remaining ingredients and allow the mixture to come to a boil for 30 seconds before reducing it to a simmer. Simmer for 30 minutes to thicken. Refrigerate leftovers in an airtight container.

Total carbohydrates: 190.25

Saoirse helps Bob set up a new bee hive.

Guide

TO GRAIN-, LEGUME-, AND DAIRY-FREE FOODS

When I wrote my first cookbook, I had pretty simple views about what comprised the ideal diet. If it was locally and sustainably produced, then it was probably fine to eat. I had blinders on when it came to considering the food needs of the massive numbers of people who were discovering that their bodies couldn't tolerate grains, legumes, or certain dairy products. In our family we lived deliciously, feasting with abandon on all these foods.

And then we got sick. Somewhat mysteriously, Bob developed diabetes, my daughters' teeth were demineralizing, and I developed a systemic fungal infection. We'd enjoyed years of raw dairy, local veggies, fruits and cheese, grassfed meat, organic and fermented grains and legumes, but it simply wasn't cutting it for us nutritionally any longer. It is a great diet for a lot of people, but for some of us, there were problems.

Over the course of two years, we've discovered that some foods react better in our systems than others, and we've learned that there are many other folks in the same boat. There is much speculation as to why this is happening. Perhaps there is increased genetic susceptibility built up over several generations' consumption of processed foods. Perhaps the problem has to do with other toxins in our culture, with the stresses confronting many Americans, with our food processing and storage practices. Either way, the simple truth is becoming more evident: grains, legumes and dairy products are fine for some folks, and problematic for others. But a local, delicious diet is still possible.

In order to assist folks who must make these choices, I have provided this quick reference guide. The **first list** contains the recipes in this book that are **grain- and**

legume-free, but which **contain dairy**. The **second list** contains the recipes that are **grain-, legume- and dairy-free**. I put these lists forward as suggestions for those folks with special dietary needs. Please remember they are only *suggestions*. This is not nutritional advice. It is always incumbent upon the home cook to read through the ingredient list and carefully consider whether substitutions must be made in order to meet the particular dietary needs of their family.

Grain- and Legume-Free Recipes that Contain Dairy

Please note: As I explored dairy-intolerance issues, I learned that not all types of dairy are problematic for all dairy-intolerant folks. Often, people who cannot tolerate casein are able to have cream and butter, and cheese is not always a problem for people who are lactose-intolerant. Dairy sensitivities can be highly individual, and some of these recipes may be perfectly fine for otherwise dairy-intolerant people. In an effort to help sort this out, I've mentioned whether a recipe contains cheese, cream, milk, butter, etc. I am partial to raw (unpasteurized) dairy products, where available, when preparing food for my family.

The recipes below are offered as suggestions. Responsibility for determining the suitability of all ingredients ultimately lies with the home cook and his or her dinner companions.

Chapter 3: Bones and Fat

Holiday Pudding with Rum Sauce (milk, and/or cream)

Chapter 4: Beef

Buttermilk Marinated Pot Roast in a Ginger Garlic Chili Sauce (buttermilk, or yogurt, or whey)

Slow-Cooked Brisket with Sweet Peppers and Caramelized Onions (butter)

Carpaccio (sauce contains milk)

Garlic-Rubbed Chuck-Eye Roast with Horseradish Cream (sour cream)

Roast Tenderloin of Beef with Goat Cheese (cheese)

Shepherd's Pie (butter, milk or cream)

Stuffed Chard with Lemon Cream Sauce (sour cream or heavy cream)

Oven-Roasted Burgers with Garlic Chive Goat Cheese (cheese)

Chapter 5: Lamb

Rack of Lamb Glazed in Balsamic Butter (butter)

Lamb Shoulder Chops in a Tarragon Cream Sauce (cream)

Easy-On-The-Cook Lamb Curry Stew (yogurt)

Lamb Meatballs and Crudités with Sundried Tomato Aioli (cheese)

Chapter 6: Pork

Slow-Cooked Pork Shoulder with Vegetables and a Creamy Red Wine Reduction (cream)

Pan-Seared Pork Chops (butter, cream)

Brined Pork Chops in a Rosemary Cream Sauce with Caramelized Pears (sour cream)

Tenderloin Medallions in Caramelized Onions and Skillet Potatoes (cream)

Maple Smoked Spare Ribs (butter in sauce)

Fresh Ham with a Shallot Dijon Reduction (butter)

Chapter 7: Poultry and Eggs

Chicken with Lemon Cream (cream)

Chicken Roasted with Caramelized Onions, Apples and Cheddar (cheese)

Turkey & Gravy: Straightforward, Simple and Delicious (butter) (gravy contains flour, but a grain-free alternative is provided)

Hollandaise Sauce (butter)

Vegetable Timbales (cream, butter, cheese)

Buttermilk Salad Dressing (yogurt, cream)

Parmesan Peppercorn Salad Dressing (cheese, yogurt, cream)

My Grandmother's Eggnog, Improved (milk, cream)

Maple Whipped Cream (cream)

Raw Milk Eggnog (raw milk, cream)

Bittersweet Fudge Pops (kefir or yogurt)

Deep Vanilla Ice Cream (cream)

Lemon Meringue Ice Cream Pie (butter, cream)

Grain-, Legume- and Dairy-Free Foods

The recipes below are offered as suggestions. Responsibility for determining the suitability of all ingredients ultimately lies with the home cook and his or her dinner companions.

Techniques

Headcheese

To stretch your organic and local produce a little further, save all the scraps (wilted leaves, stems, roots, peels, onion skins) and use them in place of fresh vegetables when making headcheese or broth.

If the cooked head is too hot to handle, use a pair of heavy-duty rubber gloves to pull the meat apart from the bone.

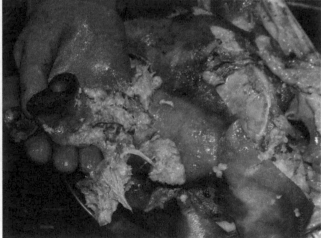

Overlook no morsels of meat; even the snout has good vittles to offer.

Finely mince the meat, fat and skin before seasoning it and adding it to the terrine.

Minced meat in the terrine will solidify once the gelatinous broth is poured over and allowed to chill.

Rendering Fat

Trim fat away from the skin before adding it to the rendering pot. Skin can then be boiled and then roasted for delicious homemade pork rinds or "cracklings" (see the recipe for Mexican Cracklings).

Diced fat for rendering.

Adding baking soda to the rendering pot.

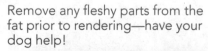

Partially cover rendering pot to allow steam to escape.

Remove any fleshy parts from the fat prior to rendering—have your dog help!

Fat is rendered and ready to strain when the cracklings are floating.

Strain rendered fat through a cheesecloth-lined colander.

Allow strained fat to cool before refrigerating.

Bountiful fat harvest!

Soap Making

Begin by melting tallow over low heat. Turn off heat once 80% of the fat has turned to liquid. Allow the residual warmth to melt the remaining fat.

Monitoring the fat's temperature is easy with an instant-read thermometer.

As the fat temperature cools and approaches 110° F, submerge the jar containing room-temperature lye solution into a hot water bath. Use 2 thermometers to simultaneously monitor the temperature of both.

Stir melted fat constantly while pouring lye solution in a slow, steady stream.

Stir the soap until it "traces," meaning it thickens to the consistency of pea soup and a spoon can visibly drizzle a trail across the surface.

Add scents or any additional ingredients once the soap has come to trace.

Spoon liquid soap into molds and cover with cardboard to enable stacking.

Stack the filled molds between layers of cardboard and wrap the stack in a blanket to slowly release its heat over 24 hours.

Homemade Farmer's Soap from grassfed beef tallow.

Candlemaking

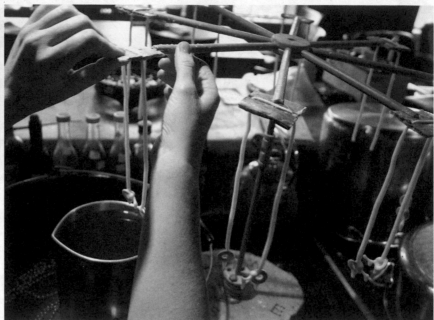

Blending equal parts tallow and beeswax results in sturdy, slow-burning, sweet smelling, economical and attractive candles.

> Our daughters' Tinker Toys were very useful for constructing a rotating rack for hand-dipped tapers.

Salves

Herbs are added to tea bags, then placed in a slow cooker with the lard and beeswax. The herbs infuse the fat for 24 hours on the lowest heat setting.

Grilling

To grill a grassfed steak: Light one side of the grill only. Once the grate is hot, sear the steaks directly over the flame for 2 minutes per side, then move them to indirect heat. Cover the grill and allow the steaks to cook indirectly for 5-7 minutes per pound for medium-rare.

Grilled chuck-eye and rib steaks

When grilled properly, muscle fibers in steaks will stay loose and full of juice.

Index

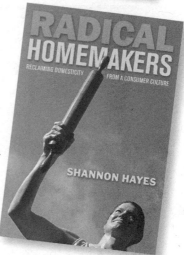